Lecture Notes in Artificial Intelligence 4760

Edited by J. G. Carbonell and J. Siekmann

Subseries of Lecture Notes in Computer Science

T0223198

Erich Rome   Joachim Hertzberg
Georg Dorffner (Eds.)

Towards Affordance-Based Robot Control

International Seminar
Dagstuhl Castle, Germany, June 5-9, 2006
Revised Papers

 Springer

Series Editors

Jaime G. Carbonell, Carnegie Mellon University, Pittsburgh, PA, USA
Jörg Siekmann, University of Saarland, Saarbrücken, Germany

Volume Editors

Erich Rome
Fraunhofer Institute for Intelligent Analysis and Information Systems (IAIS)
Adaptive Reflective Teams Department (ART)
Schloss Birlinghoven, 53754 Sankt Augustin, Germany
E-mail: erich.rome@iais.fraunhofer.de

Joachim Hertzberg
University of Osnabrück
Institute of Computer Science
49069 Osnabrück, Germany
E-mail: hertzberg@informatik.uni-osnabrueck.de

Georg Dorffner
Austrian Research Institute for Artificial Intelligence (OFAI)
Neural Computation and Robotics
and
Institute of Medical Cybernetics and Artificial Intelligence
Center for Brain Research, Medical University Vienna
Vienna, Austria
E-mail: georg.dorffner@meduniwien.ac.at

Library of Congress Control Number: 2008920268

CR Subject Classification (1998): I.2.9, I.2.10, I.2.8

LNCS Sublibrary: SL 7 – Artificial Intelligence

ISSN   0302-9743
ISBN-10   3-540-77914-0 Springer Berlin Heidelberg New York
ISBN-13   978-3-540-77914-8 Springer Berlin Heidelberg New York

Springer is a part of Springer Science+Business Media

springer.com

© Springer-Verlag Berlin Heidelberg 2008
Printed in Germany

Typesetting: Camera-ready by author, data conversion by Scientific Publishing Services, Chennai, India
Printed on acid-free paper   SPIN: 12224166   06/3180   5 4 3 2 1 0

Preface

Today's mobile robot perception is insufficient for acting goal-directedly in unconstrained, dynamic everyday environments like a home, a factory, or a city. Subject to restrictions in bandwidth, computer power, and computation time, a robot has to react to a wealth of dynamically changing stimuli in such environments, requiring rapid, selective attention to decisive, action-relevant information of high current utility. Robust and general engineering methods for effectively and efficiently coupling perception, action, and reasoning are unavailable. Interesting performance, if any, is currently only achieved by sophisticated robot programming exploiting domain features and specialties, which leaves ordinary users no chance of changing how the robot acts.

The latter facts are high barriers for introducing, for example, service robots into human living or work environments. In order to overcome these barriers, additonal R&D efforts are required. The European Commission is undertaking a determined effort to fund related basic, inter-disciplinary research in a line of Strategic Objectives, including the Cognitive Systems calls in their 6th Framework Programme (FP6, [1]), and continuing in the 7th Framework Programme. One of the funded Cognitive Systems projects is MACS ("multi-sensory autonomous cognitive systems interacting with dynamic environments for perceiving and using affordances").

In cognitive science, an affordance in the sense of perceptual psychologist J.J. Gibson [2] is a resource or support that the environment offers an agent for action, and that the agent can directly perceive and employ. Only rarely has this concept been used in robotics and AI, although it offers an original perspective on coupling perception, action, and reasoning, differing notably from standard hybrid robot-control architectures. Taking it literally as a means or a metaphor for coupling perception and action directly, the potential that affordances offer for designing new powerful and intuitive robot-control architectures is obvious.

Perceiving affordances in the environment means that perception is filtered through the individual capabilities for physical action and through the current goals or intentions, thereby coupling perception and action deep down in the control architecture and providing an action-oriented interpretation of percepts in real time. Moreover, affordances provide on a high granularity level a basis for agent interaction and for learning or adapting context-dependent, goal-directed action.

The main objective of the MACS project is to explore and exploit the concept of *affordances* for the design and implementation of autonomous mobile robots acting goal-directedly in a dynamic environment. The aim is to develop affordance-based control as a method for robotics. The potential of this new methodology will be shown by going beyond navigation-like tasks towards goal-directed autonomous manipulation in the project demonstrators.

During the MACS proposal phase in late 2003, the idea of organizing an interdisciplinary Dagstuhl seminar related to the core MACS topics emerged. The planned purpose of the seminar was threefold, namely, (1) to disseminate the MACS project ideas and concepts into related scientific communities, (2) to receive feedback on and discuss these ideas, and (3) to discuss the usage of affordances in other research areas.

The organizers saw researchers in four broad areas (philosophy and logic, artificial intelligence and computer science, psychology, and economics and game theory) addressing highly related (in some cases, the same) problems, in which work in one area in all likelihood would benefit research in another. Hence for the Dagstuhl seminar, the organizers felt that valuable interactions and contributions could be anticipated by bringing people together from these areas. The aim of the seminar was to bring together researchers from robotics, informatics, and the cognitive sciences to exchange their experiences and opinions, and generate new ideas regarding the following essential questions:

- How could or should a robot-control architecture look like that makes use of affordances in perceiving the environment?
- How could or should such an architecture make use of affordances for action and reasoning?
- Is there more to affordances than function-oriented perception, action, and reasoning?

The answers to these questions are currently wide open. Two points can be stated with certainty, however. First, an affordance-based or affordance-inspired robot-control architecture cannot simply be an extension (an "added layer," so to speak) to existing modern control architectures. The reason is that affordances would spring into existence in low-level perception, would have to pass filters in the control, such as attentional mechanisms, in order not to flood the robot's higher processing levels, and serve in some explicitly represented form of a structured result of perception as a resource for action selection, deliberation, and learning. So if there is such a thing as an affordance-based control architecture, affordances will have to play a role in all of its layers.

Second, the answers to the seminar questions do not depend on whether or not the cognitive sciences agree that Gibson is "right" in the sense that affordances exist in biological brains or minds or exist in the interaction between biological individuals and their environment. The point is, if Gibson's description of phenomena of functional coupling between perception and action is correct, then it is of high interest for robot control designers, independent of how it is best understood according to cognitive science standards. Therefore, the seminar would profit from either proponents or opponents of the affordance model. The aim here was discussion and exchange, not unanimity.

The organizers brought together 32 researchers from different scientific communities to attend the seminar. Given that the scientific background of the participants was not homogeneous, and that there was only little technical work that directly fit the seminar topic (as remarked above, there are only relatively few examples of using explicitly the concept of affordances), the program (cf. [3])

was composed of six overview talks centered around the state of the art, serving to inform the heterogeneous audience, and 13 technical presentations of mainly young researchers working in related areas.

Presentations, an abstract collection of all contributions, and an executive seminar summary can be found at the Dagstuhl Web site [3]. Twelve of the seminar contributions have been elaborated as full articles for this post-proceedings volume. Additionally, a highly relevant paper from Alex Stoytchev has been invited to complement the seminar contributions.

The organizers express their gratitude to the Dagstuhl foundation for their support and for hosting this seminar in their exceptional facilities, and to the participants for their contributions and for making the seminar successful and enjoyable. The work of organizing and conducting the seminar was partly funded by the European Commission's 6th Framework Programme IST Project MACS under contract/grant number FP6-004381. The Commission's support is gratefully acknowledged.

September 2007

Erich Rome
Joachim Hertzberg
Georg Dorffner

References

1. IST priority European Commission. 2nd call, cognitive systems, work programme 2003-4 reference (2003),
   http://cordis.europa.eu/ist/workprogramme/en/2_3_2_4.htm
2. Gibson, J.J.: The theory of affordances. In: Shaw, R.E., Bransford, J. (eds.) Perceiving, Acting, and Knowing, Lawrence Erlbaum Associates, Hillsdale (1977)
3. Dagstuhl Foundation. Towards affordance-based robot control. Dagstuhl Seminar 06231 (2006), http://www.dagstuhl.de/06231/

Table of Contents

Interpersonal Maps: How to Map Affordances for Interaction Behaviour

Verena V. Hafner[1] and Frédéric Kaplan[2]

[1] Humboldt-Universität zu Berlin, Institut für Informatik, Berlin, Germany
hafner@informatik.hu-berlin.de
[2] Ecole Polytechnique Federale de Lausanne, CRAFT, Lausanne, Switzerland
frederic.kaplan@epfl.ch

Abstract. In a study of how the concept of affordances could be applied to inter-action behaviour, we introduce the notion of "interpersonal maps", a geometrical representation of the relationships between a set of proprioceptive and hetero-ceptive information sources, thus creating a common representation space for comparing one's own behaviour and the behaviour of others. Such maps can be used to detect specific types of interactions between agents such as imitation. Moreover, in cases of strong couplings between agents, such representations per-mit to map directly an agent's body structure onto the structure of an observed body, thus addressing the body correspondence problem. These various cases are studied with several robotic experiments using four-legged robots either acting independently or being engaged in delayed imitation. Through a precise study of the effects of the imitation delay on the structure of the interpersonal maps, we show the potential of this "we-centric" space to account for both imitative and non imitative interactions.

1 Introduction

In 1977, perceptual psychologist J. J. Gibson defined an affordance as "a resource or support that the environment offers an agent for action, and that the agent can directly perceive and employ" [1]. Even though people are disagreeing about the possible ap-plications of this theory in the cognitive sciences, affordances can be seen as a useful theory of interaction for many disciplines including robotics. Affordances link percep-tion and action depending on the current goals or intentions of an agent. Gibson also stated that affordances are not classifications of objects, but rather a function-centered view, and therefore provide a more intuitive view of oneself in a certain environment or situation. An everyday example for this view are sorting systems in human environ-ments. Following Gibson's theory of affordances, putting a priority on the affordance of an object (e.g. cutting, connecting) is more intuitive than sorting objects by their name or appearance. Humans can also employ attentional processes to focus on the percep-tion of a particular affordance. This leads to joint attention [2] in the case of interaction behaviour.

Most of the research in affordances has focused on interactions between an agent and its environment [3]. However, we believe that affordances are also a relevant concept in the case of the interaction between two agents. In another research, we have explored

E. Rome et al. (Eds.): Affordance-Based Robot Control, LNAI 4760, pp. 1–15, 2008.

a novel framework permitting unsupervised activity classification [4] based on coordination patterns. Here, we introduce and explore the concept of "interpersonal maps", the application of the same idea to interaction behaviour. This concept is defined in the framework of information theory and can be applied in the context of interactions between living entities as well as between artifacts. Although information theory has historically been mainly concerned with information transmission between a sender and a receiver [5,6], several lines of research have focused on addressing issues concerning relationships between information sources [7,8,9]. In particular, it has been shown that the space of information can be equipped with a metric [10]. It is therefore possible to adapt some of the vocabulary and tools of geometry to the domain of information theory. Interpersonal maps are geometrical representations of relationships between a set of information sources.

The notion of interpersonal maps is related to several existing concepts in psychology and neuroscience. To account for early imitation, Meltzoff and Moore argue for the existence of an intermodal mapping establishing equivalence relations between different modalities such as vision or motor actions [11,12]. Such a model suggests that both perceived (self) and observed (others) behaviour could be represented in a shared neural format. Similarly, Gallese has argued that since the beginning of our life we inhabit a shared multidimensional interpersonal space. When we observe other individuals, "a meaningful embodied interpersonal link is established". Gallese refers to this form of intersubjectivity as the *shared manifold space*. Furthermore, his theory predicts the existence of "somatosensory mirror neurons" giving the capacity to map different body locations during the observation of the bodies of others [13]. However, few models try to give a precise account on how such interpersonal or intermodal mappings could be developed.

The approach presented in this article is directly inspired by several methods concerning unsupervised map building recently described in the field of artificial intelligence and autonomous robotics. Pierce and Kuipers present a method for building maps of a sensory apparatus out of raw uninterpreted sensory data [14,15]. This so-called sensory reconstruction method is based on various distances between sensors such as a normalised Hamming distance metric and a frequency metric. Sensors are clustered into subgroups based on their relative distance. The dimensionality of each subgroup can then be computed, related sensors can be projected to form a sensor map. Building on this sensory reconstruction method, Olsson, Nehaniv and Polani [16] have suggested to use the information metric defined by Crutchfield [10] as a more interesting measure of the distance between two information sources. They have conducted experiments with various sensor sets including visual and proprioceptive sensors on an AIBO robot. Related approaches were also investigated by Kuniyoshi's research team [17]. Most of these approaches interpret such sensory reconstruction methods as a way of building maps of sensors in an unsupervised manner. Some of these works make the comparison with somatosensory maps discovered in the brain.

We extend and, more importantly, reinterpret the sensory reconstruction method. The sensory reconstruction method is well-adapted to address processes underlying the emergence of behavioural complexity, but it may be misleading to interpret it only as a formation of a body map. A particular set of distances captures not only aspects of an agent's embodiment, but can also reflect the agent's current activities and the situated nature of its interaction with the environment. In particular, a specific configuration may appear in the case of couplings with other agents or in cases of remarkable coordination patterns, thus allowing the system to be interpreted as an application of the theory of affordances. We will now present the approach in a more formal manner and give results of preliminary experiments showing how this framework can be used in the context of robot-robot imitation.

2 Maps Based on Information Distances

This section reviews and illustrates the basic principles of map construction based on information distances as it is used in several other articles (e.g. [14,16,4]) . This will provide the basic elements for introducing in the next section the notion of interpersonal maps.

2.1 Definition

Distance Between Information Sources. Let us assume that the robot R_X is equipped with n sensors (proprioceptive and distance sensors). At any time t its sensory state can be captured by the vector $X(t)$

$$X(t) = (X_1(t), X_2(t), \ldots, X_n(t)) \tag{1}$$

For any sensor X_i the entropy $H(X_i)$ can be calculated as

$$H(X_i) = -\sum_{x_i} p(x_i) \log_2 p(x_i)$$

where $p(x_i)$ is the probability mass function over all possible discretised values x_i. To calculate it, the distribution of the values of X_i has to be computed with a careful choice of the number of bins (see [18]). A good solution to avoid this problem is to introduce adaptive binning [19]. In such a case, the size of the bins is variable and chosen in a way that maximises the entropy for each sensor.

The conditional entropy for two sensors X_i and X_j can be calculated as

$$H(X_j|X_i) = -\sum_{x_i} \sum_{x_j} p(x_i, x_j) \log_2 p(x_j|x_i)$$

where $p(x_j|x_i) = p(x_j, x_i)/p(x_i)$.

Crutchfield defines the information distance between two information sources as:

$$d(X_j, X_i) = H(X_i|X_j) + H(X_j|X_i) \tag{2}$$

and the normalised information distance as

$$d_N(X_j, X_i) = \frac{H(X_i|X_j) + H(X_j|X_i)}{H(X_i, X_j)} \tag{3}$$

d is a metric for the space of information sources [10]. (It can easily be shown that d_N is a metric, since the normalisation is a scale change). This means that it has the three properties of symmetry, equivalence and triangle inequality. This is its main advantage compared to mutual information $MI(X_i, X_j) = H(X_i) + H(X_j) - H(X_i, X_j)$.

- $d(X, Y) = d(Y, X)$ follows directly from the symmetry of the definition
- $d(X, Y) = 0$ if and only if X and Y are recoding-equivalent (in the sense defined by Crutchfield [10]).
- $d(X, Z) \leq d(X, Y) + d(Y, Z)$

As $H(X_i, X_j) = H(X_i) + H(X_j|X_i)$, $d_N \leq 1$. $d_N = 1$ means that the two sources are independent. In the following experiments, we will use the normalised information distance simply written as $d = d_N$.

The existence of this metric implies that the space of information has a topological structure. This permits interesting development such as the continuity of functions on information sources or the convergence of sequences of information sources. However, these properties are not central for the issues discussed here.

Other information metrics exist like Fisher information used on statistical manifolds ([20], see also [21]). These metrics are usually defined locally. To obtain the distance between two points on an information manifold, integration over geodesics is needed. In our case, Crutchfield's metric can be applied directly without such a relatively complicated intervention.

Configuration. Let us define a *configuration* as the information distance matrix $\mathbf{D}$ corresponding to the different distances between the information sources X_i

$$\mathbf{D} = \left\{ \begin{array}{l} d(X_1, X_1) \dots d(X_1, X_n) \\ d(X_2, X_1) \dots d(X_2, X_n) \\ \dots\dots\dots\dots\dots\dots\dots \\ d(X_n, X_1) \dots d(X_n, X_n) \end{array} \right\} \tag{4}$$

As $d(X_i, X_i) = 0$, elements of the diagonal are all zero. As $d(X_i, X_j) = d(X_j, X_i)$, $\mathbf{D}$ is symmetrical.

$\mathbf{D}$ summarises some important aspects about the organisation of the information sources of the system, by specifying which sources are related in terms of information and which ones are independent of the context in which the information is gathered.

Two-Dimensional Metric Projection. Going from relative positions as they are captured by a distance matrix $\mathbf{D}$ to a map representation where points $\{\mathbf{p_i}\}$ can be placed is a constraint-satisfaction problem [14]. Each couple of points $\mathbf{p_i}$ and $\mathbf{p_j}$ should satisfy:

$$||\mathbf{p_i} - \mathbf{p_j}|| = d_{i,j} \tag{5}$$

where $||\mathbf{p_i} - \mathbf{p_j}||$ is the Euclidean distance between the position of the ith and jth point and $d_{i,j}$ is the corresponding distance in the matrix $\mathbf{D}$. There are $\frac{n(n-1)}{2}$ equations to satisfy. A set of n points of dimension $n - 1$ permits to solve this equation given this set of constraints optimally, but in order to get a lower dimension representation an approximation must be taken. Pierce and Kuipers describe a method used by statisticians to determine a good dimensionality for projecting a given set of data [14]. In the rest of the article, two-dimensional projections are used for illustrative purposes although they may not be the optimal ones.

In order to create a two-dimensional map we can apply a relaxation algorithm. The algorithm is an iterative procedure of positioning the sensors in a two-dimensional space in such a way that the metric distance between two sensors in this map is as close as possible to the distance in the n-dimensional information space. Different algorithms exist in the literature [22,23,24]. Here, the algorithm of Pierce is used since it does not require any information about the relative orientation of connections between sensor nodes [24].

More precisely, the algorithm used in this paper consists of an iteration of two simple steps. Before these two steps, each sensor X_i is randomly assigned to a point $\mathbf{p_i}$ on a two-dimensional plane.

1. The force f_i on each point $\mathbf{p_i}$ is computed as:

$$f_i = \sum f_{ij}$$

where

$$f_{ij} = (\|\mathbf{p_i} - \mathbf{p_j}\| - d(X_i, X_j))(\mathbf{p_j} - \mathbf{p_i})/\|\mathbf{p_j} - \mathbf{p_i}\|$$

2. Each point $\mathbf{p_i}$ is moved according to the force f_i:

$$\mathbf{p_i} = \mathbf{p_i} + \eta f_i$$

where $\eta = 1/n$.

The energy E of the map can be calculated using the difference of the information distances d and the Euclidean distances l of sensor points in the map.

$$E = \sum_{ij} (d_{ij} - l_{ij}).$$

2.2   Example

Sensory data have been collected from an AIBO robot (Sony AIBO ERS-7, dimensions: 180 (W) x 278 (H) x 319 (D) mm) performing a slow walk while moving its head continuously from side to side. The walk was a straight movement performed in an open space (no obstacle). For this first experiment, we tried to limit the influence of the environment on the behavior. Each leg has 3 degrees of freedom, as well as the head. Infrared distance sensors are mounted on the head and on the main body[1]. The recorded sensors were:

---

[1] The robot has a colour camera mounted above its mouth, electro-static touch sensors, paw sensors, LED lights, all of which are not used in the present experiment but have been exploited in other research conducted with this robot (e.g. [25,26]).

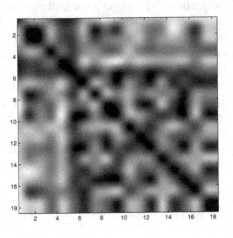

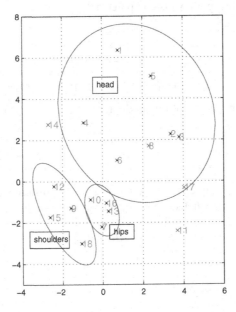

Fig. 1. Information distance matrix and bodymap. The values in the matrices range from zero (dark) to high (light). The mapping from the sensors to the position of the sensors on the robot's body is clearly visible.

1-3	distance sensors
4-6	head (proprioceptive sensors)
7-9	right front leg
10-12	right hind leg
13-15	left front leg
16-18	left hind leg

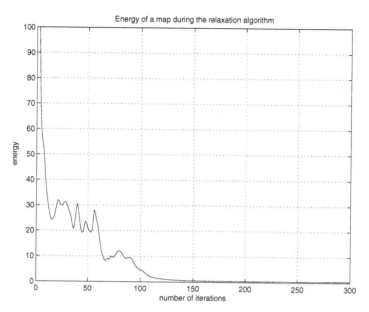

Fig. 2. Energy decrease during the relaxation algorithm

During the walk, 1000 sensor values have been collected for each of these 18 sensors. Figure 1 shows an example of the distance matrix and the maps resulting from the relaxation algorithm using the sensor measurements of the AIBO robot. In this experiment, hip and shoulder joints show remarkable coordination patterns (and also distance sensors and head joints to some extent). Figure 1 bottom shows the two-dimensional map of the robot sensors after applying the relaxation algorithm until the position of the sensor points converged. The decrease in energy of the map can be seen in figure 2. In the map of figure 1, the arrangement of the sensors in the body map already corresponds roughly to the sensor distribution on the body of the robot. Distance and head sensors are arranged in the upper right half of the map, the knee joints of all four legs on the lower right of the map and all other leg sensors on the left side. The exact map depends on the random initial conditions which are different for each run of the relaxation algorithm, but the maps have comparable structures.

The particular emergent organisation of the map results from the body structure of the robot as well as from the behavioural patterns it conducts in a particular environment. In this particular setting, embodiment constraints linking sensor information are probably the most significantly captured (e.g. spatially close similar sensors). In that sense, such maps can be interpreted as a body image. However, for other coordination patterns emergent configurations may differ greatly [4].

3   Interpersonal Maps

In this section, the maps from the previous section that represented both the body and the behaviour of one robot, will be extended to maps including the interaction with another robot. This is applied to the scenario of an imitation behaviour between robots, in which a strong coupling exists. Different interaction cases are independent behaviour, perfect imitation behaviour, and imitation behaviour with a delay in imitation.

3.1 Definition

The concept of a map can be extended to include not only internal proprioceptive sensors but also external sensors such as visual information. This permits to relate in the same format information about the robot's own body with information about other robots perceived through sensors. Let us define the state of the robot R_Y by a vector of size m:

$$Y(t) = (Y_1(t), Y_2(t), \ldots, Y_m(t)) \tag{6}$$

A possible formalisation of this situation can be obtained by supposing that the behaviour of the other robot R_Y is perceived through k new sensors in addition to the ones dedicated to proprioception. The new vector $X(t)$ of size $n + k$ can be expressed as below, where g is a potentially complex function linking the state of R_Y (dimension m) to the perceived state of R_X (dimension k).

$$X(t) = (X_1(t), \ldots, X_n(t), g_1(Y(t)), \ldots, g_k(Y(t))) \tag{7}$$

In such conditions, a map can be built using the same method as the one described in the previous section. In general, the sensors corresponding to the perceived state of R_Y will not be correlated with the activity of R_X, but they should show separated intracorrelated patterns. In such a case, the body schemas of R_X and R_Y should appear as two distinct clusters in the maps. However in some cases, some intercorrelations could be found between the two sets of sensors. This could be in particular the case when the two robots interact in a closely coupled manner, for instance during a direct imitation task. Such maps can be seen as conceptual signatures for the body correspondence problem. We will now show examples of these two situations.

For the sake of simplicity, we assume in the following examples that g offers a linear mapping linking the sensory states of the observed robot to the states perceived by the observing robot. We will discuss this assumption in the next section.

3.2 Example 1: No Intercorrelation

In this example, we used the sensors recorded from the walking robot together with the sensors of another robot it could have observed. The other robot was sitting and stretching its legs and neck. Altogether, this results in a recording of 36 sensors during 1000 time steps.

Since there is no interaction between the two robots, the two sensor groups are not directly correlated. This results in a smaller information distance on average between two sensors of the same robot than between two sensors of different robots. The interpersonal body map in figure 3 therefore shows two clusters. The first cluster has sensor indices from 1 to 18, the second cluster has sensor indices from 19 to 36. The clusters are indicated with an ellipse each that corresponds to the confidence region of the cluster assuming a Gaussian distribution. Since there are only 18 data points per cluster, this is only a rough approximation and serves the understanding of the graph. The

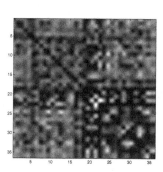 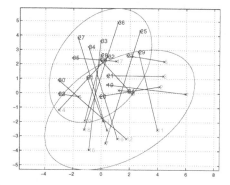

Fig. 3. Information distance matrix and interpersonal body map for a robot observing another robot behaving independently

body schemas within the two clusters are more distorted than the one in figure 1 bottom due to the interplay of the sensors, but a concentration of the head and distance sensors towards the centre of the map is still visible.

3.3   Example 2: Intercorrelation

This example studies the sensory information of one robot imitating the behaviour of the other. In this case, the robots were performing the same programmed walking pattern with a time delay of 10 recordings which corresponds to about half a second (figure 4). In this case, the interpersonal body map does not show two clusters anymore but shows a mapping between sensors of a similar type. Sensors with indices i and $i + 18$ are very close to each other on the body map. In the graphs, they are connected by lines. These lines are much shorter than in the previous graph showing that the information distances between corresponding sensors are small (e.g. X_1 and X_{19}).

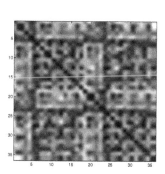 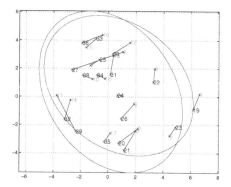

Fig. 4. Information distance matrix and interpersonal body map for a robot being imitated by another robot with a time delay of half a second

3.4 Influence of Delay on the Map Organization

In a further series of experiments, the delay in imitation of the behaviour of one robot by another robot has been varied. The experiments were performed on a robot walking behaviour of 40 seconds imitated with a delay Δ between 0 and 10 seconds. The temporal resolution was again 20 Hz.

To quantify the amount of clustering given the information distances between sensor measurements, we introduced a measurement for clustering, the *clustering factor c*.

$c = (A_1 + A_4)/(A_2 + A_3)$ where A_1, A_2, A_3, A_4 are the sums of distances in the quadrants of the distance matrix $\mathbf{D}$.

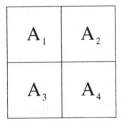

In the case of a single cluster c should be 1, in the case of two separated clusters c will be smaller than 1.

In figure 5, the clustering factor c over the imitation delay is shown. From a delay of about 1s, a shift occurs and c decreases strongly. It can also be seen that several oscillations occur with a length of about 40 data points (2s). These correspond to the oscillation pattern in the walking behaviour. However, the shift in the clustering factor and therefore in the interpersonal map around the imitation delay of 1s is more prominent than the changes due to the oscillatory behaviour.

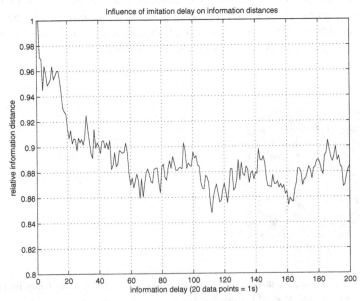

Fig. 5. Effect of the delay in imitation on the clustering of the interpersonal map

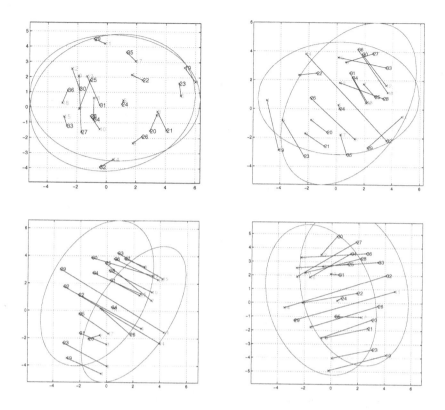

Fig. 6. Interpersonal maps for different delays in imitation: 10 (upper left), 30 (upper right), 60 (bottom left), and 120 (bottom right) data points (20dp=1s)

In figure 6, the interpersonal maps with different delays in imitation are displayed together with the two ellipses indicating the cluster of each robot's sensors as well as lines connecting corresponding sensors between the two robots. The chosen delays in imitation are $0.5s, 1.5s, 3s$ and $6s$. The clustering becomes more clear when increasing the imitation delay up to $3s$, but is similar for $3s$ and $6s$. Please note that these are examples of relaxation maps for the given imitation time delays, but they will look different for each run due to the random initialisation parameters.

As the delay increases, the configuration of the interpersonal map progressively shifts. This evolution can be represented by performing principal component analysis (PCA) in the configuration space (the space of the distance matrices) and projecting the data onto its first few principal components. The points corresponding to each configuration for an imitation delay between 0 and 100 data points (corresponding to $5s$) are plotted in figure 7 using the first three principal components. The rapid evolution for the initial high coupling imitation configurations to a cluster corresponding to low coupling situations can be clearly seen. This gives yet another view of this transition for coupled to non-coupled situations.

These different measures and representations support the idea that interpersonal maps can act as signatures of the types of coupling between interacting agents. For

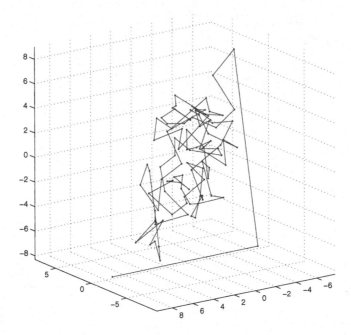

Fig. 7. Projection of the inter-robot information distances onto their first principal components

the present research, we have not implemented a way of classifying these patterns in a fully autonomous manner but we are confident that this is possible although the way to implement such an automatic process would certainly depend on the application considered.

4   Discussion

Our model makes a series of assumptions that need to be discussed. The first one is to separate sensors related to proprioception with sensors related to external perception. In practice, such a clear distinction cannot be obtained. Our embodied perception merges both internal and external stimuli without a priori discrimination. However, presenting the model this way helps clarifying the mechanism we describe.

More importantly, we assume that robot R_X's perception of the behaviour of robot R_Y can be modelled using a function g mapping the state of R_Y to R_X's perceptual state. This is a reasonable assumption in the sense that in some way or another the observation of the behaviour of R_Y can be related to R_Y's internal state. The fact that relevant information about R_Y's state can be reconstructed after this function has been applied is potentially more questionable. In our context, what counts is that some intercorrelation between Y and X can still be discovered.

We must admit that it is likely that g is a rather complex function. Even in that case intercorrelations could potentially be discovered in several circumstances. One possibility is that R_Y scaffolds the interaction to make its perceived behaviour more tuned to its own internal state. It has been well studied that adults adapt to children in order to make their overt behaviour more easily analysed [27,28].

Another possibility is that the biases of g are evaluated by a separated mechanism. More generally, the progressive awareness of self and others is likely to be linked with several other developmental processes. Other embodied developmental models suggest for instance that discrimination based on levels of predictability could play a key role in development of the animate/inanimate distinction and the self/other discrimination [29].

Here, we have deliberately chosen not to focus on these important issues in order to investigate first what could be captured by approaches based on information distance matrices. Interpersonal maps may offer a possible unified framework accounting for the structure of the agent's body schema as well as a representation of the observed behaviour of another agent. In cases of strong couplings between agents, a "we-centric" cluster can emerge in which the agent's body structure can be directly mapped onto the structure of an observed body. The system takes different features into account, such as the body, the environment, as well as the agent's behaviour and actions, thus being a perfect architecture for mapping affordances.

We strongly believe that the dynamics responsible for self-other distinction are tightly related with the ones accounting for the construction of the body schema and that both processes must be studied together. It is also clear that information available in such kinds of maps can have a direct influence on the coupling behaviour itself. Our future research will therefore investigate further the consequences of the structuring of this interpersonal space and the possible usage of this type of relational information in the larger context of robotic control architecture. In other words, we must now "close the loop" and show how such interpersonal maps can be used to structure interactions in return. The present research has explored some forms of bottom-up building of information maps, computation performed using such maps should now result in top-down influences.

Acknowledgements

Research funded by Sony CSL Paris with additional support from the ECAGENTS project founded by the Future and Emerging Technologies programme (IST-FET) of the European Community under EU R&D contract IST-2003-1940.

References

1. Gibson, J.J.: The theory of affordances. In: Shaw, R., Bransford, J. (eds.) Perceiving, Acting, and Knowing, Lawrence Erlbaum Associates, Hillsdale, NJ (1977)
2. Kaplan, F., Hafner, V.V.: The challenges of joint attention. Interaction Studies 7(2), 129–134 (2006)
3. Gibson, J.J.: The Ecological Approach to Visual Perception. Houghton-Mifflin, Boston (1979)
4. Kaplan, F., Hafner, V.V.: Information-theoretic framework for unsupervised activity classification. Advanced Robotics 20(10), 1087–1103 (2006)
5. Shannon, C., Weaver, W.: The mathematical theory of communication. University of Illinois Press (1962)

6. Cover, T., Thomas, J.: Elements of information theory. John Wiley and Sons, Inc., Chichester (1991)
7. Kullback, S.: Information theory and statistics. Dover, Mineola, NY (1968)
8. Tononi, G., Edelman, G., Sporns, O.: Complexity and coherency: integrating information in the brain. Trends in cognitive sciences 2(12), 474–484 (1998)
9. Sporns, O., Pegors, T.: Information-theoretical aspects of embodied artificial intelligence. In: Iida, F., Pfeifer, R., Steels, L., Kuniyoshi, Y. (eds.) Embodied Artificial Intelligence. LNCS (LNAI), vol. 3139, pp. 74–85. Springer, Heidelberg (2004)
10. Crutchfield, J.P.: Information and its metric. In: Lam, L., Morris, H.C. (eds.) Nonlinear Structures in Physical Systems – Pattern Formation, Chaos, and Waves, pp. 119–130. Springer, Heidelberg (1990)
11. Meltzoff, A., Gopnick, A.: The role of imitation in understanding persons and developing a theory of mind. In: Baron-Cohen, S., Tager-Flusberg, H., Cohen, D. (eds.) Understanding other minds, pp. 335–366. Oxford University Press, Oxford (1993)
12. Moore, C., Corkum, V.: Social understanding at the end of the first year of life. Developmental Review 14, 349–372 (1994)
13. Gallese, V.: The manifold nature of interpersonal relations: the quest for a common mechanism. In: Frith, C., Wolpert, D. (eds.) The Neuroscience of Social Interaction, pp. 159–182. Oxford University Press, Oxford, UK (2004)
14. Pierce, D., Kuipers, B.: Map learning with uninterpreted sensors and effectors. Artificial Intelligence 92, 169–229 (1997)
15. Kuipers, B., Besson, P., Modayil, J., Provost, J.: Bootstrap learning of foundational representations. Connection Science 18(2) (2006)
16. Olsson, L., Nehaniv, C., Polani, D.: From unknown sensors and actuators to actions grounded in sensorimotor perceptions. Connection Science 18(2) (2006)
17. Kuniyoshi, Y., Yorozu, Y., Ohmura, Y., Terada, K., Otani, T., Nagakubo, A., Yamamoto, T.: From humanoid embodiment to theory of mind. In: Embodied Artificial Intelligence, pp. 202–218. Springer, Heidelberg (2004)
18. Schreiber, T.: Measuring information transfer. Physical Review Letters 85(2), 461–464 (2000)
19. Olsson, L., Nehaniv, C., Polani, D.: Sensor adaptation and development in robots by entropy. In: CIRA 2005. Proceedings of the 6th IEEE International Symposium on Computational Intelligence in Robotics and Automation, Espoo, Finland, IEEE Computer Society Press, Los Alamitos (2005)
20. Amari, S., Nagaoka, H.: Methods of information geometry, vol. 191. Oxford University Press, Oxford, UK (2000) Translations of mathematical monographs
21. Lafferty, J., Lebanon, G.: Diffusion kernels on statistical manifolds. Journal of Machine Learning Research 6, 129–163 (2005)
22. Hafner, V.V.: Cognitive maps for navigation in open environments. In: IAS-6. Proceedings of the 6th International Conference on Intelligent Autonomous Systems, Venice, Italy, pp. 801–808 (2000)
23. Duckett, T., Marsland, S., Shapiro, J.: Fast, on-line learning of globally consistent maps. Autonomous Robots 12, 297–300 (2002)
24. Pierce, D.M.: Map Learning with Uninterpreted Sensors and Effectors. PhD thesis, The University of Texas at Austin (1995)
25. Steels, L., Kaplan, F.: Aibo's first words: The social learning of language and meaning. Evolution of Communication 4(1), 3–32 (2000)
26. Hafner, V.V., Kaplan, F.: Learning to interpret pointing gestures: experiments with four-legged autonomous robots. In: Wermter, S., Palm, G., Elshaw, M. (eds.) Biomimetic Neural Learning for Intelligent Robots. LNCS (LNAI), vol. 3575, pp. 225–234. Springer, Heidelberg (2005)

27. Schaffer, H.: Early interactive development in studies of mother-infant interaction. In: Proceedings of Loch Lomonds Symposium, pp. 3–18. Academic Press, New York (1977)
28. Kaye, K.: The mental and social life of babies. University of Chicago Press, Chicago (1982)
29. Kaplan, F., Oudeyer, P.Y.: The progress-drive hypothesis: an interpretation of early imitation. In: Dautenhahn, K., Nehaniv, C. (eds.) Models and Mechanims of Imitation and Social Learning: Behavioural, Social and Communication Dimensions, pp. 361–377. Cambridge University Press, Cambridge (2007)

Does It Help a Robot Navigate
to Call Navigability an Affordance?*

Joachim Hertzberg, Kai Lingemann, Christopher Lörken, Andreas Nüchter,
and Stefan Stiene

Universität Osnabrück, Institut für Informatik
D-49069 Osnabrück, Germany
{hertzberg,lingemann,cloerken,nuechter,
stiene}@informatik.uni-osnabrueck.de
http://www.inf.uos.de/kbs/

Abstract. Gibson's notion of affordance seems to attract roboticists'
attention. On a phenomenological level, it allows functions, which have
"somehow" been implemented, to be described using a new terminology.
However, that does not mean that the affordance notion is of help for
building robots and their controllers. This paper explores viewing an affordance as an abstraction from a robot-environment relation that is of
inter-individual use, but requires an individual implementation. Therefore, the notion of affordance helps share environment representations
and theories among robots. Examples are given for navigability, as afforded by environments of different types to robots of different under-
carriages and sensor configurations.

1 Background

Among the most basic properties that a mobile robot needs to perceive about
its environment is whether it can go someplace, i.e., drive, walk, crawl, climb—
whatever its kinematics. State-of-the-art work in indoor robot navigation typically abstracts away from many details of the problem by assuming implicitly
that any area that is not perceived as being blocked is navigable. That works
as long as you make sure your robot stays clear of staircases, glass doors and
mirrors, no drawers out of sensor height are left open, the robot fits under all
table-tops, and, of course, the floor is sufficiently flat for its undercarriage. In
a nutshell: Out of relatively protected lab environments, it is to-day non-trivial
for a mobile robot to determine whether it can physically move to some location
in its vicinity.

* Work in parts done in the projects (1) LISA, which is funded by the German Fed-
eral Ministry of Education and Research (BMBF) within the Framework Concept
"Research for Tomorrow's Production" (fund number 02PB2170-02PB2177) and
managed by the Project Management Agency Forschungszentrum Karlsruhe, Production and Manufacturing Technologies Division (PTKA-PFT); and (2) MACS,
which is funded by the European Commission's 6th Framework Programme IST
Project MACS under contract/grant number FP6-004381. The Commission's support is gratefully acknowledged.

E. Rome et al. (Eds.): Affordance-Based Robot Control, LNAI 4760, pp. 16–26, 2008.
© Springer-Verlag Berlin Heidelberg 2008

Would it then make sense to work on a Grand Theory of Navigability for mobile robots to solve the problem once and for all? Probably not, as there is no such thing as "objective navigability" in the world—whether or not a particular robot can boldly go where it has never gone before depends on its undercarriage, kinematics, geometry, control, power, and many other parameters. Considering as a zoo of robots a B21 with its small hard wheels, an outdoor Kurt3D with 20 cm diameter rubber wheels, a regular street car, and a walking machine, it is obvious that there are tremendous differences. Navigability is a *relation between a particular individual or class of robots and its environment,* much like Chemero [4] has stressed in interpreting Gibson's [9] affordances.

Does that mean that navigability, being something utterly subjective for a robot, should be deleted from the robot programmer's vocabulary? Not either! The concept is generally useful for a mobile robot, just the attribution to some area in space (the concept's implementation, to use informaticists' speak) differs among different robots. As an abstraction, it is of general use. For example, it can be communicated among fellow robots, using a uniform meaning, but relying on different implementations ("Is that area navigable for you?"). If some piece of high-level robot control software is to be exchanged between different individuals of robots, then navigability is a good candidate for an abstract concept that can be used uniformly on a high level of programming or modeling, and that may require an individual implementation or "grounding" on every individual robot.

So this informal essay interprets, from a robot designer's point of view, an affordance as an *abstraction from a robot-environment relation that is of inter-individual use, but requires an individual implementation or grounding.* Whether an affordance is currently present in some environment must be effectively determinable; perceiving it should typically require very little computation, based on available sensor data. The inter-individual use may in particular lie in sharing some abstract, high-level domain model that deals with the abstracted relation. So for example, if navigability of some connected area implies reachability between any two of its positions, then this implication remains true no matter what is navigable for a particular robot.

In the following, we will give an example, using the concept of navigability, of the use and usefulness of this view of affordances. First we give three examples from own previous work for different groundings of navigability; we will point to some other approaches from the literature. Path planning is an example for a general functionality using navigability as a basic concept and delivering different results for different navigability groundings. Sec. 3 discusses our view on the potential view of affordances in robot control. In the end, we summarize our argument in favor of using affordances, in the interpretation just sketched, in robot design.

2   Groundings of Navigability

Every computer program would yield correct results only if applied under the conditions stated in its specification. This holds for robot control systems, too.

For example, the navigation control of a mobile robot must of course be in harmony with its physical navigation capabilities—control should steer it only into areas that it can cope with. Often, the specification what a particular robot can and cannot handle physically and in terms of control is left at least partially implicit.

In this section, we will make more explicit the specifications of the autonomous driving capabilities of three different robot-plus-control systems. We will see that this leads to characterizing three different implementations or groundings of what may be labeled the affordance of navigability.

2.1 Navigability as Free Space in 2D

Our first example is a fast (up to $3.5\,m/s$) indoor robot, as described in detail in [12]. The robot is shown in Fig. 1, left.

As described in [12], its cruise control consists of a simple free-space seeking mechanism: Using very simple fuzzy rules operating on every single beam of a horizontal laser scan, it is determined in which direction is a "virtual roadway" with sufficient clearance (to set the heading), and how far away the nearest obstacle, if any, is in this virtual pathway (to set the velocity). As the involved calculations are utterly simple and the scanner delivers 180° scans with 1° resolution at 77 Hz, fast speeds as $3.5\,m/s$ can still be safely controlled in areas where, at least from time to time, space may be wide open.

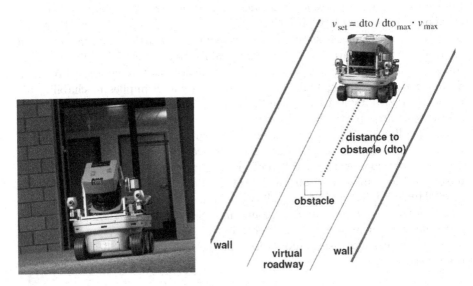

Fig. 1. The Kurt3D robot, images from [12]. Left: The robot platform. During driving, the 3D laser scanner, which is tilted downward in the image, is kept in horizontal position. Right: The "virtual roadway" used for setting velocity and heading. See text for explanations.

Fig. 2. Navigability in 3D for two different robots, applying the same criterion for their respective sizes, rendering from simulation. The simulated Pioneer in front and its bounding box fits under the table-tops; except for the table-legs, the area is completely navigable. The LISA robot (here the base platform with its correct sizes but without additional rigging, except for the navigation sensors) has table-top height, so it can navigate only in the relatively narrow aisles.

In the context of affordances viewed as relations between an individual and its environment, note that the definition and calculation of the virtual pathway does of course respect the width of the robot. Then what does this robot consider navigable, and what are the assumptions behind it? Like in many indoor lab robots, it is assumed

Space is navigable iff it is unoccupied in the virtual roadway.

This implies, in particular, that no overhanging objects exist for collision out of scan plane height, and that a sufficiently flat floor continues ad infinitum, unless framed by an obstacle perceivable in scanner height.

2.2 Navigability as Free Space in 3D

In the ongoing research project LISA [2], a robot platform of about desktop height with an additional manipulator on top is required to navigate safely in a populated lab environment. This includes tables, desks with drawers, wheeled office chairs, and other everyday objects. Part of the robot's task is to transport liquid samples. Therefore, collision with any object must be avoided under all circumstances. On the other hand, the floor is plane and flat with no steps or dents, just like in the 2D case of the Kurt3D robot before.

Under these requirements, free space in some scan plane is, of course, insufficient for navigability: We need to make sure that collision is avoided over all points of the robot surface. Given that we don't have to care about the floor, we assume

> *Space is navigable iff it does not intersect the robot's bounding box in 3D. Additionally,* accessibility *may be required: The part of space in question is connected to the current robot pose by a path through navigable space.*

Again, like in the 2D case, navigability of some area of space may differ with respect to different robot individuals, as their bounding boxes may differ. In this interpretation, it is similar to the configuration space of a navigating robot; this similarity is owed to the example of navigability, not to the concept of affordances. Note that an affordance is something in the robot's perception, whereas the configuration space is objectively given. In particular, it is possible to change the interpretation of navigability in a given robot (if the designer knows what he or she is doing), but it is not possible to change the configuration space just by an act of decision.

Technically, the required 3D geometry information about the environment is calculated on the LISA robot from small laser scanners mounted right above base plate height and pointing upward at an angle. The data fusion takes some time, but given that the velocity has to be small, in particular in the vicinity of objects, the required calculations can all be done online in real time. Figure 2 visualizes the practical difference in navigability of space for the LISA robot (or rather, a planning version of the bare navigation platform) and a Pioneer-type robot in simulation; the physical LISA robot is currently being built.

2.3   Navigability as Afforded by a 3D Surface

Out of flat lab floors, navigability depends, in addition to the absence of obstacles, on the geometry and physical structure of the ground in relation to the robot's undercarriage (wheel diameter, ground clearance, leg size etc.). This becomes an issue, e.g., in a growing number of outdoor robotics projects.

A relatively mild example is an approach to determine drivability of surface for an outdoor version of the Kurt3D robot; for details, please see [15]. The basic approach, adapted from [18], is this: Owing to its 3D laser scanner, Kurt3D builds incrementally a 3D geometry representation of its environment in the form of a scan point cloud; an example of a single scan is given in Fig. 3, left.

In a 3D scan, you can determine a sequence of scan points in the same azimuthal direction in rising vertical angles. If the angle between the cartesian projections of two subsequent measurement points is sufficiently low, then the second point is classified as a ground point. By connecting triplets of sufficiently close ground points (possibly in different azimuthal directions) to triangles, single ground points are enlarged to a ground surface; Fig. 3, middle, gives an example. Note that the ground surface need not be plane, but just "sufficiently plane", as determined by a threshold value of the allowed angle between subsequent points in ground determination.

Fig. 3. Finding navigable surface on an outdoor gravel path scene; figure imported from [15]. *Left*: A single outdoor 3D scan. Note that the path is uneven. *Middle*: Areas (triangles) between neighboring surface points all labeled drivable are shaded in blue. Note that the area in front is very dense with surface points, which are all labeled drivable. Note second that there are some disconnected patches of surface points in and behind the path shoulder. *Right*: View into the model from the same virtual view point as before, but with the next scans along the path registered. Sufficiently large areas sufficiently dense with drivable surface points are filled with blue. (Again, the area in front is completely drivable.) Note that the next scan has been taken too far away from the first to connect the drivable surface areas, so some of the objectively drivable path remains unlabeled here for lack of point density.

The time required to compute this is marginal, consisting of elementary calculations on local data. In particular, it is negligible compared to the time required to register neighboring 3D scans, which, in turn, is small compared to the $\sim 5\,s$ required to record a 3D scan in the current version of Kurt3D. Navigability is handled quite explicitly here. In full detail, we have the following assumption:

> *Space is navigable iff it corresponds to a part of surface labeled drivable in the respective 3D scan, and the robots's bounding box positioned there does not intersect with points in the 3D scan. Again, accessibility may be required in addition.*

2.4   Uses of Navigability

It is no artifact to be concerned about navigability, as can be seen in other work in the literature. As online processing of 3D geometry information is recently coming into play in robotics, it is natural to care about it. [18] is an example; we borrow the term *navigability map* from [8] (where it was called traversability map).

Reliable online determination of navigability under challenging conditions had to be pushed to some extreme in the DARPA Grand Challenge [7]. Consequently, a large part of the design effort of participating teams has gone into designing the sensor configuration and the respective algorithms for road detection (given that the Grand Challenge requires following some desert road rather than driving cross country). See [17] as an example.

Fig. 4. Tough instances of navigability decisions. Photos from the RoboCup Rescue competition, Osaka, Japan, 2005.

Navigability may even be more of a challenge in current RoboCup Rescue competitions [13], where part of the task is to navigate across extremely cluttered and ragged areas. Fig. 4 gives an impression. To our knowledge, there is no work explicitly in this context on determining navigability automatically. The reason is that current robots are mostly tele-operated in competitions and that the emphasis lies currently on physical maneuverability rather than autonomous control. So it is in fact up to the operator to decide about navigability, based on what he or she perceives on the remote user interface. Anyway, the setting presents a challenge for determining navigability, which will have to be done autonomously in the end.

Turning from these somewhat exotic examples back to mundane settings, note finally that differences in navigability in different robots have very practical consequences. Consider path planning. Standard methods work on 2D maps, see, e.g., [16, Sec. 6.2.1] and tools available in [1]. Planned paths are executable only if this map is in fact a 2D projection of the robot's navigability map; if navigability in free space in 2D is all that is needed for a particular application, the two map types would coincide.

Fig. 2 has introduced an environment where considering 3D information does become relevant: Starting from identical positions and heading towards identical target positions, the two robots may have to plan and follow completely different paths, or there may even be no executable path for the LISA robot, whereas the Pioneer may safely execute one. Fig. 5 gives an example for this environment where different robots have to find different paths, based on their different navigability maps.

3 Discussion

Then what does all that tell us about using affordances in robot control? Obviously, all cited work, including our own, has been done without affordances in mind for the respective robots, and there is no point in re-labeling existing control code as providing this and that affordance for this and that robot. So the answer to the question in the title of this paper is of course: No! But the concept of affordances, as exemplified by navigability in the previous section, could help us in another way write better robot controllers.

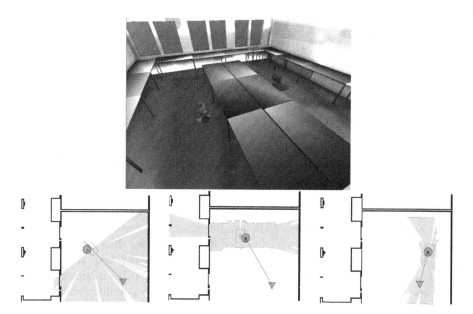

Fig. 5. An example for differences in navigability for different robots in the identical environment. **Top**: The problem is to drive from the shown pose to the target location right to the chair by the tables. **Bottom left**: The Pioneer robot shown in the top image may go straight below the tables. In light blue is the space momentarily perceived as navigable. **Bottom middle**: The taller LISA robot finds the direct path blocked (by the table-tops). **Bottom right**: After some exploration, the target position becomes part of perceived navigable space.

There is a recent trend in robotics to augment classical occupancy maps or geometry maps with certain semantic categories. This has been called *semantic mapping*, e.g., in [14], and it bears many resemblances to the classical AI problem of scene understanding or recognition [10, Sec. 16.6], to recent work on cognitive vision [5], and to symbol grounding [11] in full generality or in its more modest variant of perceptual anchoring [6].

Navigability maps, as presented in the previous section, are instances of semantic maps, if these are defined as *geometric maps that augment the geometric information by labels of data in the map* [14, p.2] – the labeling here being in terms of affordances like "navigable". Interestingly, this label is attached to no segmented object, but to part of the environment, namely, to space nearby that appears to be navigable according to the (mostly implicit) navigability definition. For the historically minded, this seems to resemble Gibson's statements that perceiving an affordance does require no object classification (and therefore, no prior segmentation).

Also somewhat in Gibson's spirit, navigability is a relation between robot and environment that is defined in terms of action on the robot's side. In happy contradiction to Gibson's view, making a local navigability *map* out of recent perceptions does of course have a gist of classifying parts of the environment, or of *reifying* a perceived relation into a classification, to use the term from knowledge representation.

What happens here is this: The robot designer has typically put much effort into making very fast the data processing that leads to the decision "navigable" or not for the particular robot – or graspable, pushable, kickable, whatever the robot's purpose in life requires. By reifying the response of these carefully tuned perception processes, a small constituent of a symbolic scene description is generated. This generation runs on-line on-board the robot, and it comes practically for free, given it is done anyway in the robot control. In a nutshell, we are solving an instance of the symbol grounding problem here *en passant*, the symbol being the rerified robot-environment relation "navigable". Given that symbol grounding is known to be one of the deep, big, and hard AI problems: Why is it so easy here?

The answer is: We have turned the symbol grounding problem upside down (or upside up insofar as it was upside down before). Rather than attempting to recognize a given symbol in the sensor data, we have started from some sensor data processing that our robot can do efficiently and reliably, as its inner control cycle relies on it, and we have then labeled its result with a telling symbol, e.g., navigability.

Is this cheating? No, as we don't claim that the robot has "invented" some new concept by itself – all creativity and insight remains on the robot designer's side.

Is it good for something? Yes, if you accept (like all the researchers in semantic mapping appear to do) that symbolic environment models may help improve robot performance, communication, robustness and engineering, then a symbol like navigability appears to be as good as others – maybe even better, as it is closely connected with the robot performance. Our argument here is to build a robot environment ontology using reified affordances, like navigability, as part of the ground concepts. Other examples of environment categories for a mobile robot might be

Recognizability: The presence of some minimal amount of reliable features or a stable appearance for its particular sensor configuration and on-line processing capabilities;

Speedability: The property of some area of being traversed with high speed (high clearance and low curvature requirements permitting);

Odometribility: The property of some area (which has to be physically traversed to determine this) of producing a low error for the used forward kinematic model on which odometry is based (high grip, low curvature needs)

Many more of the same spirit are envisable. Clearly, an environment ontology using such concepts would be different from one based exclusively on human-centered concepts. But note that these concepts are well-defined, given that they rely on the algorithms and calculations that are part of the human-made robot design. They offer themselves as a basis for an inter-individual part of a domain ontology (which will also normally be human-made): Assuming every robot has its own implementation of these environment categories based on the respective affordances, any higher-level symbolic theory in terms of them will then be grounded in the individual representations as the affordances induce. For example, based on a reification of the navigability affordance into a predicate Navigable with the respective *agent* and the perceived navigable *region* as arguments, we can use the following inter-individual axiom

$$\text{Navigable}(agent, region) \land \text{In}(loc, region) \rightarrow \text{Canmoveto}(agent, loc)$$

for deducing that *agent* can move to location *loc* (assuming the intuitive meanings of all terms invented here). Note that the Canmoveto predicate naturally involves the agent. In harmony with the navigability affordance, it has to be agent-dependent, since it allows for different agent-specific implementations of the underlying action – may it be driving, walking, crawling, or whatever. The In predicate is agent-independent, of course, representing a general spatial relation. (It may be necessary or useful to give the Navigable and Canmoveto predicates another argument for time or situation, as they may be time-varying. This is out of the scope of the simple example here.)

There are singular examples in the literature where properties like the ones named have been used for tackling particular problems in robot control; for example, something similar to speedability has been used in [3] for improving the estimation of the time needed for completing a list of delivery tasks. Environment theories or ontologies using such reified robot-environment relations, whose individual grounding comes nearly for free in every individual robot controller, do not seem to exist yet.

4   Conclusion

So it does *not* help a robot navigate to call navigability an affordance – not too surprising. However, every efficient robot control system includes highly tuned sensor data processing modules whose purpose it is to perceive within short control cycle times particular robot-environment relations that are necessary for the robot's intended function: navigability has been the running example for such a relation in this essay.

It may or may not be in Gibson's spirit to call these relations affordances. Anyway, their reifications seem to offer some potential for a particular form of symbol grounding in robot control – in fact, the grounding is given, all that needs to be done is define fitting and useful robot domain theories or ontologies making use of the respective concepts. We have no such robot domain theory or ontology yet. We are just convinced they would make sense.

References

1. The player project (2006), http://playerstage.sourceforge.net/
2. Project LISA (2006), http://www.inf.uos.de/kbs/LISA.html
3. Belker, T., Beetz, M., Cremers, A.B.: Learning of plan execution policies for indoor navigation. AI Communications 15(1), 3–16 (2002)

4. Chemero, A.: An outline of a theory of affordances. Ecological Psychology 15(2), 181–195 (2003)
5. Christensen, H.I., Nagel, H.-H. (eds.): Cognitive Vision Systems. LNCS, vol. 3948. Springer, Heidelberg (2006)
6. Special issue: Perceptual anchoring. J. Robotics and Autonomous Systems 43(2-3) (2003)
7. DARPA. Grand challenge 2005 – harnessing american ingenuity (2005), http://www.grandchallenge.org/
8. Doherty, P.: Personal communication (2006)
9. Gibson, J.J.: The Ecological Approach to Visual Perception. Houghton Mifflin, Boston, MA (1979)
10. Ginsberg, M.: Essentials of Artificial Intelligence. Morgan Kaufmann, San Mateo, CA (1993)
11. Harnad, S.: The symbol grounding problem. Physica D 42, 335–346 (1990)
12. Lingemann, K., Nüchter, A., Hertzberg, J., Surmann, H.: About the control of high speed mobile indoor robots. In: ECMR 2005. Proc. 2nd Europ. Conf. Mobile Robotics, pp. 218–223 (2005)
13. NIST. Urban search and rescue robot competitions and arenas (2006), robotarenas.nist.gov/competitions.htm
14. Nüchter, A.: Semantische dreidimensionale Karten für autonome mobile Roboter. PhD thesis, Bonn University, Inst. f. Informatics (May 2006)
15. Nüchter, A., Lingemann, K., Hertzberg, J.: Extracting drivable surfaces in outdoor 6D SLAM. In: ISR 2006. 7nd Intl. Symposium on Robotics and 4th German Conf. Robotik 2006 (2006)
16. Siegwart, R., Nourbakhsh, I.R.: Introduction to Autonomous Mobile Robots. MIT Press, Cambridge, MA (2004)
17. Thrun, S., Montemerlo, M., Dahlkamp, H., Stavens, D., Aron, A., Diebel, J., Fong, P., Gale, J., Halpenny, M., Hoffmann, G., Lau, K., Oakley, C., Palatucci, M., Pratt, V., Stang, P., Strohband, S., Dupont, C., Jendrossek, L.-E., Koelen, C., Markey, C., Rummel, C., van Niekerk, J., Jensen, E., Alessandrini, P., Bradski, G., Davies, B., Ettinger, S., Kaehler, A., Nefian, A., Mahoney, P.: Stanley: The robot that won the DARPA Grand Challenge. J. Field Robotics 23(9), 661–692 (2006)
18. Wulf, O., Arras, K.O., Christensen, H.I., Wagner, B.A.: 2D Mapping of Cluttered Indoor Environments by Means of 3D Perception. In: ICRA 2004. Proc. IEEE Int. Conf. Robotics and Automation, pp. 4204–4209 (April 2004)

Learning Causality and Intentional Actions*

Somboon Hongeng and Jeremy Wyatt

School of Computer Science
University of Birmingham
Edgbaston, B15 2TT, United Kingdom
{s.hongeng,j.l.wyatt}@cs.bham.ac.uk

Abstract. Previous research has shown that human actions can be detected and classified using their motion patterns. However, simply labelling motion patterns is not sufficient in a cognitive system that requires the ability to reason about the agent's intentions, and also to account for how the environmental setting (e.g. the presence of nearby objects) affects the way an action is performed. In this paper, we develop a graphical model that captures how the low level movements that form a high level intentional action (e.g. reaching for an object) vary depending on the situation. We then present statistical learning algorithms that are able to learn characterisations of specific actions from video using this representation. Using object manipulation tasks, we illustrate how the system infers an agent's goals from visual information and compare the results with findings in psychological experiments. In particular we show that we are able to reproduce a key result from the child development literature on action learning in children. This provides support for our model having properties in common with action learning in humans. At the end of the paper we argue that our action representation and learning model is also suitable as a framework for understanding and learning about affordances. An important element of our framework is that it will allow affordances to be understood as indicative of possible intentional actions.

1 Introduction

There has been increasing interest in recent years in the development of systems that are able to recognise human actions. Our goal is to develop such systems for use as part of a cognitive system such as a robot assistant. Such a robot requires the ability not only to recognise human actions with objects, but also to learn to recognise new actions. Moreover, a truly flexible robot needs to able to characterise actions so that it can distinguish what is an essential component of the action, and what is superfluous. One way to achieve this is to separate the high level intention of the human in acting to achieve the goal from the precise low level movements of body and objects required to achieve that intention. In this paper we present a model containing just such a division.

---

* This research was supported by the EU FP6 IST Cognitive Systems Integrated Project Cognitive Systems for Cognitive Assistants "CoSy" FP6-004250-IP.

E. Rome et al. (Eds.): Affordance-Based Robot Control, LNAI 4760, pp. 27–46, 2008.

In this paper we assume that our primary source of information is visual, the robot must be able to learn about and recognise actions from video sequences. There are a number of existing approaches for learning and recognition from video sequences. Probabilistic graphical models such as Bayesian Belief Networks [4], hidden Markov models (HMM) and their extensions [10,5] are one class of approaches already widely used to encode, detect and label patterns of trajectories and motion vectors (often in an image space or on a 2D ground plane). However, labelling motion patterns alone is not sufficient to reason about the agent's intentions, or to understand how the shape of an object, and the environmental setting affect the way an action is performed or what its results are. This leads in turn to the issue of affordances, which we think of as features that are easily computable functions of images, and that reliably indicate a possibility for an intentional action, and perhaps allow us to modulate or control that action. In this paper we will not show how to learn affordances, but we will argue that affordance learning needs to be integrated with learning about actions.

In this paper, we develop a cognitive vision system designed to be part of a robot system that will interact with a human agent who manipulates objects on a table top (e.g., "grasping", "pushing"). Object manipulation is considered to be goal-directed and we have developed a probabilistic graphical action model that explicitly represents the causal links between the agent's goals, its hand movements, and the scene structure. Such graphical structures allow us to factorize features computed for a given sequence into hand motion features and environment state features. During the course of manipulative actions that achieve a goal state g^i (which is pre-determined during the training), there can be many hand manoeuvring acts a, which depend on the state s of the environment. We generate training data by performing an action in different environmental conditions. For example, to get to the state g^i where the hand is near the object, "reaching for an object" is performed while there are varying number of objects nearby that may cause collision if the hand directly moves to the target. From the training sequences, we learn the optimal feature sets with the most discriminative power and cluster them into classifiers for a and s. We then learn the goal-specific action selection policy by constructing causal networks between a and s based on the estimation of causal strength.

After training, an action goal g^i is recognized in a Bayesian formalism by accumulating the evidence at each time frame that the agent's choice of hand manoeuvre a matches with the choice one would make to achieve the goal g^i given the observed world state s. At the end of the paper, we present some preliminary results for both action learning and recognition. We believe that while HMMs and other pattern-based action representations may be used to detect these actions, action representations that integrate goal-specific action selection policies are more suitable to a cognitive system that requires reasoning about intentions and object affordances [1].

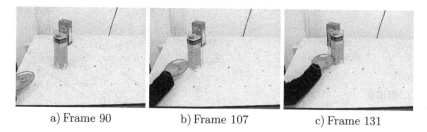

a) Frame 90   b) Frame 107   c) Frame 131

Fig. 1. Pushing steps in "Reach for-Push-Retract" sequence

2   System Overview

Figure 1 shows the environment that we use to train and analyze action sequences. It involves an agent, his hand, two inanimated objects, and a table top, which are collectively called objects when no specific context is given. Objects to be manipulated have approximately simple geometric shapes (e.g., rectangular) and distinctive color distributions. In this paper, we assume that actions of our interest are perceived based on changes of 3D object poses and relations in the scene. We capture actions with two static cameras (frontal and side views) generating two synchronized video streams, from which rough estimates of the 3D object poses can be obtained by triangulation. We note that it is possible to obtain 3D scene information with varying degrees of accuracy using other camera configurations. For example, a 3D model of a textured object can be partially reconstructed from a stereo rig using standard stereopsis or from a mobile single-camera setting using Structure from Motion. For learning simple object manipulation, we found that rough estimates of 3D poses are sufficient.

We consider an intentional action to be composed of action steps, each of which is executed such that the precondition of the succeeding step is achieved. In general, the goal of an action step is observable as one or more scene features (e.g., object relations) that occur at the end of the step. For instance, if the action were "push a box", an agent may reach out his hand toward a box (Fig. 1(a)), such that the hand becomes close enough to make contact with the box. While there are various ways of making contact through grasping, touching, etc., in Fig. 1, he moves his hand further to touch the middle of the box (Fig. 1(b)). Given that the hand is now in contact with the box, moving the hand forward makes the box translate and change its location (Fig. 1(c)). We are interested in developing a system that learns the models of these kinds of actions. After training, the system should be able to recognize an instance of actions in a different environment, and also predict what will happen at the end of an action step. We also expect that the system could be used for exploratory action planning in a robot.

Figure 2 shows the overview of our action analysis system. From the video streams, we detect and track objects (including hands) to obtain 3D bounding boxes and 2D shapes in each view. At each frame t, visual features of the scene O_t are computed based on quantization of attributes related to object motion

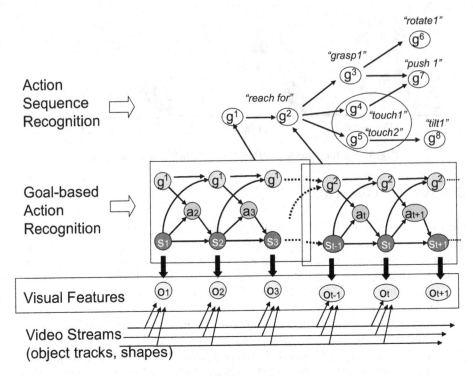

Fig. 2. System architecture

and poses, as well as inter-object relations. An action step (e.g., "reach for") is modeled using a causal graphical model (shown as a graph in a rectangular box in Fig 2) consisting of three types of nodes (g an agent's goal, a a hand maneuvering act, and s a world state). Scene features O provide visual evidence for recognizing these nodes as represented collectively by thick arrows towards visual features. For example, features representing motion vectors of the hand provide evidence for hand maneuvering acts. More complex features that represent relative locations and orientations of the hand, the target object and other landmark objects provide evidence for a world state (or a snapshot of scene configuration). The links between nodes in the graphical models illustrate how we assume an agent acts during $t = 0, ..., t_{g^i}$ to achieve a goal g^i. At time t, the agent chooses to perform a maneuvering act a_t. We assume that the agent not only bases this decision on the desire to achieve the goal g^i, but also considers the environmental state s_{t-1}. For example, while trying to reach for an object, the agent also needs to avoid collision with other objects. As a result of a_t, s_t changes to s_{t+1}. This process is repeated until the relevant part of the world state $s_{t_{g^i}}$ satisfies g^i, at which point the agent switches to another another action to achieve goal g^{i+1}. The network of goals (NG) above the boxes shows various possible human behaviors, in which a human acts to achieve one goal after another. For instance, an agent may reach out his hand for a mug (i.e., *reachfor*), and then touch the top part (*touch*$_2$). At this point, if the agent moves his hand further, the mug will lean forward (*tilt*$_1$) due to the fact that the contact point is high. Alternatively, if the agent touches the middle of the mug (*touch*$_1$), the mug may be pushed away (*push*$_1$).

Our action recognition algorithm is based on a Bayesian formalism, in which probability distributions are defined over all possible acts, environmental states, and action selection policies for a given graphical casual network g^i (shown in the box). Across time frame t, we gather and combine the evidence for g^i by computing $P(a_t|O_t)$ and $P(s_t|O_t)$ and combining them with $P(a_t|s_t, g^i)$ and $P(s_{t+1}|s_t, a_t)$. In Section 4.3, we describe how to learn the structure and parameters of the g^i network. While not the focus of this paper, the system also learns to expand the NG ontology for sequences of actions from the individually learned action models.

3 Detecting and Tracking Objects

Our approach to modelling a hand that is performing certain actions such as picking up a mug is based on the 3D trajectories and change of orientation of objects during the course of action. This section explains our two-view (frontal and side) object tracking system, where our goal is to track and reconstruct 3D bounding boxes of objects using two calibrated cameras. We assume that typical views of all objects (e.g., hand, mug, milk bottle) that may appear in the scene are known. This allows us to learn object-specific color distributions and to make assumptions about shapes.

Our tracking algorithm begins by tracking objects in each view independently based on Particle Filtering (PF) [6]. In both views, hand and mug are represented as an ellipsoid blob with 5 parameters, and the milk bottle as a rectangular blob with 5 parameters. These 5D variables constitute the object state spaces. In PF-based probabilistic tracking, the probability distribution over the object state space is represented by point mass and can be propagated and updated dynamically by a weighted resampling technique, allowing for accurate, on-line modelling of the non-linearity and non-Gaussianess of the dynamics. An object is tracked by finding the most likely state, where the likelihood of an object state is evaluated based on color and shape outlines. The PF-based tracking results are shown for the side view in Fig. 1. We successfully tracked all objects throughout the video in spite of 2D rigid motion and a small change in scale and color. However, tracking was not successful when the hand moved too quickly and the system located the hand at the same location as the mug or the box of tomato juice due to the similarity of color distributions or ellipse templates. This problem can be solved by using a more articulated shape model at the cost of increased computational complexity. Our probabilistic tracker has also shown to be robust to partial occlusion, or instances where shape and/or color evidence were not completely available.

Given the contours of an object in two views, we compute the 3D pose by projecting a 3D cone from the camera center over the 2D contour on the image plane for each view. The 3D bounding box is then computed by intersecting the 3D cones. At each time-frame t, we track all known objects i to obtain the 3-part object pose description : $op_i^t = $ (objId, objType, BoundingBox). We note that the origin of a world coordinate is fixed at one of the table corners such that the x-y plane is aligned with the table surface. As discussed in Section 4.2, the world coordinate system provides a frame of reference (FOR) for computing many features in the table top scene. Later, we also introduce an agent-based FOR, constructed by aligning the y-axis of the world's FOR with the vector from the agent to a location that we assume the agent directs its attention to. One pre-defined, natural attended location is the center of the table, but it could be any object of interest. Figure 3 (a) shows the 3D tracking results of hand and box in "push a box" sequence. The dots and the polygons are, respectively, the projection of the centroid of the hand and the bottom surface of the box on to the world x-y plane. We notice that while the tracking of object centroids is relatively reliable, the reconstruction of the 6 planes of the 3D bounding boxes is highly sensitive to the errors from the 2D view-based object detection (as can be seen from the noisy blue polygons). Such 3D tracking errors are one of the major issues in action detection, where by a probabilistic action recognition framework that combines various sources of evidence (especially from top-down) and averages out errors across time frames can offer an optimal (or near optimal) solution.

4   Learning Intentional Actions

4.1   Object Representation

In section 3, we represent an object by a color and shape based appearance model that is useful for tracking. To learn actions, more abstract representation is needed, which may require high-level segmentation of an object into parts. In this paper, we propose to segment object regions to allow localization of motion patterns on object surfaces, as well as the distribution of contact points of the hand and the object, which can be useful for understanding action and object structures. We first compute the principal axis of symmetry (A_S). The blob is segmented using n control points $cp_i, i = 1, ..., n$, which are uniformly sampled along A_S. For each cp_i, a line is drawn across A_S to partition the blob. In Fig. 3(b), a line is drawn across cp_1, segmenting the bounding box into 4 segments. For each segment, we compute various local shape features such as the average length of cross section, the curvature of the outline, and the distribution of velocity vectors. Other local 3D information may also be included. We describe object features in greater detail in Section 4.2

4.2   Features

Given the 3D tracks and view-based object representations, we compute various features useful for analyzing the agent's behaviors. Each feature is a real value

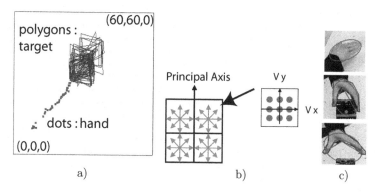

Fig. 3. a) Tracking of hand and box in "push" sequence. b) Segmented-2D blob representation ($n = 1$) and motion vector distributions. c) Hand states.

(between 0 and 1), computed as a response to a Gaussian receptive (G-receptive) field that corresponds to a quantized attribute of the tracked entities. We organize features into four groups: $F = (f_u, f_h, f_{hu}, f_{uv})$, where h refers to *hand*, and u and v refer to two different objects. In the following, subscripts p and m refer to pose and motion attributes.

- Object features (f_u): The state of object u is described by *motion features* (f_{u_m}) and *pose features* (f_{u_p}). For each segmented-blob, we quantize the distribution of motion vectors in each segment by computing its responses to nine G-receptive fields (Fig. 3(b)). These features provide information about motion patterns on object surfaces. Pose features of an object are computed from the 3D object orientation relative to the world's FOR. We project the principal axis of the 3D bounding box onto the vertical and horizontal planes, and compute the responses of the projected vectors to eight directional G-receptive fields that correspond to the prototypical directions similar to those shown in Fig. 3(b).
- Hand features (f_h): We model a hand as a gripper, as we are interested in pose features (f_{h_p}) related to approaching directions and opening angles. The approaching direction of a hand is computed from the deepest defect point of the convex hull of the outline of hand region. Otherwise, the principal axis of the hand region is computed. The gripper's direction is then quantized in the same way as object orientation. Using three G-receptive fields, we also quantize the gripper's opening angle to be either minimal (e.g., when only the back of the hand is seen), average and large as illustrated in Fig. 3(c).
- Hand-object relational features (f_{hu}): To describe the relative position of h to u, we construct a graded discretization of the 3D space around u based on three G-receptive fields with the mean distance at: $\mu_1 = r_u + r_h$, $\mu_2 = sep(u)/2$, and $\mu_3 = sep(u)$, where r_u and r_h are respectively the radius of the smallest ball containing the 3D bounding box of u and h, and $sep(u)$ is the minimum distance from u to other objects (v). The distance d_{hu} between the centroids of h and u is then computed and applied to these three distance

G-receptive fields. We also compute the change of d_{hu} as being positive, negative and zero. Also, the 3D directional vector from h to u is projected on the agent's FOR, and applied to eight directional receptive fields.

Features related to the contact areas of h and u include the shortest distance between the outlines of the gripper and object, and the spatial distribution of the contact region (computed as the normalized overlap region of h with the segmented blob of object u). For grasping direction, we compute the angle between the gripper's direction and the principal axis of the object and measure its responses to the eight directional G-receptive fields.

For relative motion features, we compare the velocity vector of h (vel_h) to the directional vector from h to u ($vel_{h,u}$). by computing the responses of the angle between vel_h and $vel_{h,u}$ to eight directional G-receptive fields. If u is moving, we also compare vel_h to vel_u in a similar fashion, but replacing $vel_{h,u}$ with vel_u.

- Object-object relational features (f_{uv}): For object-object relations, we compute the relative poses (f_{uv_p}) of a pair of objects and exclude multi-object relations. Similar to the hand-object relative pose features (f_{hu_p}), we construct a graded discretization of the space around object v. The distance and direction from u to v, change of distance, and contact features are computed and applied to the appropriate G-receptive fields.

4.3   Goal-Based Probabilistic Action Model

The number of features computed for an action sequence can be very large and we represent the same features in various ways using different frames of reference (e.g., world's, agent's and object's FORs). In a scene consisting of four objects (agent, hand, and two objects), there could be at least 415 features per frame. However, typically only a small number of features are goal-relevant, and there also exists dependencies among them. Taking advantage of this fact, we construct a compact action model for robust recognition.

We propose to model goal-based actions in a Bayesian framework that allows for statistical reasoning in a graphical structure that explicitly represents the dependency between hand movement a, world states s, and goals g (as illustrated in Fig. 2). For simplicity, we assume that there is only one intentional agent and that the agent chooses a_t to execute from a set of all possible acts $n(a)$ based on $P(a_t|s_{t-1}, g^i)$, a *probabilistic action selection policy*. As a result of a_t, the world state s_t changes to s_{t+1} according to $P(s_{t+1}|a_t, s_t)$. This section first describes how to recognize an action, given these action models. Later, we describe how to detect goal-invariant features and learn action models.

Action Recognition and Goal Inference. In a particular environment, there can be many goals $g^i \in G$, and one of the observer's task is to infer g^i from the agent's behavior. Let $O_{1...T}$ be a time series of observations, where $O_t = (f_h, f_u, f_{hu}, f_{uv})_t$ is the set of features computed for the scene at frame t. By applying Bayes' rules, one can compute $P(g^i|O_{1...T}) \simeq P(g^i)P(O_{1...T}|g^i)$ as follows.

$$P(g^i|O_{0...T}) = P(g^i) \sum_{a_{1...T}} P(O_{0...T}|s_{0...T}, a_{1...T})P(s_{0...T}, a_{1...T})|g^i) \tag{1}$$

$$= P(g^i) \prod_{t=1}^{T} \sum_{a_t} P(O_t|s_t, a_t)P(s_t, a_t|s_{t-1}, g^i)P(O_0|s_0) \tag{2}$$

$$= P(g^i)P(O_0|s_0) \prod_{t=d_t=A}^{T} \sum P(O_t|a_t)P(O_t|s_t)P(s_t|s_{t-1}a_t)P(a_t|s_{t-1}, g^i) \tag{3}$$

In Eq. 1, the likelihood is marginalized only over possible maneuvering acts, as we only keep track of the most likely state sequences, which can be estimated at time T. Equation 2 is derived based on the assumption that 1) a_t depends on s_{t-1}, and 2) given s_t and a_t, O_t is independent of s and a at other time frames. Equation 3 is derived by 1) expanding $P(s_t, a_t|s_{t-1}, g^i)$ according to the structure in Fig. 2, and 2) the assumption that features produced by s_t are independent of a_t and vice versa. Also in Eq. 3, A is expanded to be $a_j^i \in n(a^i)$, where $n(a^i)$ are the set of all possible maneuvering acts associated with g^i. Similarly, s_t can be expanded as $s_k^i \in n(s^i)$. In general, we assume that the state transition is deterministic, and $P(s_t|s_{t-1}a_{t-1})$ can be disregarded, when comparing g^i and g^j. An action can be recognized by its associated goal g_i that maximizes $\max_i P(g^i|O_{0...T})$.

To recognize a sequence of actions (e.g., (g^i, g^j)), we propagate the probabilities of actions along the network as
$P(g^ig^j|O_{0...t_{ij},...T}) = P(g^i|O_{0...t_{ij}})P(g^j|g^i)P(g^j|O_{t_{ij}+1,...T})$, where t_{ij} is the time frame in which the goal switching occurs. An optimal t_{ij} can be found by maximizing $\max_{t_{ij}} P(g^ig^j|O_{0...t_{ij},...T})$. This paper, however, focuses only on the learning and recognition of individual actions.

Training. To compute Eq. 3, the system needs to learn $P(O|a^i)$, $P(O|s^i)$, and action selection policies $P(a^i|s^i, g^i)$. In other words, we aim to learn, in Bayesian terminology, hand maneuvering act models $P(a^i|O)$ and environment state models $P(s^i|O)$. Our learning strategy is illustrated in Fig. 4(a), where by a separate model is learned for each action. The network of three nodes in the box on the top-left is a compact representation of those in Fig. 2. The three nodes provide prior knowledge for factorizing features F into two groups: F_a and F_s. Features in $F_a = f'_{h_m}, f''_{h_m}, ..., f'_{hu_m}, f''_{hu_m}, ...$ are related to hand motion and used for learning $P(a^i|O)$ (as shown by arrows from a^i nodes to features in F_a) The rest of the features F_s are world-state features and used for training $P(s^i|O)$ (as shown by arrows from s^i nodes to features in F_s). The dotted arrows from s^i to a^i indicate the need to learn causal networks for $P(a^i|s^i, g^i)$.

Our learning technique is based on causal induction between binary variables. Using a likelihood threshold (e.g., 0.5 for two quantization levels), we convert all feature values (F_t) computed for the positive and negative training sequences into binary features. We note that all training sequences are pre-segmented and the negative training sequences are the sequences whose final states are not g^i. By slightly abusing the symbols, we represent the negative positive and negative training sequences as g^{i+} and g^{i-}. The training starts by selecting optimal

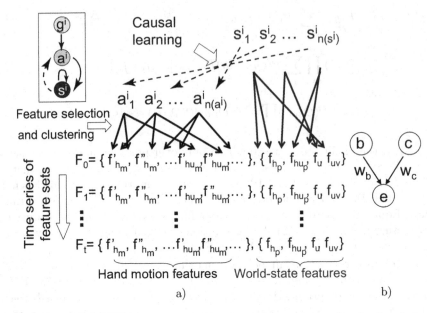

Fig. 4. (a) Learning action models from sequences of features $(f_h, f_u, f_{hu}, f_{uv})$. (b) Generative causal network.

feature sets of a^i with most discriminative power, and then constructing classifiers based on the selected features. We compute the frequencies of each feature appearing in g^{i+} and g^{i-}. For $f_a \in F_a$, we estimate:

$$P(f_a|g^{i+}) = \frac{N(f_a^+, g^{i+})}{(N(f_a^+, g^{i+}) + N(f_a^-, g^{i+})} \qquad (4)$$

$$P(f_a|g^{i-}) = \frac{N(f_a^+, g^{i-})}{(N(f_a^+, g^{i-}) + N(f_a^-, g^{i-})}, \qquad (5)$$

where f_a^+ and f_a^- refer to the presence and absence of f_a, and $N(f_a^+, g^{i+})$ refers frequencies of f_a being present in g^{i+} and so on. The feature f_a is selected as a salient feature for recognizing a^i, if the ratio of $P(f_a|g^{i+})$ and $P(f_a|g^{i-})$ is greater than δ_h, a threshold value. In our experiments, $\delta_h = 2$ has been used. This process is repeated for all features in F_a. After feature selection, we cluster the selected features into $n(a^i)$ groups using co-occurrence as a criterion. That is, features that are frequently present at the same time frame are grouped into the same classes a_j^i. A classifier for a_j^i is constructed based on the Bayes' classifier assumption that all selected features f are independent given a_j^i. $P(O|a_j^i)$ can then be computed as the product of $P(f|a_j^i)$, which is used to evaluate $P(O_t|a_t)$ in Eq. 3. After learning the models for a_j^i, we detect the salient features of s^i that may have been used to determine the selection of a_j^i. Similar to the learning of a_j^i, we perform feature selection and clustering, and learn the classifier for each s_k^i in $n(s^i)$.

Finally, we learn the action selection policies $P(a^i|s^i, g^i)$ by constructing causal networks between a^i_j and s^i_k (shown by dotted arrows). We compute causal power (CP) for each cause s^i_k (or c) and effect a^i_j (or e) as:

$$CP = \frac{P(e^+|c^+) - P(e^+|c^-)}{1 - P(e^+|c^-)} \tag{6}$$

CP corresponds to the probability that, for a case in which c was not present and e did not occur, e would occur if c was introduced (or "sufficient cause") [8]. The presence of a causal link is accepted if CP is higher than a threshold. As have been shown by [3], CP also corresponds to a maximum-likelihood estimate of the causal strength parameter w_c in the noisy-OR parameterization of the generative causal network shown in Fig. 4(b). In this causal network, when both b and c are generative causes, and independently increase the probability of the effect, which is similar to the case where multiple environmental states have generative causal effects on the choice of action a^i_j. The likelihood of the effect given causes can be computed as:

$$P(e^+|b, c; w_b, w_c) = 1 - (1 - w_b)^b (1 - w_c)^c, \tag{7}$$

where w_b and w_c are CP's of b and c, respectively, and $b^+ = c^+ = 1, b^- = c^- = 0$ for arithmetic operations.

5   Preliminary Experiment Results

5.1   Recognition of Intentional Actions

We validate the effectiveness of our causal graph-based action models by recognizing four actions: "reach for (an object)", "push", "pull ", and "retract (hand)". We implemented a total of 123 features, which are a subset of those described in Sec. 4.2. Most features are derived from the projection of 3D trajectories and velocity onto the horizontal planes of the world's and agent's FORs. These features are sufficient for recognizing our target actions due to the fact that the movement of objects and hand occurs mostly along the table top. The structure and parameters of each graph-based action model are learned separately using three positive and three negative action sequences. Each sequence has approximately 20 data samples of hand maneuvering act instances. The learned action models are tested on eight ground truth sequences (two for each action class).

At each video frame, we combine the probabilities of hand maneuvering acts, environmental states and action selection policies, and compute the likelihood of the actor performing a particular goal. The probabilities of the four action goals are normalized such that they sum up to one. An action is correctly detected if the most likely action goal matches the ground truth. We evaluate the effectiveness of our action models based on 1) frame-by-frame detection rates, and 2) the detection rate of an action goal given the observation of the whole sequences. For frame-by-frame detection rates, we obtained the average detection rate of 84.6%, 85.7%, 90.9% and 90.9% for "reach for", "push", "pull ", and "retract", respectively. In contrast to frame-by-frame detection, when probabilities are combined across time frames using Eq. 3, we obtained a 100% detection rate on all test sequences.

Recognizing Actions in Continuous Videos. It is more natural for a robot to observe various actions in a long un-segmented video stream such as "Reachfor-Push-Retract" shown in Fig. 1. Figure 5 shows the frame-by-frame analysis results of this sequence, which match with the ground truth, where by "reach for" (solid) occurs during Frames 94 and 110, "push" (dotted) during Frames 131 and 137, and "retract" (dashed) during Frames 141 and 150. The likelihood of "pull" is never above 0.25 and not shown in the figure. During Frames 111 and 130, the hand either pauses or pushes the object very slowly so that none of the actions are detected. During frames 94 and 110 of "reach for", we notice occasional detection errors (sudden drops in probabilities), which are caused by tracking errors typical of real video analysis. While the detection of "reach for" can be improved as described earlier by combining probabilities across time frames during the action using Eq. 3, the video needs to be segmented appropriately. In our experiments, we rely on zero-velocity frames as segmentation points. When such conditions cannot be guaranteed, computational models with dynamic time warping properties such as a HMM and its variants [5] can be used.

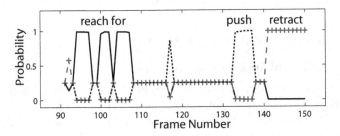

Fig. 5. Analysis of "Reach for-Push-Retract". The four color-coded graphs show the probabilities of action goals.

Recognizing Actions with a Cluttered Scene. Figures 6 and 7 show a more challenging scenario, where the scene is cluttered with multiple objects, each of which is a potential target of interest. Humans can quickly perceive that the agent first reaches for the green ball (object 1), pushes it, and retracts the hand to the initial state. The agent then pushes and pulls the blue bottle (object 2), and then attempts to pull the football (object 3). However, since the blue bottle now locates between the agent and the football (and obstructs the direct path), the agent needs to reach around it. This video shows that the environmental setting can be dynamic and the agent needs to adapt his course of actions accordingly. Variations in environmental settings can also affect the learning and recognition of intentional actions, which we analyze in Sec. 5.2.

Action recognition results of the video in Figures 6 and 7 are shown by bar graphs along the side of each frame. For each potential target object, we calculate the likelihood ($l_i = P(g^i|O_{0\hat{T}})$) of the four actions (from top to bottom: "reach for", "retract from", "push", and "pull") using Eq. 3. For a clear view of the comparison of action recognition results across target objects, instead of normalizing the likelihood values per target object per frame as in Fig. 5, we compute $(nll_{max} - \log(l_i))$, where nll_{max} is the maximum value of negative log-likelihood computed for the sequence. The length of bars varies according to these values, whereby the longer the bar is, the more likely the action. For motion-less frames with zero-velocity (i.e., action segmentation points), the bar length is reset to the maximum. The bar length then decreases as time progresses due to multiplication of probabilities. At each frame, for each target object we highlight the bar with the longest length.

As indicated by the highlighted bars, most actions are correctly recognized even when the agent needs to extend the arm around the obstacle (blue bottle) to reach for and pull the football in Frames 278 and 305. The system, however, fails to detect the "pushing" (Frame 182) and "pulling" (Frame 235) of the blue bottle due to unstable localization of its 3D poses. We note that noise-level in videos is not the only source of tracking errors. Our tracker can become unstable for high-dimensional object poses (e.g., there are 5 free parameters for a box-shape, 3 for a circle), which can be improved by increasing the number and the quality of searches for correct poses at the cost of computational-complexity.

We also notice the lack of attention mechanism in our action recognition framework. This results in interpretation of actions involving each target object independently. In Fig. 7 at Frame 305, when actions are analyzed independently the system also indicates that the agent is retracting his hand from the green ball. While visual features for such interpretation may be present, they are most likely suppressed by the fact that that attention is being given to "pulling the football". It has been widely known in neuroscience that an attention mechanism drives human perception of complex object motion [9] We believe that an attention mechanism also plays an important role in learning and understanding intentional actions. It remains a research issue as to when and how perception of hand movements and state configurations are selectively modulated.

5.2   Understanding Human Intentions

Recent research has indicated that infants as young as twelve months old are able to interpret actions as means to goals and generate systematic inferences to identify relevant aspects of the situation to justify the actions. To account for such observations, Csibra et. al. [2] propose that one-year old infants maintain teleological representations of actions which relate goal states, actions, and situation constraints to one another via the rationality principle. Although unable to represent intentional mental states, counterfactual and fictional realities (which are believed to develop at much later ages), teleological representations provide explanations and predictions for the observed actions based on the principle that goals states are realized by the most rational action available to the actor within the constraints of the situation. By comparison, the links between three node types (a, s, g) in our graphical representation of action, model causality relations and play a similar role to the rationality principle in teleological representations. This section demonstrates the use of our action models to explain precocious understanding of goal-directed actions by one-year old infants.

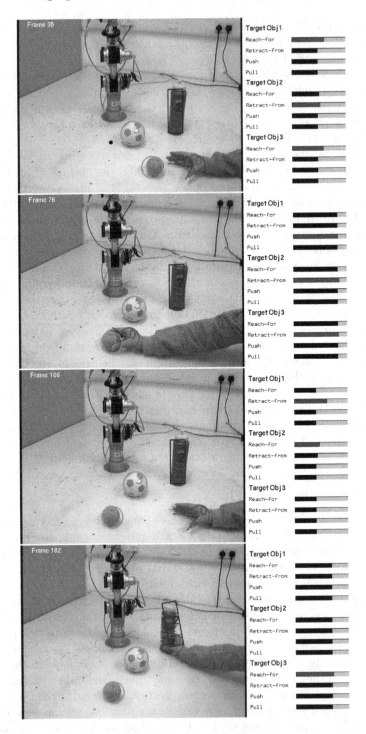

Fig. 6. Evaluating four actions on three objects at Frames 35, 76, 106 and 182

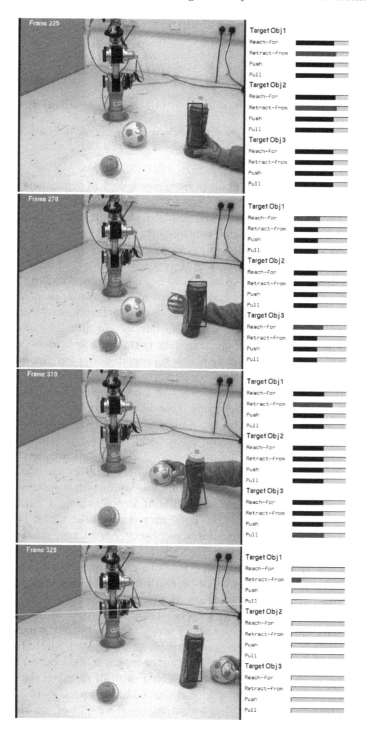

Fig. 7. Evaluating four actions on three objects at Frames 235, 278, 305 and 328

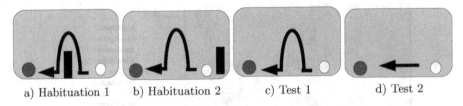

a) Habituation 1   b) Habituation 2   c) Test 1   d) Test 2

Fig. 8. The experimental events to test the understanding of goal-directed actions by one-year old infants

We start by summarizing the findings from psychological experiments by Csibra et. al. [2]. In these experiments, infants were separated into two groups. Infants in one group were habituated to events depicted in Fig. 8 (a) ("jumping over an obstacle"), and the other to events depicted in Fig. 8 (b) ("jumping over nothing"). After habituation, they were shown events in Figures 8 (c) and (d), and the looking time was measured. The results have shown that on average the infants habituated to Fig. 8 (a) spent almost 5 seconds longer looking at Fig. 8 (c) than Fig. 8 (d). That is, they find the event in Fig. 8 (c) more incompatible with their interpretation (or expectation). In contrary, the infants habituated to Fig. 8 (b) spent an equal amount of time (around 1 sec difference) looking at Figures 8 (c) and (d). That is, "jumping over nothing" is considered to be an inefficient way to get to the end state and is represented as a movement pattern executed on purpose.

Instead of modelling the "jumping over" actions, we train the action model "reach for an object". We collect eight ground-truth sequences as shown in Fig. 10 and Fig. 11(a), where by 3D hand trajectories are projected on the world's x-y plane for clarity. The projected hand trajectories (shown as solid lines) are marked with different numbers (e.g., 1,2,3) to indicate that they are separate training instances. The beginning of the trajectories are marked with triangles and the targets are shown by rectangles. We use six sequences to train the models in two contexts, either with or without an obstacle. In a "no obstacle" condition (Fig. 10(a)), we observe the hand move toward the target or make a slight curve. In an "obstructed" condition, we observe curved trajectories around an obstacle (*obs*) shown as a circle in Fig. 10(b). We use three negative training sequences (e.g., "retract hand", "push") for both conditions.

Figure 9 illustrates how salient motion features are selected and associated with a nodes after the training and how the causal strength between a and s nodes is established. The grey nodes with two branching arrows at the bottom of Fig. 9(a) are hand motion features, each of which indicates how the hand moves (solid arrows) relative to the directional vector to the target (dotted arrows). Since the hand either moves toward the target or makes a slight curve, the hand motions corresponding to a_1^i and a_2^i are selected most often given the environmental state s_1^i, as shown by the solid and dashed arrows from s_1^i to a_1^i and a_2^i respectively. Other motion types (e.g., a_3^i) that are the result of tracking errors or random acts are associated with much less causal strength (shown in dotted). The environmental state s_1^i is associated with pose- and location-based features

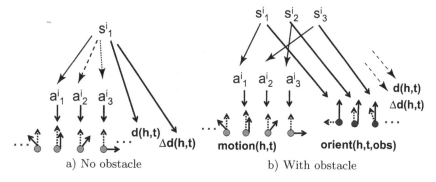

a) No obstacle   b) With obstacle

Fig. 9. Action models learned from two training conditions

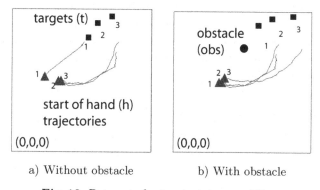

a) Without obstacle   b) With obstacle

Fig. 10. Data sets for two training conditions

such as the distance to the target $d(h,t)$ and the change of distance $\Delta d(h,t)$. Alternatively, when trained in an "obstacle" condition, s_1^i, s_2^i, s_3^i are detected to correspond to various types of feature $orient(h,t,obs)$, each representing a configuration of the directional vectors (h,t) and (h,obs). For examples, s_2^i corresponds to the case where the direct path from h to t is obstructed by obs. These environmental states influence different choices of hand acts as shown in Fig. 9(b). For example, a_3^i (moving the hand sideways) is a preferred choice when obstruction is present. We note that s_1^i includes all cases where the angle between (h,t) and (h,obs) is more than 90 degrees, as well as when no obs is present.

We use the learned models to evaluate the likelihood of two test sequences shown in Fig. 11(a) using Eq. 3. Both sequences are 20 frames long showing a hand reaching for a target object without any obstacle. Figure 11(b) shows the negative log-likelihood of the observed events (straight and curved tracks), given the trained models of "reach for" (with and without obstruction).

As shown by the two bar graphs on the right of Fig. 11(b), based on the model learned from events with the "obstruction" condition, the curved trajectory is less likely (i.e., the bar labeled "curved" is higher), due to the lack of environmental structure that would account for the non-straightness. This is in

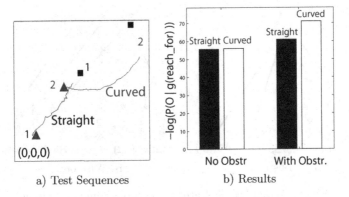

a) Test Sequences   b) Results

Fig. 11. (a) Testing sequences. (b) Recognition of two ways to reach an object: *Straight* and *Curved*.

agreement with the results reported in [2], where by the infants who are habituated to the "jumping over obstacle" events indicate a sign of surprise, by looking longer at "jumping over nothing", as the jumping movement is un-accounted for. When the test trajectories are evaluated by the model learned from events with the "no obstruction" condition, the gap in the likelihood between the two paths is reduced as shown by the two bar graphs on the left of Fig. 11(b). This is because the system has been trained to associate the curved trajectories as an action performed on purpose (against the rationality principle).

6   Conclusion

Our experiments have shown that a goal-based action model can be used for classifying intentional actions effectively in a controlled environment. Arguably, other action models such as coupled-HMMs [7] can also be trained to recognize the sequences used in our experiments based on patterns of coupled-motion between hand and all potential target objects. However, we believe that recognizing actions by action-selection policies enables a cognitive system to better reason about environmental structures and human intentions. We have shown support for it as a model that has some of the same properties as learning about actions in infants. Still, there are other factors involving human learning about actions that are not addressed in this paper.

First, our action representations are based on 3D spatial features of the scene that are estimated using stereopsis. Extracting 3D scene structure reliably from visual input is, however, known to be a difficult problem in computer vision and there is a need for rigorous testing to see how robust our action analysis system is against various levels of noise. Second, it is possible that action recognition and understanding is based on different kinds of features to those used here. For example, from the viewpoint of neuroscience features that are relevant to perception of object and movement on the retinal images gradually become more abstract (e.g., becoming position and scale invariant) along ventral and dorsal pathways in the primate cerebral cortex. Action representations that are based on such features (abstract but view-based) would be more biologically plausible than ours, but it is not clear how 3D information is induced from such representations. One hypothesis is that humans do not rely on precise 3D information, but integrate information from other modalities (e.g. proprioception) to enable both perception and action. Finally, perception of cluttered scenes containing *many* objects of various shapes (such as in Figures 6 and 7) requires an attentional mechanism. It would be interesting to investigate when and how attention should play a role in action perception and learning.

Finally we turn to the issue of affordances. Affordances, on a reductionist view, can be thought of as visually derived features that are strongly indicative of a potential for action. Some may be merely conventional, some may concern several objects, some static relations between objects, and others dynamic ones. On the assumption that many affordances are learned by observation, one approach to identifying affordances is to apply machine learning techniques to observed sequences of action. This is our intended approach, building on the model of action we have presented here. We aim to couple the learning of an affordance (the visual features associated with the possibility of action) with learning about actions in general. For us the benefit of a learned affordance in a robot system will be for it to act as a computationally cheap short cut to identifying potential actions and complex sequences of actions. We suggest that the problem of learning which visual features of a scene are associated with the possibility of an action is in general the same as the problem we have solved in this paper: that of learning which visual features of a sequence of scenes are associated with the execution of an action. Of course, the types of features available to the learning system will need to be broader. If we are interested in identifying whole range of possible actions with an object or set of objects then we will need features that describe surface shape. Extracting these from an image using current vision techniques is no simple task.

In this paper we developed a representation of actions, and methods for learning using this representation that enable us to identify the specific visual features associated with an action during its execution. Our approach, as with many learning approaches to computer vision, is to extract a large number of features automatically from an image or image sequence. Having gathered these the system learns which visually derived features are indicative of an action being performed. At the moment our system only learns about visual features taken during the action course itself. The next step will be to show that it can learn which visual features of a static scene prior to the action occurring can be reliably associated with a particular action.

References

1. Bajcsy, R.: Object concepts and action: Extracting affordances from objects parts. Acta Psychologica 115(1), 69–96 (2004)
2. Gergely, G., Csibra, G.: Teleological reasoning in infancy: the naive theory of rational action. Trends in Cognitive Sciences 7(7), 287–292 (2003)

3. Glymour, C.: Learning causes: Psychological explanations of causal explanation. Minds and Machines 8, 39–60 (1998)
4. Gong, S., Xiang, T.: Recognition of group activities using dynamic probabilistic networks. In: IEEE Proceedings of the International Conference on Computer Vision, pp. 742–749 (2003)
5. Hongeng, S., Nevatia, R.: Large-scale event detection using semi-hidden markov models. In: IEEE Proceedings of the International Conference on Computer Vision, Nice, France, pp. 1455–1462 (2003)
6. Isard, M., Blake, A.: Icondensation: Unifying low-level and high-level tracking in a stochastic framework. In: Burkhardt, H.-J., Neumann, B. (eds.) ECCV 1998. LNCS, vol. 1406, pp. 893–908. Springer, Heidelberg (1998)
7. Oliver, N., Rosario, B., Pentland, A.: A bayesian computer vision system for modeling human interactions. IEEE Transactions on Pattern Analysis and Machine Intelligence 22(8), 831–843 (2000)
8. Pearl, J.: Causality: Models, Reasoning and Inference. Cambridge University Press, Cambridge, UK (2000)
9. Tsotsos, J.K., Liu, Y., Martinez-Trujillo, J.C., Pomplun, M., Simine, E., Zhou, K.: Attending to visual motion. Journal of Computer Vision and Image Understanding 100, 3–40 (2005)
10. Vogler, C., Metaxas, D.: A framework for recognizing the simultaneous aspects of american sign language. Journal of Computer Vision and Image Understanding 81, 358–384 (2001)

GrAM: Reasoning with Grounded Action Models by Combining Knowledge Representation and Data Mining

Nicolai v. Hoyningen-Huene, Bernhard Kirchlechner, and Michael Beetz

Intelligent Autonomous Systems Group
Technische Universität München, Munich, Germany
{hoyninge,kirchlec,beetz}@in.tum.de
http://ias.cs.tum.edu

Abstract. This paper proposes GrAM (Grounded Action Models), a novel integration of actions and action models into the knowledge representation and inference mechanisms of agents. In GrAM action models accord to agent behavior and can be specified explicitly and implicitly. The explicit representation is an action class specific set of Markov logic rules that predict action properties. Stated implicitly an action model defines a data mining problem that, when executed, computes the model's explicit representation. When inferred from an implicit representation the prediction rules predict typical behavior and are learned from a set of training examples, or, in other words, grounded in the respective experience of the agents. Therefore, GrAM allows for the functional and thus adaptive specification of concepts such as the class of situations in which a special action is typically executed successfully or the concept of agents that tend to execute certain kinds of actions.

GrAM represents actions and their models using an upgrading of the representation language OWL and equips the Java Theorem Prover (JTP), a hybrid reasoner for OWL, with additional mechanisms that allow for the automatic acquisition of action models and solving a variety of inference tasks for actions, action models and functional descriptions.

1   Introduction

Marvin L. Minsky stated 1986 in "The Society of Mind": "we need to combine at least two different kinds of descriptions. On one side, we need structural descriptions for recognizing chairs when we see them. On the other side we need functional descriptions in order to know what we can do with chairs" [1, p. 123]. These two kinds of descriptions mirror the bifocal perspectives of all agents: the perceptual and the acting view. In the first one, objects are grouped into concepts according to similarities in the sensory input like appearance or shape, we call these a structural concept. The categories of the second are clustered by similarities of their use or function and therefore, we call them functional concepts. Even these two constructs seem orthogonal, there must be a mapping

E. Rome et al. (Eds.): Affordance-Based Robot Control, LNAI 4760, pp. 47–62, 2008.
© Springer-Verlag Berlin Heidelberg 2008

between them in our mind or otherwise we could not categorize things we see into a functional concept like seats.

Functional concepts are based on the (typical) behavior of agents. Imagine, which things we would categorize as seats for elephants as opposed to men, or the meaninglessness of such a category for fish. Action models that describe the preconditions and typical output of an action according to a class of agents are essential for this type of descriptions. Functional concepts fit ergo perfectly to planning tasks because of their relatedness to preconditions of actions.

In this paper we describe a knowledge representation language and a system based on it, that is able to handle structural and also functional descriptions. We exemplify the system by an information agent that performs no action itself, but is capable to perceive actions of other agents and their environment as facts within a given structural concept hierarchy. This suffices to explain the intent and usage focusing on the main idea. The system could easily be utilized for active agents.

To handle functional and structural descriptions we equip agents with GrAM (Grounded Action Models) that provides means for automatically acquiring action models and for reasoning about subsumption of individuals under functional and structural concepts. GrAM provides the following principles.

1. GrAM is a representation language that uses OWL (Web Ontology Language), a knowledge representation language based on description logics. GrAM provides a basic ontology with *GrAM:actions*, *GrAM:situations*, and *GrAM:agents*, as well as action models as additional entities. Domain ontologies can easily be adapted to use GrAM's representational power. To apply GrAM to a particular application domain, we import an OWL ontology and assert that concepts in this ontology are specializations of *GrAM:actions*, *GrAM:situations*, and *GrAM:agents*. Through these assertions, the domain concepts inherit the properties of the respective GrAM concepts and GrAM inference mechanisms become applicable to these concepts. It also provides constructors for functional concepts in terms of action models.

2. GrAM represents action models as sets of Markov logic rules that correlate situation and action properties with a probability distribution. Definitions of action models can be explicit specifying the rule set extensional or implicit specifying a set of executed actions and the situations that the actions were executed in or that resulted from their execution.

3. GrAM provides a number of inference mechanisms for actions and their models which allow for the automatic acquisition of action models, predicting action properties, subsumption under functional concepts, assessing the predictive accuracy of a model, etc. Stated implicitly an action model defines a data mining problem that, when executed, computes the respective set of prediction rules that is the explicit model.

GrAM is the only knowledge representation mechanism we know of that covers action models together with the symbol grounding problem and reasons about them in sophisticated ways. GrAM integrates data mining as a key inference mechanism and provides a seamless transition between action models and data mining tasks and results. Resource intensive inferences are performed in a demand driven and therefore resource efficient way.

GrAM is implemented extending the OWL Web Ontology Language. Actions and situations are specified as OWL classes, action models are introduced as new entities and the extended language offers new constructors for functional concepts. To realize GrAM's reasoning mechanisms we have extended JTP, a hybrid reasoner for OWL, with additional reasoning mechanisms that allow for the automatic acquisition of the explicit representation of action models and solving a variety of inference tasks about actions and action models.

In the remainder of the paper we proceed as follows. The next section introduces the representation of football games as our example application domain. We give an overview for OWL and describe GrAM's extensions including a basic action ontology in section 2 as well as action models and functional concept constructors in section 3. By means of scoring chances we illustrate the strength of GrAM's representation language. GrAM's inference mechanisms to handle these terms are detailed afterwards in section 4. Implementational aspects contain a short guidance, how to adapt GrAM into any agent system (see 5). An overview of related work (6) and conclusions (7) complete this paper.

2   Representing Football Games

For the purpose of this paper we consider a particular application domain: the analysis of games in simulated robot football ([2], [3]). Each year more than 30 research groups participate in a competition for simulated robot football teams in the context of the RoboCup world championship. Each participating research group programs a team of simulated football players that have, at a very abstract level, fairly realistic perception and action capabilities. The competition games are logged by the simulator writing the positions and motions of all players and the ball, and the time stamped referee decisions such as offside and corner kick into log files. The ball motion implied by the ball position data is segmented into ball actions. Recognized ball actions are classified into shots, passes, and dribblings. These data form the observations of a game that are used in this paper.

Building models of ball actions in simulated football games is an interesting research task for several reasons. First, these actions are in several dimensions more realistic than models typically used in AI applications such as AI planning [4]. The spatio temporal properties are often very important. Ball actions have many different parameters: passes can be played hard or soft, deep or sideways, safe or risky, played to different receivers, etc. The effects of actions are typically affected by interactions and therefore highly situation-dependent. The outcomes are typically nondeterministic and the actions have high probability of failing. Many of these features are shared with other physical actions that are carried out by humans and animals. A consequence is that the appropriate modeling of ball actions requires particularly rich representation means.

2.1 OWL (Web Ontology Language)

We represent and reason about actions and action models using an extension of the OWL Web Ontology Language [5]. OWL is a knowledge representation language based on description logics. The basic representational means are classes and individuals, the subclass relationship and the properties of objects. Classes define a group of individuals that belong together because they share some properties. The classes together with the subclass relationship form a specialization hierarchy on classes: the ontology. Properties represent binary predicates, and can be used to state relationships between individuals or from individuals to data values. An example class definition is represented in section 2.3, figure 2 and 3 exemplify the assertions of individual facts.

The selection of description logics as representation language for structural concepts is driven by mainly two aspects: structural and relational knowledge can be naturally described and inference can be done efficiently. The particular use of OWL has several advantages over other description languages. It is specialized for ontologies in the web and proposed as a recommendation of the world wide web consortium. The exchange of knowledge and the use of existing information will become more and more important for all kinds of agents. For our demonstration domain a number of OWL ontologies are accessible through the World Wide Web including football ontologies with information about football players, teams, management, as well as time and action ontologies. We have also included concepts of the upper ontology of openCyc (http://www.opencyc.org/), which offers an OWL export, into our ontology.

As OWL is based on XML, taxonomies and logical expressions can be transformed into hypertext documents for browsing customized using XSLT style sheets. Comprehensive software toolboxes for processing OWL documents including APIs and parsers like Jena are available. Editors such as Protege including browsers for ontologies rendered as graphs like OntoViz ease the creation and modification of OWL knowledge bases. Using these tools, knowledge bases and action models can easily be published in the semantic web in human and machine readable form. Queries to GrAM can be stated in OWL-QL (OWL Query Language) [6].

2.2 Football Ontology

Figure 1 shows an excerpt of a football ontology including the three key classes ball action, player and situation. The graph displayed in UML notation shows subclass relationships and the most important properties of actions, players and situations. Subclass relationships are represented by arcs with hollow arrow heads and properties by those with filled arrow heads. As already mentioned the class hierarchy reuses concepts like *PurposefulAction* of the openCyc upper ontology.

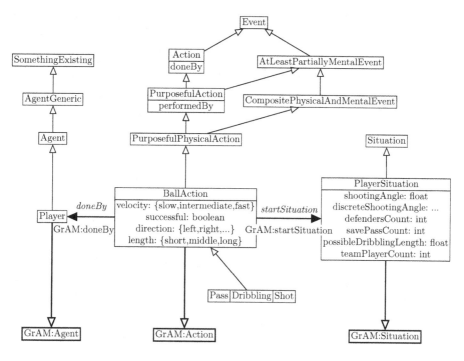

Fig. 1. Excerpt of the ontology representing the football domain and its integration in GrAM

The most important interactions between ball actions, situations and players are the following ones. Ball actions are *doneBy* a player in a *startSituation* that correspond to a *PlayerSituation* observed by the player closest to the ball. Subclasses of ball actions are modelled as dribblings, shots, or passes. Ball actions can be *successful* if and only if the team of the performer of the ball action keeps possession in the resulting situation or that team scored a goal. In addition, a number of parameters of the ball actions are shown as data valued properties like the velocity, direction or length.

Situations are completely determined by the properties *position*, *velocity*, and *acceleration* of the ball and the performing player. To reason about situations effectively we use, however, additional user defined situation abstractions, such as the distance of the ball to the goal (*goalDistance*), the number of possible save passes (*savePassCount*), etc. These properties of (start) situations are typically much better correlated to properties of actions such as the action outcome and are therefore needed to learn prediction models for these action properties effectively.

Figure 2 and 3 show example situations in a simulation league game. Beside an image of the scene the action and situation individuals are stated in terms of the football ontology of figure 1.

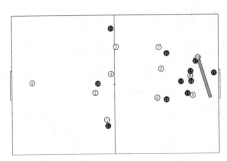

Individual(ballaction256 type Pass
 value(occurs [2536,2545]^^Interval)
 value(byPlayer player10)
 value(successful true^^xsd:boolean)
 value(length long^^xsd:string)
 value(velocity fast^^xsd:string)
 value(direction right^^xsd:string)
 value(startSituation pS2536_10)
Individual(pS2536_10 type PlayerSituation
 object: player10
 position: penaltyAreaAway
 defendersCount: 1
 goalDistance: 16509.65
 possibleDribblingLength: 1912.5471
 savePassCount: 9
 teamPlayerCount: 2
 shootingAngle: 0.5218
 discreteShootingAngle: tinyAngle)

Player 10 passes to player 9.

Fig. 2. Situation in a simulated RoboCup game stated in OWL using terms of the football ontology

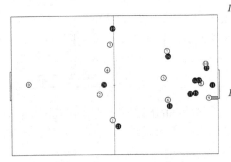

Individual(ballaction257 type Shot
 value(occurs [2545,2546]^^Interval)
 value(byPlayer player9)
 value(successful true^^xsd:boolean)
 value(length short^^xsd:string)
 value(velocity medium^^xsd:string)
 value(direction forward^^xsd:string)
 value(startSituation pS2545_9)
Individual(pS2545_9 type PlayerSituation
 object: player9
 position: penaltyAreaAway
 defendersCount: 1
 goalDistance: 7108.3555
 possibleDribblingLength: 5535.4663
 savePassCount: 5
 teamPlayerCount: 0
 shootingAngle: 6.122713
 discreteShootingAngle: wideAngle)

Player 9 scores a goal.

Fig. 3. Shot at the goal and (successful) scoring chance for *player9* stated in OWL

2.3   Defining Scoring Chances

There are a lot of other concepts in the football domain not represented in the ontology excerpt. For the rest of this paper we focus on the concept of scoring chances. This concept is obviously a subclass of situations. Stating which situations belong to scoring chances in a general form is difficult because of the high dependency of the definition in respect to the player skills. So a situation could be a scoring chance for a professional player but not for a rookie.

In description logics it is straightforward to define successful scoring chances i.e. situations that lead to observed goals if the definition is based on structural concepts only. Let us look to a definition of successful scoring chances stated in OWL. It would have the following form:[1]

---

[1] We use just the abstract syntax in this paper and forbear from spearheading the XML notation because of clarity, compactness and readability, the translation is obvious indeed.

Class(*ScoringChance complete*
  intersectionOf(
  Situation
  restriction(
    startSituation^{-1}
    allValuesFrom(
      intersectionOf(
      Shot
      restriction(successful value(true)) *)))))*

An instance of this class is stated in figure 3. In contrast to this compact definition it is difficult or not even possible to incorporate also the unsuccessful scoring chances under the concept. Scoring chances in their full meaning can only be described in a functional way: they could be defined as the situations in which some football players *tend* to shoot the ball and are *likely* to score if they shoot. The wording already suggests a probabilistic notion of the concept and we need action models, external to OWL, to be able to express intention and typical behavior of players and thus cover the whole meaning of scoring chances. This definition task will illustrate GrAM's abilities as our running example for the rest of the paper.

3   Representation Language

Because of the limited representational power of OWL in respect to action models we need additional language constructs. GrAM's representation language constitutes an extension of OWL by a basic ontology and constructors for action models and functional concepts, which are determined by the behavior of some agent. To equip the representation language with action models, some basic concepts and relations are necessary in advance.

3.1   GrAM's Basic Action Ontology

We consider actions as state transitions analogously to the situation calculus [7]. The class *Action* is therefore related to a *start* and *end situation*. Also an action is supposed to be done by some agent as an intended event. Figure 4 visualizes the three key classes and their relationships with the namespace prefix *GrAM*.

The specific concepts of the domain of interest have to be linked to these classes by stating a subclass or equivalent class or property relationship to be processable by GrAM. This is already done for our football ontology shown in figure 1, the respective classes and relations are highlighted in the excerpt illustration.

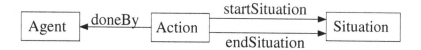

Fig. 4. The ontology representing predefined concepts and relations

3.2   Action Models

The intention or typical behavior of an agent or agent group is represented by an action model. More precisely it corresponds to the correlation between property values of an action and its start situation with a probability distribution. The probability distribution is mostly necessary because of a not fully observable or modelled environment and the nondeterminism of action outcomes. The correlation i.e. an action model is represented as a set of Markov Logic rules.

Markov Logic. Markov logic [8] is a first order predicate logic language where probabilities can be assigned to formulas. Probabilities are stated as weights that specify how strong a contradiction to the individual formula diminishes the worlds probability. Markov logic has the expressive power to represent a wide range of probabilistic representations that can be learned using statistical relational learning methods including decision and regression trees. We will state our action models explicitly in Markov logic. A Markov logic rule set for an action model can be written as

$$rule_j = \textbf{condition}_j \xrightarrow{prob_j} \textbf{conclusion}_j.$$

Thus, rules for predicting properties of actions that are contained in the rule set of an explicit action model have the following form:

$\forall ba.\ startSituation(ba, sit)$
$\qquad \land\ cond_{situationProperty_k}(sit) \land \ldots$
$\qquad \land\ cond_{situationProperty_n}(sit)$
$\xrightarrow{prob}\ actionProperty_i(ba, value_i) \land \ldots$
$\qquad \land\ actionProperty(ba, value)$

The rule states that if situation sit is the enabling situation of ba and satisfies the conditions for the given properties $cond(sit)$ then the action ba will typically have the declared property values with a probability of $prob$. Predictable action properties contain also the type of an action i.e. the membership to a class.

Explicit Definition of Action Models. The set of rules of action models predict the characteristics of actions in situation specific ways. We define for example an action model $exampleAM$ consisting of just one rule:

$\forall ba.\ startSituation(ba, sit)$
$\qquad \land\ \forall x.distanceToGoal(sit, x) \land x \leq 10000)$
$\qquad \land\ \forall x.defendersCount(sit, x) \land x \leq 1)$
$\xrightarrow{0.8}\ successful(ba, true)$

It describes the shot behavior and states that a shot would succeed with a probability of 80 percent in a situation, where the shooter is closer than 10.000 mm to the goal and there is at most one defender in the direction to the goal.

The condition $startSituation(ba, sit)$ is contained in every rule and needs not to be assigned explicitly. In abstract syntax the definition would look like the following:

ExtensionalActionmodel(exampleAM
  withRule(Rule(Body(
    restriction(distanceToGoal lessThanOrEqual(10000))
    restriction(defenderCount lessThanOrEqual(1))
    Head(restriction(successful value(true)))
    withProbability(0.8)))

Implicit Definition of Action Models. The explicit definition of action models can be quite cumbersome because the behavior has first to be analyzed to extract a rule representation. Also even one agent could show different behaviors depending on the environment like the performance of an expert player versus a beginner differs ¿from its performance against an opponent of equal strength. GrAM allows an action model to be defined implicitly by a set of actions and their start situations. This set is assumed to contain observed examples of the behavior that should be described by the action model. The action model is asserted to hold for this set i.e. the model describes the correlations in the given set correctly. To focus only on some aspects of the correlation the situation and action properties can optionally be narrowed down by enumerating only the relevant.

Suppose we want to define the scoring chances for a particular player, say '*player9*'. The specialization of this situation class requires a model of the typical shot behavior of *player9*, the respective definition of the implicit action model has the following form:

IntensionalActionModel(typicalBehavior9
  forAction(restriction(doneBy value(player9)))
  observable(goalDistance position teamPlayerCount
    savePassCount possibleDribblingLength defendersCount)
  predictable(type successful))

This model named *typicalBehavior9* represents the correlation between the stated observable situation properties on the one side and the *type* of action that is chosen and its outcome (*successful*) based on all observed actions of *player9* (denoted by *forAction*) on the other.

3.3 Functional Concept Definitions and Action Related Concepts

GrAM allows to construct specific subclasses of *Situation* functionally according to an action model and a set of actions. A subclass, constructed by this way, contains the start situations of the action set for which the given action model predicts the respective action property values correctly according to a specified threshold. This threshold declares the minimal probability for the truth of the Markov logic rules combined with the action and situation values as facts. So the subsumption of a situation individual under a specific situation class has no probability distribution but is assigned only to a boolean value. That is fundamental to integrate the constructed concept into the description logic which does not deal with probability distributions in its inference. For this reason

GrAM has the strength to handle nondeterministic action models on the one side and to include concepts based on these models in a description logic like OWL on the other side.

Other action related concepts offered by GrAM are agent class constructors and predictions. Agent classes describe agents that show the same behavior as represented in a given action model for a specified set of actions. A threshold for minimal probability as in the definition of situation classes is also obligatory and is used with the same semantics.

Predictions are primarily used in queries to find out which action property values would be typical for a given behavior in a specified situation.

Using the functional situation class constructor we are able to define scoring chances for *player9* as the class of situations that would lead with a probability higher than 70 percent to a successful shot according to the typical behavior of *player9* (defined in section 3.2). The situation class constructor has the following form:

> *SituationClass(ScoringChance*
>   *byActionmodel(typicalBehavior9)*
>   *forAction(Shot restriction(successful value(true)))*
>   *minProbability(0.7))*

To examplify the use of agent class constructors as an additional functional description, we define the concept *ExampleAgent* as all agents showing a specific behavior namely *exampleAM*, which was introduced in section 3.2, for actions in the first half of a football game:

> *AgentClass(ExampleAgent*
>   *byActionmodel(exampleAM)*
>   *forAction(ActionsFirstHalf)*
>   *minProbability(0.6))*

GrAM offers also constructors for predictions, which make only sense as incomplete definitions in premises of queries and are introduced therefore in the next section 4.

4   Inference

GrAM offers not only a representational framework for action models and related concepts but also mechanisms to automatically infer explicit representations of action models, subsumption for related concepts, and predicted values.

The subsumption of individuals under situation classes is inferred by application of Markov rules with a higher probability than the given threshold to start situations of the given actions and by comparison of the produced action property values with the asserted ones. If they are equal, the situation individual is assumed to be a member of the situation class.

The situation shown in figure 2 would be classified as scoring chance for *player9* because there exists an applicable Markov Logic rule of action model *typicalBehavior9*. For example,

$\forall ba.\ startSituation(ba, sit)$
$\qquad \wedge \forall x.distanceToGoal(sit, x) \wedge x \le 17203.732)$
$\qquad \wedge \forall x.defendersCount(sit, x) \wedge x \le 1)$
$\qquad \xrightarrow{0.8}\ type(ba, Shot)$
$\qquad\quad \wedge successful(ba, true)$

applies to this situation and has a higher probability than the specified threshold of 0.7: The closest player to the ball in the considered situation is not further away than seventeen meter from the goal and there are no defenders towards the goal, so *player9* would perform a successful shot in this situation.

Membership of agent individuals to an agent class is inferred in a similar way. An agent belongs to an agent class if it conforms to the behavior specified by the respective action model in all considered actions. The inference process ensures this by verifying that the property values of all actions of the specified set done by the agent equal the ones, generated by application of the action model rules with higher probability than the threshold.

The predictions are inferred also via application of Markov Logic rules. A generated action with predicted properties and the probability of the used rule is appended to the prediction individual and can be queried. Only those values are generated that are predicted by an applicable rule.

Say we want to examine, how *player9* would act in a specific situation named *hypoSituation*, where *player8* failed to score. First, an incomplete definition of a prediction individual is made:

Individual(examplePred Prediction
*   byActionmodel(typicalBehavior9)*
*   forSituation(hypoSituation))*

Then, the most likely values together with their probability can be received. An OWL-QL query to achieve the outcome would be stated as follows:

(and (toAction examplePred ?predAction)
*   (withProbability examplePred ?probability)*
*   (successful ?predAction ?outcome))*

The variable *?outcome* would be bound to *true* or *false* according on which Markov logic rule of the action model *typicalBehavior9* would be applicable for *hypoSituation* to predict the outcome. The probability of the prediction will be assigned to *?probability*, *?predAction* contains just a generated name identifying the predicted action.

For all deductions concerning action related concepts the inference process needs an explicit representation of the action model. The Markov Logic rules are therefore needed to be available also for implicitly defined action models. GrAM is able to extract the rules out of implicit definitions of action models by solving a data mining problem. All observed action and start situation pairs form the training data for that problem. The inference process first builds a matrix filled with all predictable action and respective situation property values. Decision tree learning [9] is applied to these data if action properties are discrete. Because we can not assume the action properties to be uncorrelated in general, the prediction of action property values is not learned separately for every property but at once. The learned decision tree is flattened to rules that belong to every possible path in the tree, taking the conjunction of the inner nodes as condition and the leaf as conclusion. The corresponding probability value is computed by multiplying confidence and support of the classification in the leaf (which can also be transformed to Markov logic weights). For continuous action properties GrAM infers the rules by REPTree regression tree learning [10] and analogous transformation of the resulting tree.

The mentioned inference mechanisms in combination with a calculus for OWL are sound in respect to the defined semantics of the concepts. Completeness, however, can not be ensured because of the rule generation process by data mining, where a lot of rule sets that holds for the training data exist but only one specific is mined.

We provided the introduced inference mechanisms by extending a theorem prover for first order logics called Java Theorem Prover (JTP). JTP is an object-oriented modular hybrid reasoning system implemented in Java [11]. It has a simple and general reasoning architecture consisting of modules called reasoners. The modular character of the architecture makes it easy to extend the system by adding new reasoners. JTP is equipped with special purpose reasoners for OWL expressions and knowledge bases, satisfiability in interval temporal logics, and others.

We have added inference mechanisms for action models in the form of reasoners. Namely we have equipped JTP with reasoners for solving data mining tasks, prediction by data mining models, and subsumption of individuals under functionally defined and action related concepts.

All inferences in GrAM including the generation of the explicit rule form are computed in a lazy manner or on demand. That is the respective data mining tasks are only solved if the respective explicit model has been queried directly or indirectly.

5   Work with GrAM

Starting from an existing knowledge base of an application domain which contains an ontology and facts, GrAM offers an easy way to build an information system based on this knowledge, that can be integrated into agent systems. The implemented system architecture of GrAM is shown schematically in figure 5. To adapt a domain to GrAM, the domain ontology has to be linked to GrAM's action ontology (see the arrow marked with 1 in figure 5). The facts representing the observed agent behaviors and additional knowledge can be transferred without modification (see arrow 2). Facts and extended ontology form the knowledge base of an information system, which offers a web service interface to answer queries. The answer is inferred by GrAM's inference mechanisms including data mining and Markov rule application (see arrows 3 and 4). The web service interface via SOAP over HTTP offers a flexible interface independent of programming languages and platforms.

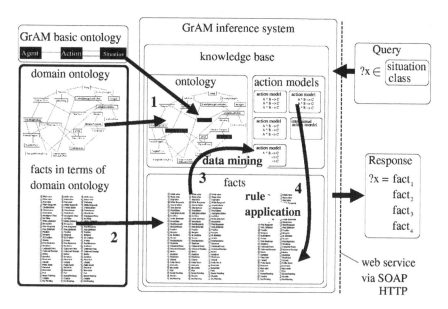

Fig. 5. GrAM's system architecture

We implemented a servlet as graphical user interface to GrAM, that can be used for human interaction with GrAM. A screen shot of a web browser showing the query input mask is depicted in figure 6.

6 Related Work

Our research on GrAM is part of a larger research effort in which we investigate computational models of embedded intelligent systems that "know what they are doing" [12]. Having action models that cover a wide range of behavior and its rationale is a necessary capability of such systems. Research on action modeling has been mainly performed in the area of reasoning about action using first-order predicate and nonmonotonic logics [13]. Those representations have only covered a small subset of the models proposed here. Symbolically specified action models yield the so-called symbol grounding problem: assigning meaning to symbols based on perception and action mechanisms of agents. While symbol grounding is not addressed in this research branch GrAM proposes a solution for it consisting of implicit and explicit action models.

The acquisition of models of physical actions has so far received surprisingly little attention. Oates et al. [14] have learned models of action effects expressed in the sensor data space. Pasula et al [15] learn probabilistic Strips like rules from examples. Stulp and Beetz [16] use learned performance models in order to optimize chains of abstract actions. This branch of research does not focus on the representational issues of model acquisition.

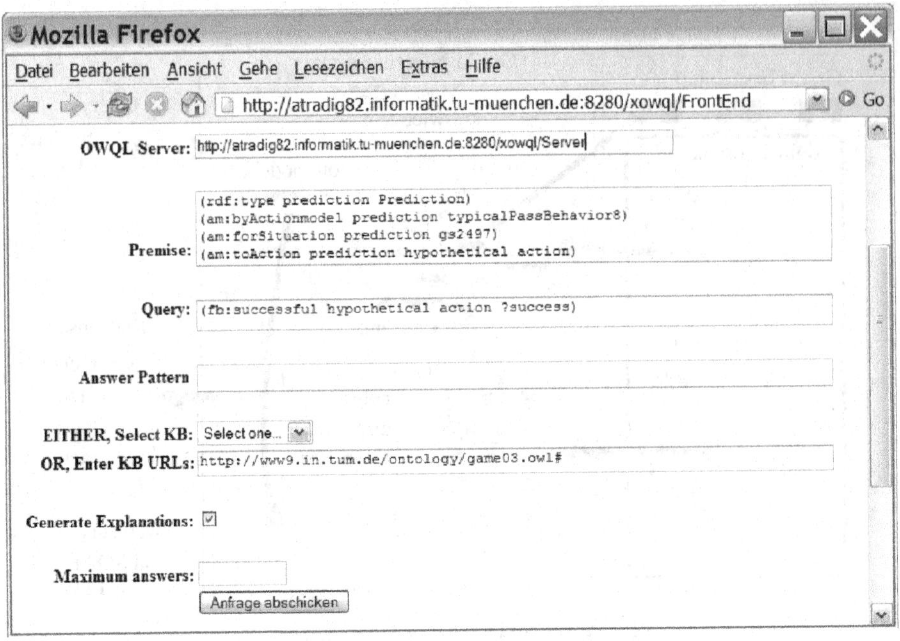

Fig. 6. Web interface to GrAM

We know of no other practical knowledge representation mechanisms that cover the range of action models and reasons about them as GrAM does. As well the combination of structural and functional descriptions was not be addressed before. Also, GrAM's integration of the data mining mechanism and its seamless transition between action models and data mining tasks and results is, as far as we know, novel.

7   Conclusions

In this paper we have proposed GrAM as an extension of a knowledge representation system that makes action models, their acquisition and reasoning about them as an integral part of the knowledge representation system of an intelligent agent. GrAM can be used for various domains where the behavior of agents needs to be embedded into the reasoning apparatus of the system. Functional descriptions are adapted to the behavior of agent groups to learn a structural representation of the same concept.

In a companion research project we use GrAM to represent and reason about a range of action models including causal and outcome models, action selection models, parameterization models, derived models, and others [3]. We believe that the representation languages that are capable of grounding action models and acquire them through data mining will be of key importance in the development of embedded intelligent systems that "know what they are doing".

We are also starting to apply GrAM in the context of autonomous robot learning. For this purpose GrAM is integrated into the robot learning language ROLL [17] and used to make robots "action aware" [18]. GrAM will furthermore be used in context-aware intelligent environments, especially in the kitchen scenario where we try to achieve models for everyday activities [19,20].

References

1. Minsky, M.L.: The society of mind. Simon and Schuster (1986)
2. Beetz, M., Flossmann, S., Stammeier, T.: Motion and episode models for (simulated) football games: Acquisition, representation, and use. In: Kudenko, D., Kazakov, D., Alonso, E. (eds.) AAMAS 2004. LNCS (LNAI), vol. 3394, Springer, Heidelberg (2005)
3. Beetz, M., Kirchlechner, B., Lames, M.: Computerized real-time analysis of football games. IEEE Pervasive Computing 4, 33–39 (2005)
4. Smith, D., (ed.): Special Issue on the 3rd International Planning Competition. Journal of Artificial Intelligence Research 20 (2003)
5. Bechhofer, S., van Harmelen, F., Hendler, J., Horrocks, I., McGuinness, D., Patel-Schneider, P., Stein, L.: OWL Web Ontology Language Reference, W3C Recommendation (2004)
6. Fikes, R., Hayes, P., Horrocks, I.: OWL-QL: A Language for Deductive Query Answering on the Semantic Web. Technical Report KSL 03-14, Stanford University, Stanford, CA, Technical Report (2003)
7. McCarthy, J.: Situations, actions and causal laws. Technical report, Stanford University (1963) Minsky, M. (ed.): Semantic Information Processing. MIT Press, Cambridge (Reprinted 1968)
8. Domingos, P., Richardson, M.: Markov logic: A unifying framework for statistical relational learning. In: Proceedings of the ICML 2004 Workshop on Statistical Relational Learning and its Connection to Other Fields, Banff, Canada, IMLS, pp. 49–54 (2004)
9. Quinlan, J.R.: C4.5: programs for machine learning. Morgan Kaufmann Publishers Inc., San Francisco (1993)
10. Witten, I.H., Frank, E.: Data Mining: Practical machine learning tools and techniques, 2nd edn. Morgan Kaufmann, San Francisco (2005)
11. Frank, G., Fikes, R., Jenkins, J.: JTP: A system architecture and component library for hybrid reasoning. In: Procs. of the 7th World Multiconf. Systemics, Cybernetics, and Informatics, Orlando, Florida, USA (2003)
12. Brachman, R.: Systems that know what they're doing. IEEE Intelligent Systems, 67–71 (2002)
13. Allen, J., Ferguson, G.: Actions and events in interval temporal logic. Journal of Logic and Computation 4, 531–579 (1994)
14. Oates, T., Schmill, M., Cohen, P.: Identifying qualitatively different outcomes of actions: Gaining autonomy through learning. In: Proceedings of the Fourth International Conference on Autonomous Agents, Barcelona, Spain, pp. 110–111. ACM Press, New York (2000)
15. Pasula, H., Zettlemoyer, L., Kaelbling, L.: Learning probabilistic relational planning rules. In: Procs. of the 14th International Conference on Planning and Scheduling (2004)

16. Stulp, F., Beetz, M.: Optimized execution of action chains using learned performance models of abstract actions. In: IJCAI. Proceedings of the Nineteenth International Joint Conference on Artificial Intelligence (2005)
17. Beetz, M., Kirsch, A., Müller, A.: RPL-LEARN: Extending an autonomous robot control language to perform experience-based learning. In: AAMAS. 3rd International Joint Conference on Autonomous Agents & Multi Agent Systems (2004)
18. Stulp, F., Beetz, M.: Action awareness – enabling agents to optimize, transform, and coordinate plans. In: AAMAS. Proceedings of the Fifth International Joint Conference on Autonomous Agents and Multiagent Systems (2006)
19. Kranz, M., Rusu, R.B., Maldonado, A., Beetz, M., Schmidt, A.: A player/stage system for context-aware intelligent environments. In: Dourish, P., Friday, A. (eds.) UbiComp 2006. LNCS, vol. 4206, pp. 17–21. Springer, Heidelberg (2006)
20. Rusu, R.B.: Acquiring models of everyday activities for robotic control in current PhD research in pervasive computing. Technical Reports - University of Munich, Department of Computer Science, Media Informatics Group LMU-MI-2005-3 (2006)

Affordance-Based Human-Robot Interaction

Reinhard Moratz and Thora Tenbrink

Transregional Collaborative Research Center "Spatial Cognition"
University of Bremen
{moratz,tenbrink}@informatik.uni-bremen.de

Abstract. In our targeted scenario, humans can flexibly establish joint object reference with a robot entirely on the basis of their own intuitions. To reach this aim, the robot needs to be equipped with the kind of knowledge that can be matched in a cognitively adequate way to users' intuitive conceptual and linguistic preferences. Such an endeavour requires knowledge about human spatial object reference under consideration of object affordances and functional features. In this paper we motivate our approach by reviewing relevant insights gained in the field of Spatial Cognition, and we discuss the suitability of our robotic system to incorporate these findings. In our context, affordances are visually perceivable functional object aspects shared by the designer of the recognition module and the prospective robot user or instructor.

1 Introduction

Human-robot interaction centers on events in which human instructors expect robots to perform desired actions on specified objects [Zhang and Knoll, 2003]. A shared goal across contexts is therefore to establish joint reference to one or several objects present [Moratz et al., 2001]. This goal can be achieved successfully in one of several ways: for example, instructors could specify exact metric measures, knowledge about all potentially needed objects could be implemented or successively taught to the robot, or users could be provided with a list of object names or class IDs that the robot can understand. However, each of these methods comes with its own problems. In more complex settings or open scenarios, and whenever generic tasks need to be formulated, the limits of predefined referring strategies become obvious. Generic tasks need to be specified by a set of rules comprising complex robot commands.

An everyday example involving a future service robot is the following. The robot could be taught by an untrained user to set the table as follows: Each cutlery piece (knives, forks etc.) is placed at the side of the plate which corresponds to the side where the human hand is that will use the tool. If pasta is served, the fork would be on the right side of the plate, otherwise it would typically be on the left side. If these principles are taught to the robot as a set of functional rules, the robot can generalize to a new scenario in a sensible manner. For example, if a guest for some reason can use only one arm, all cutlery needs to be placed at the corresponding side. Also, culturally diverse habits can easily be accounted for. Such generic rules can be formulated by linguistic functional propositions as instruction representations.

The problem addressed in this paper is how to let the service robot acquire coarse, underspecified knowledge from the environment, which is functionally motivated

E. Rome et al. (Eds.): Affordance-Based Robot Control, LNAI 4760, pp. 63–76, 2008.

[Hois et al., 2006] and matches natural human strategies of spatial reference. Since we consider it essential to avoid the use of forced unnatural communication methods, we present a cognitively inspired approach to establish joint object reference using only simple, natural linguistic means. Our approach makes use of natural object classification by an affordance-based recognition module. In our context, affordances are functional aspects shared by the designer of the recognition module and the prospective robot user or instructor. We start by discussing the general motivation for this approach via pursuing a classification and characterization of generalizable human-robotic interaction scenario types and features associated with them. Then we outline relevant findings on natural and function-based human object reference. Finally we present the current status of our robotic system and elaborate the affordance-based approach.

2   Linguistic Human-Robot Interaction

In the first subsection we motivate and structure different settings/domains for linguistic human-robot interaction. The second subsection sketches our empirical approach and results concerning users' conceptual and linguistic strategies when interacting with robots.

2.1   Contexts and Motivation for Linguistic Human-Robot Interaction

The contexts for human-robot interaction can be classified with respect to the spatiotemporal coupling between instructor and robot. We sketch here a classification into three levels.

In the simplest variant, which can be called "on-line instruction scenario", the human and the robot share the spatiotemporal context. This may be the case either by being co-present, or by radio transmission of video or laser range scans. In these cases, the human can control the robot directly; the robot works in a tele-operated fashion. In these settings direct control means like joysticks or graphical interaction can achieve near optimal results even without the need for linguistic modules [Tsuji and Tanaka, 2005]. However, spoken commands can enhance the graphical interface in a multimodal manner. Considerable progress in this direction is currently documented by major research projects such as COSY, e.g., [Kruijff et al., 2007], and COGNIRON, e.g., [Spexard et al., 2006].

On the second level, called "in advance instruction scenario", a human instructs a robot to perform in a remote place where the specific details are not known, and no further ad-hoc communication between the robot and the human is possible after the instruction. This scenario involves underdetermined qualitative knowledge about spatial arrangements [Habel et al., 1999]. In this case, the instructed robot has no perception of the relevant parts of the scene at the time of instruction [Webber et al., 1995]. Here, the fact that natural language can express *underspecified* knowledge can be used as an advantage. A gesture or pictorial interface would deliver details to the robot which are possibly not part of the knowledge available at the moment of the instruction and could lead to serious inconsistencies between the command and the scene/configuration in which to execute the command.

Finally, a long term goal of linguistic human-robot interaction is to enable naive (un-informed) users to program mobile robots in an intuitive manner [Lauria et al., 2001]. This idea encompasses "generic scenarios", our third level, in which commands are in-tended to be applicable across diverse contexts after they have been issued in a general fashion. For example, an airport security officer could program a mobile robot how to behave with respect to unattended luggage via a command to the robot such as "ask the person on the closest seat whether this piece belongs to somebody". Here, the meanings of 'closest', 'seat', and 'person' have to refer to generalizable categories that the robot can interpret across contexts. Spatial prepositions like 'closest' are of special interest in those scenarios [Moratz and Tenbrink, 2006], [Moratz, 2006] because they can be applied solely on the basis of spatial features, without presupposing knowledge about further situational details. Furthermore, an expression like 'seat' should be interpreted functionally, i.e., based on the affordances that a seat offers for the user, rather than based on specific perceptual details that may vary widely across contexts.

While our approach is motivated by the third, generic level of instructions, the actual scenarios we (like most other approaches) use to explore natural human-robot interac-tion empirically take place on the first level (on-line, face-to-face scenarios). This makes sense because a comprehensive linguistically enabled robot system capable of interpret-ing generic instructions would also need a simple direct linguistic control module. Also, users might like to start their experience with a linguistic robot interface in simple joint attention scenarios before moving into generic instructions. Here we address the ques-tion of how the findings at this stage of research can be generalized towards application in the more advanced scenarios.

2.2 Investigating and Modelling Features of Linguistic Human-Robot Interaction

In our empirical approach, we use simple human-robot interaction settings to establish how speakers react when confronted with a robot with certain functionalities that they do not know the details of [Fischer, 2003]. Such a situation resembles a future scenario in which human users expect a service robot to function based on their intuitions con-cerning how to instruct the robot, rather than based on a need to read a complex and detailed manual.

In a typical setting used in our work [Moratz and Tenbrink, 2006], several similar ob-jects are placed on the floor together with the robot, and the experimental participants' task is to make the robot move towards one of these objects. This scenario captures the specific need to establish joint object reference, which is a crucial aspect of many generalizable complex situation types.

A crucial element of this approach is the realization that speakers' strategies when addressing a robot are based entirely and systematically on their concepts of the robot. Such concepts are not always directly accessible; for example, asking the users about their expectations may often only lead to vague generalizations. But speakers display their concepts of the robot by their linguistic choices [Fischer, 2006]. To begin with, users' utterances reflect their previous expectations of the robot. The features of human language directed towards artificial communication partners has been shown to differ systematically from that of language used in human to human communication [Doran et al., 2001]. This phenomenon is related to long recognized principles of *recipient design* [Sacks et al., 1974]. In our scenario, participants seemed to deduce the robot's behavioral functionalities from the robot's communicative capabilities; they did not appear to expect the robot to be able to do something that it could not communicate about [Fischer and Moratz, 2001]. Of course, this contrasts with the actual circumstances, since speech and behavior modules may be quite unrelated in a robot. Gradually, throughout the discourse, the users adapt their concepts (as reflected in their language) to the actual situation and the experience they have gained [Fischer and Moratz, 2001, Amalberti et al., 1993]. Accordingly, our data show that users tend to re-use syntactic and conceptual schemas after experiencing success with certain kinds of constructs [Moratz and Tenbrink, 2006]. Users try out a number of different strategies and then rely systematically on positive experience.

From these findings, the following observation can be gained, which is crucial for our approach. Even if users start out by expecting the robot to have fundamentally different functionalities as compared to humans, they can adapt quickly to the robot's actual features. Therefore, users confronted with a robot that is able to recognize objects on the basis of their function will soon be able to utilize this specific capability to a great extent. This expectation includes the humans' ability to realize, and adapt flexibly to, the robot's limitations: some objects will be recognized easily by the robot, while others are more difficult due to situational factors such as partial occlusion, scanner resolution limitations, or less easily detectable object features. Accordingly, speakers can use jointly identified objects for future reference, also in order to refer to other, more difficult objects, based on their relation to the identified ones. Spontaneous instructions such as "Go to the (unknown) object in front of the (known) chair" then represent a natural way of communicating.

Another important insight supported by our empirical findings is that the users' instructions do not need to rely on spoken language. Typing text into an interface is nowadays common and widespread; many people are quite content to use reduced keyboards such as those available on mobile phones. Therefore it can be expected that this does not impose undue cognitive load on the user. Also, our findings show that - contrary to what might have been expected - users' written instructions did not differ fundamentally in any crucial respect from their spoken instructions to robots in our face-to-face scenario [Moratz and Tenbrink, 2003]. For the system and for the success of the communication, using typed language has considerable advantages. Current speech recognition systems work well, but still not well enough to avoid recurring misinterpretations and failures to understand the spoken input. These can then lead to severe misconceptions concerning the robot's capabilities and functionalities on the part of the user [Moratz and Tenbrink, 2003], since users may fail to realize that it is simply the level of speech recognition that is responsible for miscommunication. Especially with users that are not familiar with technological details, it is essential for the robot to react suitably to all input the user gives, which is only possible if speech recognition problems are ruled out.

3   Human Spatial Object Reference in Natural Settings

As stated above, our focus for successful human-robot communication centers on joint object reference as a crucial element across scenarios. This section summarizes earlier findings from the literature and from our own research that are relevant for this endeavour.

In a situation involving a configuration of various objects, how do speakers refer to them? Trivially, if only different objects are present, speakers can use class names. If joint reference can successfully be achieved by this method, no further investigations are necessary. Another possibility is to rely on obvious object features such as colour, shape, or size. This option is only available if the interlocutors share the ability to recognize these features unproblematically in an object. Speakers then choose a feature for reference that is best suited for establishing contrast [Herrmann and Deutsch, 1976]. If these methods fail, it is feasible to rely on descriptions of spatial object relations. For example, speakers can make use of proximity or distance terms such as *near, far* [Tenbrink, 2005]. These terms are appropriate if the intended object is closer to, or farther away from, the object it is specified in relation to (that is, the *relatum*) than other objects are. Also depending on the spatial situation, other terms such as *on, in, at, between, amid* may or may not be applicable. These terms rely on the presence of one or more other objects (relata) situated in a certain kind of spatial and/or functional relation to the intended object (from now on called the *locatum*). For example, a locatum *between* two relata would be situated within a spatial region delimited by the positions of the two relata. A locatum *in* a relatum entails a relationship of functional containment involving location control; the relationship may or may not involve geometric enclosure in addition [Coventry and Garrod, 2004]. All of these options are therefore fairly situation-dependent and cannot be applied in all cases.

In the case of the so-called *projective expressions*, the case is different. Terms like *left, right, in front of, behind* can be applied in almost any situation involving the spatial position of an object: one of these terms will always be applicable for a spatial description. However, projective terms are more complex than other spatial expressions in that they involve not only a relatum but also an *origin*, a position from which a visual perspective or (view or movement) direction is derived. Here, the notion of spatial *reference systems* comes into play [Levinson, 2003]. In the case of the so-called *intrinsic* reference systems, the origin is conflated with the relatum. An example for an intrinsic description is, "The ball is to my left." Here, although the perspective is not mentioned explicitly, it can be assumed that the speaker uses her own view direction to describe the ball's position in relation to herself. Objects with intrinsic sides can also serve as the relatum and origin of an intrinsic reference system. In *relative* reference systems, the origin differs from the relatum. A speaker could say: "The ball is to the left of the table from my point of view." However, perspectives are typically not given explicitly. The perspective used is typically that of the interlocutor if the speaker wishes to facilitate the task for the listener or if actions are involved on the part of the listener [Herrmann and Grabowski, 1994], both of which is the case in human-robot instruction tasks. In fact, our speakers do consistently employ the robot's perspective [Moratz et al., 2001].

Now, the question remains how speakers choose which objects they can rely on in order to describe the position of other objects; what determines the choice of a suitable relatum? In his well-known approach to cognitive semantics, Talmy proposes that they do so based on a number of systematic principles, most of which pertain to the features of the objects available for reference [Talmy, 2000]. Crucially, while the locatum is an object with unknown spatial properties (since the aim is to describe its position in relation to the relatum), the relatum "acts as a reference entity, having known properties that can characterise the primary object's unknowns" [Talmy, 2000, p183]. Typically, therefore, the relatum will be less movable or more stable than the locatum, it will be larger and more easily recognizable, more immediately perceivable, and so on.

If the positions of the interactants present in a scenario are stable, they can be used as relata (as in a robot instruction like "Go to the object to your left"). However, as discussed in section 2.1, this may not always be the case, especially if a spatial relation should be applicable generically. Then, it will be more feasible to use salient, already recognized objects as relata for the identification of a new locatum. This can happen in one of two ways: speakers can use a relative reference system involving the perspective of one of the interlocutors, or they can employ an intrinsic reference system based on the object's intrinsic features. But only the intrinsic case can truly be used generically, since this implies that the actual presence of a person is not required, or (in the case of a generic robot instruction) the robot's position does not need to be specified. Here, the object's intrinsic or functional features and axes become crucial, since it is only possible to say that something is "in front of the table" (without an additional perspective) if the table has an intrinsic front.

In order to determine an object's internal regions, several different aspects come into play, most of which are not physically determined but rather based on human cognition and behavioural conventions [Herrmann, 1990, p120]. In animate beings the part containing perceptual organs defines the intrinsic front. In other cases, typical direction of motion and orientation to the observer play a role [Miller and Johnson-Laird, 1976, p 400f.]. Thus, arrows have an intrinsic front because of their associated direction of motion, and a desk's front is defined by its usual orientation to a person. Intrinsic tops are dependent on an entity's characteristic orientation on the vertical axis. Often, functional features come into play that are derived from humans' characteristic uses of the objects. For example, the front side of a television is the side that humans look at when watching TV, and the back side of objects is often the one that is less accessible. Functional aspects are also decisive for the determination of the spatial regions for which spatial terms are applicable in context [Coventry and Garrod, 2004]. Whether an umbrella is referred to as being *over* a person depends on where the rain comes from. Furthermore, there is some evidence that intrinsic reference frames are preferred in situations involving functional features of (familiar) objects, while relative reference frames are more likely in non-functional situations [Carlson-Radvansky and Radvansky, 1996].

From these findings, we can conclude the following generalizations in relation to our human-robot interaction scenario. Spatial reference using projective terms is a flexible method of establishing joint object reference especially when other methods fail or when generalizable options are called for. Corresponding to their natural preferences, speakers will often use the robot's position as relatum, employing intrinsic reference systems. If this is not feasible because of the general circumstances (for example, in generic instructions) or because a suitable spatial relation cannot be straightforwardly described, it becomes crucial to rely on salient objects within the scenario as relatum, using a relative reference system (employing the robot's perspective in non-generic situations) or an intrinsic reference system using the object's intrinsic features. In the latter case, which stands out as the best option available for generalizable reference, object recognition using natural object categories and the identification of functional features becomes essential. In the following, we turn to the technological requirements involved here.

4   Object Recognition Using Natural Object Categories

The problem of object recognition has a long tradition in computer vision research. One approach is to perform a model-based interpretation in a priori known environments. There are fast algorithms that use CAD models for the recognition of rigid objects [Lanser et al., 1997]. The CAD models are used to generate 2D views (multi-view representation) which are compared with features of the perceived scene. Articulated objects can be represented as a composition of rigid components which are explicitly connected by specific kinematical constraints, e.g., rotational and/or translational joints [Hauck et al., 1997].

Approaches that use precise geometrical prior knowledge of objects are designed to unify a currently sensed object with an object already known. A more complex task is to categorize unknown, novel objects by interpreting them with respect to semantic concepts (e.g. "chair", "door"). Solutions for this problem would be very helpful in the context of human-robot interaction. A cognitive theory ("Recognition by Components") about how humans find natural categories from visual input was proposed by Biederman [Biederman, 1987]. It partitions objects into a set of 3D primitives (geons) that are generalized cylinders. A semantic object category comprises a prototypical relative spatial arrangement of specific geons.

Such a semantic interpretation demands the model-driven segmentation into volumetric parts. The recovery of volumetric shape descriptions from range data is central to the approach of Dickinson, Metaxas, and Pentland [Dickinson et al., 1997]. The target representation in this approach is a qualitative vocabulary of 3D parts (generalized cylinders) and their qualitative relative orientation. An alternative approach is the use of super-quadrics with parameterized global deformations [Solina and Bajcsy, 1990] [Leonardis et al., 1994] [Wu and Levine, 1994]. However, the above mentioned approaches do not perform a semantic interpretation. The context of these systems typically is the task of determining grip positions for manipulators. The ambitious goal of assigning natural categories to novel objects for human-robot interaction was first approached by Louise Stark and her group [Stark and Bowyer, 1996].

Our approach (described below) is very similar to Stark's function-based recognition. It is based on an idea which originates from Gibson [Gibson, 1979] and is developed further by the geo-informatics research community [Kuhn, 1996] [Jordan et al., 1998] as well as theories of language understanding [Gorniak and Roy,]. Objects are characterized by the "services" (affordances) they offer a user. As an example, stairs are characterized by a ratio of height to width of their steps that allow for climbing them comfortably [Mark, 1987]. These affordances are often closely related to the spatial arrangement of their components. This is the link to the component based approach of Biederman [Biederman, 1987] mentioned above. In our approach we start by investigating which feature-detectors are powerful enough to detect invariant features of object categories which are important for humans in office scenarios. Therefore we first focus on the design of the feature detectors and only aim to add learning capabilities to the system in a second step.

Based on the insight that objects have certain forms resulting from their functions, object shape can be used to help identify the object's function and ultimately the object itself. We developed an object recognition system that can handle the input data, render it, and perform our object recognition algorithms. Details of an earlier version of the system have previously been presented in [Wünstel and Moratz, 2004]. Figure 1 shows an experimental scene together with the scanning equipment. The scene consists of two chairs, a waste paper basket, and a briefcase. During a tilt pass of its pan-tilt unit the scanner generates a point cloud of the scene (cf. figure 2).

Fig. 1. Scene together with the scanning equipment on the left

In our scenario free-form objects in an office environment have to be identified. In the current version, we mainly focus on the concept of the *supporting plane*. When the function of an object part is to support a potential other object, this part has to be parallel to the ground.

A specific difficulty for our system is based on the fact that it perceives the scene from one perspective only (see figure 3). A supporting plane which is occluded too much cannot be detected reliably anymore. We therefore chose an anthropomorphic perspective (the scanner is placed in a similar height as a human head) to minimize this problem.

The three-dimensional surface points resulting from the laser range image are separated into up to four layers (see figure 4 for images of the layers). We then project each

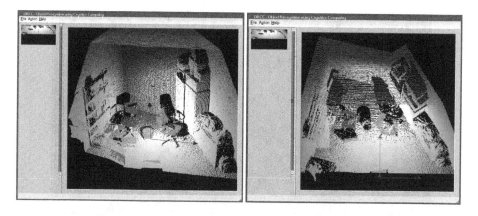

Fig. 2. Rendered range data - the identified objects and segments are colored

Fig. 3. Scene nearly from the perspective of the scanner

layer into a two-dimensional plane. Within this plane we can now robustly segment object parts by using standard methods. These segments, representing object parts in certain heights, are then used to identify the whole three-dimensional object.

The approach performs best for objects having strong functional constraints at the system's current perceptual granularity (e.g. desks, tables, chairs, open doors, and empty book shelves). However, smaller objects on the ground (e.g. waste paper baskets, briefcases etc.) can be detected but not classified reliably by our current system. These objects can however be referred to by a human, and furthermore they can be referred to by reference to other objects in the environment (e.g. "the briefcase to the left of the chair") [Moratz, 2006]. This utterance could be interpreted in various ways, depending on the underlying reference system. In the case of figure 3, it represents the robot's point of view in a relative reference system. Since the robot is able to detect the chair's intrinsic features, an intrinsic reference system is equally possible. In [Moratz and Tenbrink, 2006] we show how the robot can disentangle various options for reference systems in a situated interaction situation. In cases of true referential

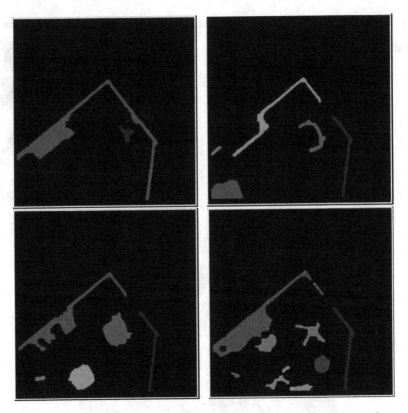

Fig. 4. Resulting segments of the four levels beginning with the highest. Sitting surfaces at the second lowest level (third subfigure).

ambiguity, a clarification procedure would need to be initiated. Thus, joint object reference can be achieved successfully for the full scenario consisting of easily and less easily recognizable objects. The system recognizes the more salient, functionally interpretable objects and is then able to interpret the human's reference to other, less salient objects using the successfully identified objects as relata. As outlined above, this approach corresponds well to humans' intuitive methods of spatial object reference. Taking this basic idea as a starting point, it is a promising endeavour in future research to combine the automatic detection of those objects that are functionally salient to the user with elaborate models of spatial reference resolution. In this way, users' intuitive focus of attention as well as basic linguistic reference strategies can be suitably accounted for as well as exploited advantageously.

5   Integration of Affordance-Based Recognition and Linguistic Modules

Advanced linguistic human-robot interaction as sketched in subsection 2.1 requires the integration of the semantic knowledge of a linguistic module and the conceptual knowledge of the sensorical component (e.g. the object recognition module described in section 4). Therefore we adopt an architecture/design principle which allows for the necessary interactions and is applicable to the different domains [Habel et al., 1999]. It integrates several knowledge components and is suitable for solving the matching problem between underdetermined conceptual representations and sensorical input.

The experimental system focuses on the object recognition module. Our goals in realizing this system were twofold, scientifically and application oriented: On the one hand, the system serves as the experimental means to test theoretical hypotheses about the interaction of underdetermined conceptual representations and sensorical input of spatial environments, on the other hand, natural language interfaces, which allow to give affordance-based object reference instructions, can make robot applications accessible for non-expert users.

The system consists of the following interacting modules: the syntactical component, the semantic component, the spatial reasoning component, and the sensing and action component. A typical interaction of the human instructor with our robot system in the scenario depicted in figure 3 could be the following. The instructor gives the command: "Zeige mir den Gegenstand hinter dem Hocker" ("Show me the object behind the stool"). The robot highlights the briefcase on its screen.

The system performs in the following way. The syntactical component parses the command. The affordance-based recognition module is the main part of the sensing and action component. It categorizes a seat without a backrest as stool. The spatial preposition *hinter* (behind) is interpreted by the spatial reasoning component (see [Moratz, 2006] for details). The semantic component decides about the most appropriate integrated interpretation and decides which object to highlight.

A specific option relevant for our design methodology is using a knowledge representation scheme for reasoning processes which is structured according to affordance-based criteria. In Raubal and Moratz (this volume) we sketch a suitable technology consisting of a specifically designed operator set in a robot architecture. This operator set is used by the high-level control module for the robot, which performs the planning process about the operator sequences. The operators themselves have a functional meaning shared by instructor and robot since the set of operators is designed according to affordance-based criteria.

6 Conclusion and Outlook

We have outlined our approach to affordance-based joint object reference both from a theoretical and a technological perspective. The theoretical motivation focuses on allowing uninformed users to communicate with robots about previously unidentified objects by using their intuitive strategies for object reference in spatial scenarios. For this purpose, we have outlined possible human-robot interaction scenarios in relation to human speakers' conceptual options for achieving reference. We then briefly presented our system under development that employs a function-based object recognition module, utilizing $2\frac{1}{2}$D laser range data. Focusing on functional rather than strictly perceptual aspects is a promising approach since humans typically interact with objects in systematic ways, thus delimiting the range of aspects that the robot needs to take into account.

In our system new affordances cannot be learnt by the robot itself but need to be designed by the developer of the recognition module. An interesting aim for future research is to arrange affordances in a functional ontology. Then new affordances could be derived in a systematic high-level way. In the next step the robot should learn new affordances by itself.

Acknowledgements

The authors would like to thank Michael Wünstel, Kerstin Fischer, and John Bateman for their contributions to the general enterprise. Michael Wünstel implemented the main part of the object recognition system. This work is part of the Transregional Collaborative Research Center SFB/TR 8 Spatial Cognition: Reasoning, Action, Interaction (Bremen / Freiburg, Germany); funding by the DFG is gratefully appreciated.

References

[Amalberti et al., 1993] Amalberti, R., Carbonell, N., Falzon, P.: User Representations of Computer Systems in Human–Computer Speech Interaction. International Journal of Man–Machine Studies 38, 547–566 (1993)

[Biederman, 1987] Biederman, I.: Recognition-by-components: A theory of human image understanding. Psychological Review 94, 115–147 (1987)

[Carlson-Radvansky and Radvansky, 1996] Carlson-Radvansky, L.A., Radvansky, G.: The influence of functional relations on spatial term selection. Psychological Science 7, 56–60 (1996)

[Coventry and Garrod, 2004] Coventry, K.R., Garrod, S.C.: Saying, seeing and acting: The psychological semantics of spatial prepositions. Essays in Cognitive Psychology series. Psychology Press (2004)

[Dickinson et al., 1997] Dickinson, S., Metaxas, D., Pentland, A.: The role of model-based segmentation in the recovery of volumetric parts from range data. IEEE Transactions on Pattern Analysis and Machine Intelligence 19(3), 259–267 (1997)

[Doran et al., 2001] Doran, C., Aberdeen, J., Damianos, L., Hirschman, L.: Comparing several aspects of human-computer and human-human dialogues. In: Proceedings of the 2nd SIGdial Workshop on Discourse and Dialogue, Aalborg, Denmark, pp. 1–2 (September 2001)

[Fischer, 2003] Fischer, K.: Linguistic methods for investigating concepts in use. Methodologie in der Linguistik (2003)

[Fischer, 2006] Fischer, K.: What Computer Talk Is and Is not: Human-Computer Conversation as Intercultural Communication. AQ, Saarbruecken (2006)

[Fischer and Moratz, 2001] Fischer, K., Moratz, R.: From communicative strategies to cognitive modelling. In: Workshop Epigenetic Robotics, Lund (2001)

[Gibson, 1979] Gibson, J.: The Ecological Approach to Visual Perception. Houghton Mifflin Company, Boston (1979)

[Gorniak and Roy,] Gorniak, P., Roy, D.: Situated language understanding as filtering perceived affordances. Cognitive Science (in press)

[Habel et al., 1999] Habel, C., Hildebrandt, B., Moratz, R.: Interactive robot navigation based on qualitative spatial representations. In: Wachsmuth, I., Jung, B. (eds.) Proceedings Kogwis 1999, St. Augustin. infix, pp. 219–225 (1999)

[Hauck et al., 1997] Hauck, A., Lanser, S., Zierl, C.: Hierarchical recognition of articulated objects from single perspective views. In: IEEE International Conference on Computer Vision and Pattern Recognition, pp. 870–876. IEEE Computer Society Press, Los Alamitos (1997)

[Herrmann, 1990] Herrmann, T.: Vor, hinter, rechts und links: das 6H-Modell. Psychologische Studien zum sprachlichen Lokalisieren. Zeitschrift für Literaturwissenschaft und Linguistik 78, 117–140 (1990)

[Herrmann and Deutsch, 1976] Herrmann, T., Deutsch, W.: Psychologie der Objektbenennung. Hans Huber Verlag, Bern u.a (1976)

[Herrmann and Grabowski, 1994] Herrmann, T., Grabowski, J.: Sprechen: Psychologie der Sprachproduktion. Spektrum Verlag, Heidelberg (1994)

[Hois et al., 2006] Hois, J., Wünstel, M., Bateman, J.A., Röfer, T.: Dialog-based 3d-image recognition using a domain ontology. In: Proc. International Conference Spatial Cognition, September 24–28, 2006 Bremen, Germany (2006)

[Jordan et al., 1998] Jordan, T., Raubal, M., Gartrell, B., Egenhofer, M.: An affordance-based model of place in GIS. In: Eight International Symposium on Spatial Data Handling, pp. 98–109 (1998)

[Kruijff et al., 2007] Kruijff, G.-J.M., Zender, H., Jensfelt, P., Christensen, H.I.: Situated dialogue and spatial organization: What, where... and why? International Journal of Advanced Robotic Systems, Special Issue on Human and Robot Interactive Communication 4(2) (to appear, 2007)

[Kuhn, 1996] Kuhn, W.: Handling data spatially: Spatializing user interfaces. In: SDH 1996. Advances in GIS Research II, Delft. International Geographical Union, pp. 13B.1–13B.23 (1996)

[Lanser et al., 1997] Lanser, S., Zierl, C., Munkelt, O., Radig, B.: Moral - a vision-based object recognition system for autonomous mobile systems. In: Sommer, G., Daniilidis, K., Pauli, J. (eds.) CAIP 1997. LNCS, vol. 1296, pp. 33–41. Springer, Heidelberg (1997)

[Lauria et al., 2001] Lauria, S., Bugmann, G., Kyriacou, T., Bos, J., Klein, E.: Training personal robots using natural language instruction. IEEE Intelligent Systems 16(5), 38–45 (2001)

[Leonardis et al., 1994] Leonardis, A., Solina, F., Macerl, A.: A direct recovery of superquadric models in range images using recover- and select paradigm. In: Eklundh, J.-O. (ed.) ECCV 1994. LNCS, vol. 800, pp. 309–318. Springer, Heidelberg (1994)

[Levinson, 2003] Levinson, S.C.: Space in language and cognition: explorations in cognitive diversity. Cambridge University Press, Cambridge (2003)

[Mark, 1987] Mark, L.: Eye height-scaled information about affordances: A study of sitting and stair climbing. Journal of Experimental Psychology: Human Perception and Performance 13, 361–370 (1987)

[Miller and Johnson-Laird, 1976] Miller, G., Johnson-Laird, P.: Language and Perception. Cambridge University Press, Cambridge (1976)

[Moratz, 2006] Moratz, R.: Intuitive linguistic joint object reference in human-robot interaction. In: Proceedings of the Twenty-First National Conference on Artificial Intelligence (AAAI), pp. 1483–1488 (2006)

[Moratz et al., 2001] Moratz, R., Fischer, K., Tenbrink, T.: Cognitive Modeling of Spatial Reference for Human-Robot Interaction. International Journal on Artificial Intelligence Tools 10(4), 589–611 (2001)

[Moratz and Tenbrink, 2003] Moratz, R., Tenbrink, T.: Instruction modes for joint spatial reference between naive users and a mobile robot. In: Proceedings of RISSP IEEE International Conference on Robotics, Intelligent Systems and Signal Processing, Special Session on New Methods in Human Robot Interaction, pp. 8–13. Changsha, China (2003)

[Moratz and Tenbrink, 2006] Moratz, R., Tenbrink, T.: Spatial reference in linguistic human-robot interaction: Iterative, empirically supported development of a model of projective relations. Spatial Cognition and Computation 6(1), 63–106 (2006)

[Sacks et al., 1974] Sacks, H., Schegloff, E., Jefferson, G.: A simplest systematics for the organization of turn-taking for conversation. Language 50, 696–735 (1974)

[Solina and Bajcsy, 1990] Solina, F., Bajcsy, R.: Recovery of parametric models form range images: The case for superquadratics with global deformations. IEEE Transactions on Pattern Analysis and Machine Intelligence 12(2), 131–146 (1990)

[Spexard et al., 2006] Spexard, T., Li, S., Wrede, B., Fritsch, J., Sagerer, G., Booij, O., Zivkovic, Z., Terwijn, B., Kröse, B.: BIRON, where are you? Enabling a robot to learn new places in a real home environment by integrating spoken dialog and visual localization. In: Proceedings of the IEEE/RSJ International Conference on Intelligent Robots and Systems (IROS) (2006)

[Stark and Bowyer, 1996] Stark, L., Bowyer, K.: Generic Object Recognition using Form and Function. World Scientific, Singapore (1996)

[Talmy, 2000] Talmy, L.: Towards a cognitive semantics. A Bradford Book, M.I.T. Press, Cambridge, MA (2000)

[Tenbrink, 2005] Tenbrink, T.: Identifying objects on the basis of spatial contrast: an empirical study. In: Freksa, C., et al. (eds.) Spatial Cognition IV. LNCS (LNAI), vol. 3343, pp. 124–146. Springer, Heidelberg (2005)

[Tsuji and Tanaka, 2005] Tsuji, T., Tanaka, Y.: Tracking control properties of human-robotic systems based on impedance control. IEEE Transactions on Systems, Man, and Cybernetics, Part A 35(4), 523–535 (2005)

[Webber et al., 1995] Webber, B.L., Badler, N.I., Eugenio, B.D., Geib, C.W., Levison, L., Moore, M.: Instructions, intentions and expectations. Artif. Intell. 73(1-2), 253–269 (1995)

[Wu and Levine, 1994] Wu, K., Levine, M.: Recovering parametric geons from multiview range data. In: Proc. IEEE Conf. Computer Vision and Pattern Recognition, pp. 159–166. Seattle (1994)

[Wünstel and Moratz, 2004] Wünstel, M., Moratz, R.: Automatic object recognition within an office environment. In: Canadian Conference on Computer and Robot Vision (CRV2004) (2004)

[Zhang and Knoll, 2003] Zhang, J., Knoll, A.: A two-arm situated artificial communicator for human-robot cooperative assembly. IEEE Transactions on Industrial Electronics 50(4), 651–658 (2003)

Reinforcement Learning of Predictive Features in Affordance Perception

Lucas Paletta and Gerald Fritz

Joanneum Research Forschungsgesellschaft mbH,
Institute of Digital Image Processing, Computational Perception Group,
Wastiangasse 6, Graz, Austria

Abstract. Recently, the aspect of visual perception has been explored in the context of Gibson's concept of affordances [1] in various ways [4-9]. In extension to existing functional views on visual feature representations, we focus on the importance of *learning* in perceptual cueing for the *anticipation of opportunities for interaction* of robotic agents. Furthermore, we propose that the originally defined representational concept for the perception of affordances - in terms of using either optical flow or heuristically determined 3D features of perceptual entities - should be generalized towards using *arbitrary* visual feature representations. In this context we demonstrate the learning of causal relationships between visual cues and associated anticipated interactions, using visual information within the *framework of Markov Decision Processes (MDPs)*. We emphasize a new framework for cueing *and* recognition of affordance-like visual entities that could play an important role in future robot control architectures. Affordance-like perception should enable systems to react to environment stimuli both more efficiently and autonomously, and provide a potential to plan on the basis of relevant responses to more complex perceptual configurations. We verify the concept with a concrete implementation of learning visual cues by reinforcement, applying state-of-the-art visual descriptors and regions of interest that were extracted from a simulated robot scenario and prove that these features were successfully selected for their relevance in predicting opportunities of robot interaction.

1 Introduction

The concept of affordances has been coined by J.J. Gibson in his seminal work on the ecological approach to visual perception [1]. In the context of ecological perception, visual perception would enable agents to experience in a direct way the opportunities for action. However, Gibson remained unclear about both how this concept could be used in a technical system and which representation to use. Neisser [2] replied to Gibson's concept of direct perception with the notion of a perception-action cycle that shows the reciprocal relationship of the knowledge (i.e., a schema) about the environment directing exploration of the environment (i.e., action), which samples the information available for pick up in the environment, which then modifies the knowledge, and so on. This cycle describes how knowledge, perception, action, and the environment all effectively interact in order to achieve goals.

E. Rome et al. (Eds.): Affordance-Based Robot Control, LNAI 4760, pp. 77–90, 2008.

Our work on affordance-like perception is in the context of technical, i.e., robotic systems, based on a notion of affordances that *'fulfill the purpose of efficient prediction of interaction opportunities'*. We extend Gibson's ecological approach under acknowledgment of Neisser's understanding that *purposive* visual feature representation on various hierarchies of abstraction are mandatory to appropriately respond to environmental stimuli. We take advantage of a refined concept of affordance perception by representing (i) an interaction component (*affordance recognition*: recognizing relevant events in interaction via perceptual entities) and (ii) a predictive aspect (*affordance cueing*: predicting interaction via perceptual entities). This conceptual step enables firstly to investigate the functional components of perception that make up affordance-based prediction, and secondly to lay a basis to identify the causal relation between predictive features and predicted events via machine learning technology.

The particular contribution of this work is to demonstrate that reinforcement learning provides the appropriate concept to enable purposive - in particular, *affordance based* - perception which is consequently structured into cueing, behavior, and outcome related components. Learning is mandatory to enable agents to autonomously develop their characteristic embodied perception through interaction with the environment. *Reinforcements* guide the development through *exploration without external supervision*.

The outline of this paper is as follows. Section 2 describes the relevance of structured affordance-like representations in robot perception and argues for the importance to learn the features of perceptual entities. Section 3 presents the concept of predictive features in the context of probabilistic decision making, in particular, with respect to reinforcement learning. Section 4 illustrates the experimental results that strongly support the proposed hypothesis on the relevance of generalized features that can be learned using reinforcement for successful affordance-like cueing in robot control systems. Section 5 concludes with an outlook on future work.

2 Affordance Perception and Predictive Features

Affordance-like perception aims at supporting control schemata for perception-action processing in the context of rapid and simplified access to agent-environment interactions. In this Section we argue for the relevance of learning in cue selection, and present a framework on functional components that enables the system to identify relevant visual features.

2.1 Related Work

Previous research on affordance-like perception focused on heuristic definitions of simple feature-function relations to facilitate sensor-motor associations in robotic agents. The MIT humanoid robot Cog was involved in object poking and proding experiments that investigate the emergence of affordance categories to choose actions with the aim to make objects roll in a specific way (Fitzpatrick et al.[6]). The research of Stoytchev [7] analyzed affordances on an object level, investigating new concepts of object-hood in a sense of how perceptions of objects are connected with visual events that arise from action consequences related to the object itself. However, these experiments involve computer vision still on a low level, and do not consider complex sensor-motor representation of an agent interaction in less constrained, even natural environments. In the biologically motivated cognitive framework of Cos-Aguilera et al. [15], object based affordances are set in the context of motivation driven behavior selection. In contrast to our work, they do not learn visual feature extraction in a purposive manner (Section 2.2) but rather match sensory input with stored object features in a classical sense and then associate object identities with appropriate interaction patterns.

Affordance based visual object representations are per se function based representations. In contrast to classical object representations, functional object representations (Stark and Bowyer [7], Rivlin et al. [8]) use a set of primitives (relative orientation, stability, proximity, etc.) that define specific functional properties, essentially containing face and vertex information. These primitives are subsumed to define surfaces from the functional properties, such as 'is sittable' or 'provides stable support'. Bogoni and Bajcsy [9] have extended this representation from an active perception perspective, relating observability to interaction with the object, understanding functionality as the applicability of an object for the fulfillment of some purpose. However, so far function based representations have been basically defined by the engineer, while - in contrast - it is particularly important in affordance based recognition to *learn* the structure and the features themselves *from experience* (Section 4).

2.2 Predictive Features in Purposive Vision

Fig. 1 depicts the concept of feature based affordance perception as outlined in [14]. We first identify the functional component of *affordance recognition*, i.e., the recognition of the affordance related visual event that causally anticipates a relevant interaction, e.g., the capability of lifting (*lift-ability*) an object using an appropriate robotic actuator. The recognition of this event should be performed in identifying a process of evaluating spatio-temporal information that leads to a final state. This final state should be unique in perceptual feature/state space, i.e., it should be characterized by the observation of specific feature attributes that are abstracted from the stream of sensory-motor information.

The second functional component of *affordance cueing* encompasses the key idea on affordance based perception, i.e., anticipating the opportunity for interaction from causally relevant features, i.e., the *predictive features*, that can be extracted from the incoming sensory processing stream. In particular, this component is embedded in the perception-action cycle of the robotic agent. The agent is receiving sensory information in order to build upon arbitrary levels of feature abstractions, for the purpose of recognition of perceptual entities. In contrast to classical feature and object recognition, this kind of recognition is *purposive* in the sense of selecting exactly those features that efficiently support the evaluation of identifying an affordance, i.e., the perceptual entities that possess the capability to predict an event of affordance recognition in the feature time series that is immediately following the cueing stage of affordance based perception. The outcome of affordance cueing is in general a probability distribution P_A on all possible affordances (Section 4.1), providing evidence for a most confident affordance cue by delivering a hypothesis that favors the future occurrence of a particular affordance recognition event. This cue is *functional* in the sense of *associating* to the related feature representation a specific *utility* with respect to the capabilities of the agent and the opportunities provided by the environment, thus representing *predictive features* within the affordance based perception system.

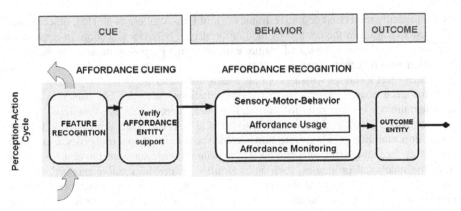

Fig. 1. Concept of affordance perception, depicting the key components of affordance cueing and recognition embedded within an agent's perception-action cycle (most left). While affordance cueing (left) provides a prediction on future opportunities of interaction on the basis of related predictive features, affordance recognition (right) identifies the convergence of a sensory-motor behavior towards the identified outcome of the overall interaction pattern.

The relevance of attention in affordance based perception has first been mentioned by developmental psychologist E.J. Gibson [3] who recognized that attention strategies are learned by the early infant to purposively select relevant stimuli and processes in interaction with the environment. In this context we propose to understand affordance cues and affordance hypotheses as fundamental part in human attentive perception, claiming that – in analogy – purposive, affordance based attention could play a similar role in machine perception as well. There are affordances that are explicitly innate to the agent through evolutionary development and there are affordances that have to be learned [1]. Learning chains of affordance driven actions can lead to learning new, more complex affordances. This can be done, e.g., by imitation, whereby it is reasonable to imitate goals and sub goals instead of actions [10]. In the context of the proposed framework on affordance based perception (Fig. 1), learning should play a crucial role in determining predictive features.

In contrast to previous work on functional feature and object representations [7,8], we stress the fact that functional representations must necessarily contain *purposive features*, i.e., represent perceptual entities that refer to interaction patterns and thus must be selected from an existing pool of generic feature representations. Feature selection (and, in a more general sense, feature extraction) must be performed in a machine learning process and therefore avoid heuristic engineering which is always rooted in a human kind understanding of the underlying process, a methodology which is necessarily both, firstly, error prone due to failing insight into statistical dependencies and, secondly, highly impractical for autonomous mobile systems.

3 Predictive Features and Probabilistic Decision Making

3.1 Predictive Features for Affordance Cueing

Early awareness of opportunities for interaction is highly relevant for autonomous robotic systems. Visual features are among the multiple modalities from sensory processing that operate perception via optical rays and therefore support early awareness from rather remote locations. Although the necessity of affordance perception from 3D information recovery, such as optical flow, has been stressed in previous work [1], we do not restrict ourselves to any specific cue modality and intend to generalize towards the use of arbitrary features that can be derived from visual information, restricting only on the constraint that they enable reliable prediction of the opportunity for interaction processes from an early point in time.

Affordance Hypotheses. The outcome of the affordance cueing system is in general expected to be – given a perceptual entity in the form of a multimodal feature vector - a probability distribution over affordance hypotheses,

$$P_{Ai} = P(A_i \mid F_t),$$

with affordance hypothesis A_i, and feature vector F_t at time t. It is then appropriate to select an affordance hypothesis $A_{max} = arg\ max_i(P(A_i))$, with Maximum A Posteriori (MAP) confidence support for further processing.

Scenario. The scenario for the experiments (Fig. 2) encompassed a mobile robotic system (Kurt2, Fraunhofer AIS, Germany), equipped with a camera stereo pair and a magnetizing effector, and some can-like objects with various top surfaces, colors and shapes. The purpose of the magnetizing effector was to prove the nature of the individual objects by lowering its rope-end effector down to the top surface of the object, trying to magnetize the object (only the body, *not* the top surface of the can are magnetizable) and then to lift the object. Test objects with well magnetizable geometry (with slab like top surfaces, in contrast to those with spherical top surface) are subject to a *lifting interaction*, while the others were not able to be lifted from the ground. This interaction process was visualized for several test objects and sampled in a sequence of 250 image frames. These image frames were referenced with multimodal sensor information (e.g., size of magnetizing and motor current of the robot, respectively).

Visual Features. From the viewpoint of a technical system using computer vision for digital image interpretation, we particularly think that complex features, e.g., local descriptors, such as the Scale Invariant Feature Transform (SIFT [11]), could support well the construction of higher levels of abstraction in visual feature representations. Fig. 3 shows the application of local (SIFT) descriptors for the characterization of regions of interest in the field of view. For this purpose, we first segment the color based visual information within the image, and then associate integrated descriptor responses sampled within the regions to the region feature vector. The integration is performed via a histogram on SIFT descriptors that are labeled with 'rectangular' (a) and 'circular' (b) attributes, respectively. The labeling is derived from a k-means based unsupervised clustering over all descriptors sampled in the experiments, then by selecting cluster prototypes (centers) that are relevant for the characterization of corresponding rectangular/circular shaped regions, and finally by determining histograms of relevant cluster prototypes that are typical in a supervised learning step (using a C4.5 decision tree [12]).

Fig. 2. Scenario of affordance based robot simulation experiments (Section 3). Bird's view illustrating robot Kurt2 within a scene of objects of colored cans, using a magnetic effector at the end of a rope for interaction with the scene, described in more detail in Section 5. The lower left/right corner shows the field of view of the left and right camera, respectively.

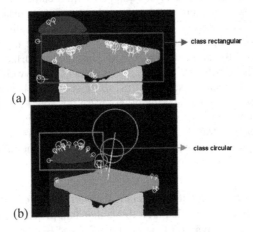

Fig. 3. Categories of local descriptor classes supporting affordance cueing. Classes of SIFT descriptors [11] occurring on (a) *rectangular* and (b) *circular* region boundaries, respectively.

Cue-Feature Value Matrix. Fig. 4 shows a sample cue-feature value matrix (in the context of the experiments, see Section 5) that visualizes dependencies between feature attributes of the region information and a potential association to results of the affordance recognition process. We can easily see that the SIFT category information (*rectangular=R* and *circular=C* region characterization) together with a geometric feature (*top=T* region, i.e., representing a region that is located on top of another region) provides the discriminative feature that would allow the system to predict the future outcome (e.g., *lift-able/non lift-able*) of the affordance recognizer. The latter therefore represents the identification of the affordance and thereby the nature of the interaction process (and its final state) itself.

colour	G	R	M	R	Y	B	Bl	Gr
SIFT category	R	R	C	C	R	R	R	N
shape L/W	L	L	L	L	P	P	P	L
T/B	T	T	T	T	B	B	B	N
LIFTABLE	Y	Y	N	N	Y	Y	N	N
NOT LIFTABLE	N	N	Y	Y	Y	Y	Y	N

Fig. 4. Cue-feature value matrix depicting attribute values of 2D features (color G/green, R/red, M/magenta, etc.), or SIFT category (R/rectangular, C/circular, etc.) and interaction results (left column, bottom) in dependence on various types of visual regions (top row). From this we conclude a suitable feature value configuration (i.e., SIFT categories to discriminate *lift-able/non lift-able* predictions) to support the hypothesis on *lift-able* object information.

3.2 Reinforcement Learning of Predictive Features

The importance in the selection of purposive features for the cueing of affordance relevant features has already been argued in Section 2.2. The key idea about our idea of applying learning for feature selection is based on the characterization of extracted perceptual entities, e.g., *segmented regions* in the image,

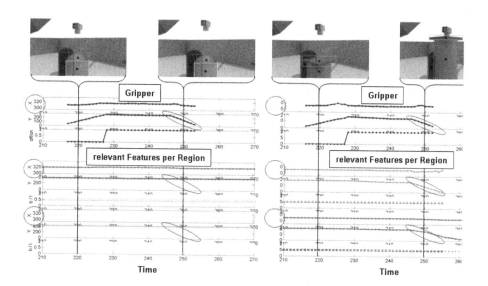

Fig. 5. Example of an *affordance recognition process* (here referring to '*lift-able*'): The upper image shows the right camera views of the robot while trying to lift a test object by means of a magnetizing effector at the lower end of a rope. The diagrams visualize the observation of robot relevant sensor information (e.g., status of gripper, magnet [on/off] and various features of test objects within the focus of attention. Using this sensor/feature information, the relevant channels to discriminate regions of interest that are associated to *lift-able* and *non-lift-able* objects are identified (highlighted by ellipsoids).

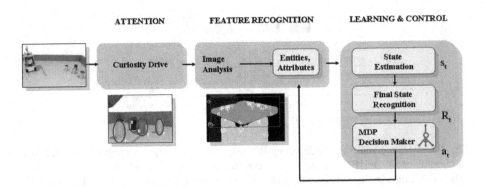

Fig. 6. Closed-loop processing in affordance-based feature recognition. On the basis of attentive image segmentation (curiosity drive), feature entities are recognized, build up a perceptual state and fed into the decision making component. Different perceptual states will anticipate different trajectories in state space; those that are highly rewarded since they anticipate targeted outcome states (the outcome event), will eventually represent a 'cue' status.

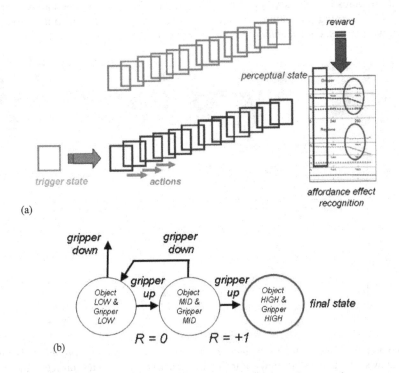

Fig. 7. Structure of the Markov decision process. (a) Perceptual states that represent the outcome (effect) status can be traced back to 'early' perceptual states that enable anticipation of future perceptual states, on the basis of a particular behavior based interaction between agent and environment (sequence of perceptual states and actions).

via a feature vector representation. Each region that would be part of the final state within the affordance recognition process can be labeled with the corresponding affordance classifications. The regions can be back-tracked using standard visual tracking functionality to earlier stages in the affordance perception process. The classification label together with the feature attributed vectors of the region characterization build up a training set that can be input to an exploratory machine learning methodology, such as, reinforcement learning.

Markov decision processes (MDPs [16]) have already been introduced in the context of object recognition (e.g., in [17,18]), in the sense of optimal selection of visual procedures or selected foci of attention to integrate visual information for decision making. Here, the MDP will provide the general framework to outline a multi-step behavioral task under the viewpoint of state based prediction, i.e., cueing, of future outcomes of that task. Fig. 6 shows a schematic outline of closed-loop learning of the behavioral task within the robot scenario presented in Sec. 3.1, together with the extraction of early cues (feature recognition) from a selection of relevant attributes.

An MDP is defined by a tuple $(S;A;\delta;\Re)$ with state recognition set S, action set A, probabilistic transition function δ, and reward function $\Re$: $S{\times}A \rightarrow \Pi(S)$. This describes a probability distribution over subsequent states, given action $a{\in}A$ executable in state $s{\in}S$. In each transition, the agent receives reward according to $\Re{:}S{\times}A{\rightarrow}R$, $\Re_t{\in}R$. In our experimental scenario, the agent must act to maximize the utility $Q(s,a)$, i.e., the expected discounted reward

$$Q(s,a) \equiv U(S,a) = E\left[\sum_{n=0}^{\infty}\gamma^n R_{t+n}(s_{t+n},a_{t+n})\right],$$

where $\gamma{\in}$ [0,1] is a constant controlling contributions of delayed reward. We formalize a sequence of action selections a_1, a_2, ..., a_n as an MDP and are searching for optimal solutions with respect to finding action selections so as to maximizing future reward with respect to the affordance task. With each action, an estimate on the cumulative reward gives feedback about the direction towards the goal of the task. With each action, the reward is received per action by $R(s,a) := \Omega$, with $\Omega{=}1$ if the goal event is reached (object lifted into goal image zone), and $\Omega{=}0$ if not (Fig. 8). Since the probabilistic transition function $\Pi(.)$ cannot be known beforehand, the probabilistic model of the task is estimated via reinforcement learning, e.g., by Q-learning [19], which guarantees convergence to an optimal policy applying sufficient updates of the Q-function Q(s; a), mapping recognition states (s) and actions (a) to utility values. The Q-function update rule is

$$Q(s,a) \equiv (1-\alpha)Q(s,a) + \alpha\left[R + \gamma\left(\max_{a'} Q(s',a')\right)\right],$$

where α is the learning rate and γ controls the impact of an action on future policy returns. The decision process is determined by the sequence of actions. The agent selects then the action with largest Q(s,a), i.e.,

$$a_T = \arg\max_{a'} Q(s_T,a')$$

so as to maximize the cumulative expected reward $Q(s,a)$. In the selected scenario, actions and states are defined as described in Fig. 7 and 9, respectively.

4 Experimental Results

The experiments were performed in a simulator environment with the purpose of providing a proof of concept of successful learning of predictive 2D affordance cues and characterizing affordance recognition processes.

4.1 Simulation

The scenario is split up into two phases (a) a *cueing phase,* i.e., the robot is moving to the object, and (b) a *recognition phase,* i.e., the robot tries to lift an object as depicted in Fig. 2. In both phases, parts of the objects are described by their regions and any region has different features like color, center of mass, top/bottom location and the shape description (rectangular, circular) already described in Section 3. These features are extracted from the robot camera imagery. Additional information, such as effector position, are provided by the robot. Regions are the entities used in the experiment, i.e. no explicit object model is generated for the can-like objects.

4.2 Affordance Recognition

The *recognition* of an affordance is crucial for verifying a hypothesis about an affordance A associated with a entity E. These entities are extracted out of the images as follows. Firstly, a watershed algorithm is used to segment regions of similar color together. After merging of smaller parts, every entity is represented by the average color value, the position in the image and the relation to adjacent regions (top/bottom). This information is also used for tracking entities over time. To verify whether or not an entity becomes '*lift-able*', the magnetizable effector of the robot is lowered until the top region of the object under investigation is reached, the magnet is switched on and the effector is lifted up. Fig. 5 shows the features of the effector (position and magnet status) over time (diagram of gripper features). If the entity is *lift-able* (Fig. 6, right column), a common motion between effector and region can be recognized. Additionally the magnet has to be switched on and the effector has to be placed in the center of the top region. These rules build up the affordance recognizer looking for *lift-able* entities in the recognition phase of the experiment.

4.3 Reinforcement Learning of Predictive Features

Cueing and recognition can require extraction of different kinds of features. Section 3 already emphasized the need for some structural description of the top region, to separate the unequal shape of the top regions. In order to get structural information about an entity, a histogram over prototypical SIFT descriptors is used to discriminate between circular and rectangular regions.

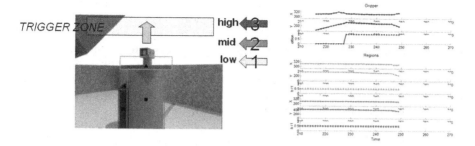

Fig. 8. Reinforcement issued for an object being captured into different zones of the image. If the object is captured and brought into the 'trigger zone' (high, zone '3'), then a reinforcing reward of $\Omega=1$ is delivered, otherwise it is $\Omega=0$ (Sec. 3.2).

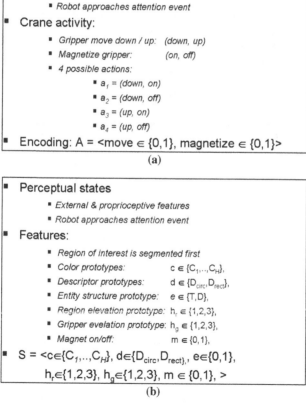

■ Curiosity drive:

　　■ *Attention event in field of view*

　　■ *Robot approaches attention event*

■ Crane activity:

　　■ *Gripper move down / up:　(down, up)*

　　■ *Magnetize gripper:　　　(on, off)*

　　■ *4 possible actions:*

　　　　■ a_1 = *(down, on)*

　　　　■ a_2 = *(down, off)*

　　　　■ a_3 = *(up, on)*

　　　　■ a_4 = *(up, off)*

■ Encoding: A = <move $\in \{0,1\}$, magnetize $\in \{0,1\}$>

(a)

■ Perceptual states

　　■ *External & proprioceptive features*

　　■ *Robot approaches attention event*

■ Features:

　　■ *Region of interest is segmented first*

　　■ *Color prototypes:*　　　　$c \in \{C_1,..,C_H\}$,

　　■ *Descriptor prototypes:*　　$d \in \{D_{circ}, D_{rect}\}$,

　　■ *Entity structure prototype:*　$e \in \{T,D\}$,

　　■ *Region elevation prototype:*　$h_r \in \{1,2,3\}$,

　　■ *Gripper elevation prototype:*　$h_g \in \{1,2,3\}$,

　　■ *Magnet on/off:*　　　　　$m \in \{0,1\}$,

■ S = <$c\in\{C_1,..,C_H\}$, $d\in\{D_{circ},D_{rect}\}$,, $e\in\{0,1\}$,

　　$h_r\in\{1,2,3\}$, $h_g\in\{1,2,3\}$, m $\in \{0,1\}$, >

(b)

Fig. 9. Descriptions of components and entities of the reinforcement learning task within the denoted robot scenario. (a) Definition of the action set. (b) Definition of the perceptual state vector S.

Classification of Relevant Descriptors. All local SIFT descriptors extracted in the region of the entities are clustered using the k-means (k = 100) method. For each specific entity, we generate a histogram over cluster prototypes, using a NN-approach to get the cluster label for each SIFT descriptor in that region. In a supervised learning step, every histogram is labeled whether it is or isn't associated with a rectangular or circular entity. A C4.5 decision tree of size 27 is then able to distinguish between these two classes. The error rate on a test set with 353 samples is ~ 1.4%. Table 1 shows the resulting confusion matrix for the test set.

Table 1. Confusion Matrix for C4.5 Based Structure Classification

Classified as			
Rect.	Circ.		
256	1	Rect.	Class
4	92	Circ.	

Q-learning, decisive states, and affordance based cueing. The objects tested for the affordance '*lift-able*' in the recognition phase are members of the training set. The outcome of the recognition provides the class label ('*lift-able*' or '*non lift-able*'). The bottom region of the object is marked 'unknown' because this entity is not tested directly. As mentioned earlier, there exists no object model yet, therefore only *entities* exist in the system. Backtracking the object's entities over time allows additional training samples to be used with little additional memory effort to remember the data. In our experiment, 30 frames are used from the beginning of the affordance recognition back, for a recall of ~2.5 seconds from the past (12 fps are captured by the robot during simulation). The entity representation for the cueing phase contains the following features: (a) average color value of the region in the image, (b) top/bottom information, (c) the result of the structure classification, and (d) the size of the segmented region. Fig. 10 depicts the learning curve resulting from the reinforcement learning phase, with respect to the average cumulative predicted reward associated to

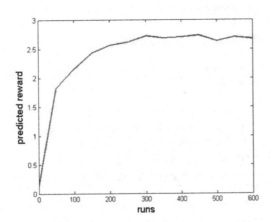

Fig. 10. Learning curve resulting from the reinforcement learning phase, with respect to the average cumulative predicted reward associated to an early perceptual state that is verified to represent a 'cueing' state

- Predictive cue:
  - $E(R) = 2,73$ for a[lift-event]
    $S = <c=green, d=D_{rect}, e=top, h_r=1, h_g=3, m=0>$
- Non-predictive perceptual state (1):
  - $E(R) = 0,23$ for a[lift-event]
    $S = <c=green, d=D_{circ}, e=top, h_r=1, h_g=3, m=0>$
- Non-predictive perceptual state (2):
  - $E(R) = 1,71$ for a[lift-event]
    $S = <c=yellow, d=D_{rect}, e=down, h_r=1, h_g=3, m=0>$

Fig. 11. Different results for cumulative predicted rewards (E(R)), reflecting different evaluation of states towards 'cueing' and 'non-cueing' states, and one intermediate type of state that eventually should not be interpreted as 'cueing' state, as it is characterized as delivering ambiguous information about the anticipatory potential of the referred perceptual state. The features of the predictive cue (top) describe the segmentation of a sample color region at the top of a region configuration that is particularly characterized by the rectangular SIFT descriptors (D_{rect}). In contrast, a non-predictive perceptual state is characterized by the associated circular SIFT descriptors (D_{circ}). No decisive information can be derived from a perceptual state (bottom) that represents a region at the bottom (e=down) of a region configuration.

an early perceptual state that thereby is verified to represent a 'cueing' state. Fig. 11 depicts different results for cumulative predicted rewards reflecting different evaluation of states towards 'cueing' and 'non-cueing' states, and one intermediate type of state that eventually should not be interpreted as 'cueing' state but rather characterized as delivering ambiguous information about the anticipatory potential of the referred perceptual state.

5 Conclusions

This work presented the framework of reinforcement learning for perceptual cueing to opportunities for interaction of robotic agents. The framework for cueing and recognition of affordance-like visual entities is verified with a concrete implementation using state-of-the-art visual descriptors on a simulated robot scenario and demonstrates that features can be successfully selected that are relevant for prediction towards affordance-like control in interaction. The simulation was chosen in a realistic way so that major elements of a real world scenario, such as shadow events, noise in the segmentation, etc., characterized the results and thus enable a scaleable verification of the theoretical assumptions.

Future work will focus on extending the feature based representations towards object driven affordance-based interaction, grounding the work on the visual descriptor information presented here, and demonstrating the generality of the concept. Further-more, we believe that the presented reinforcement learning paradigm provides the appropriate methodology to motivate the learning of functional object recognition on the basis of the reward driven cost function. This implies that the categorization of predictive perceptual states into a classification of predictive object features, grounding the object notion in a concept of predictive feature abstractions.

References

[1] Gibson, J.J.: The Ecological Approach to Visual Perception, Boston, Houghton Mifflin (1979)

[2] Neisser, U.: Cognition and Reality. Principles and Implications of Cognitive Psychology Freeman & Co, San Francisco (1976)

[3] Gibson, E.J.: Exploratory behavior in the development of perceiving, acting and the acquiring of knowledge. Annual Review of Psychology 39, 1–41 (1988)

[4] Faillenot, I., Toni, I., Decety, J., Grégoire, M.-C., Jeannerod, M.: Visual pathways for object-oriented action and object recognition: functional anatomy with PET. Cerebral Cortex 7, 77–85 (1997)

[5] Fitzpatrick, Paul, Metta, G., Natale, L., Rao, S., Sandini, G.: Learning About Objects Through Action - Initial Steps Towards Artificial Cognition. In: ICRA. Proc. IEEE International Conference on Robotics and Automation, Taipei, Taiwan (May 12–17, 2003)

[6] Stoytchev, A.: Behavior-Grounded Representation of Tool Affordances. In: ICRA. Proc. IEEE International Conference on Robotics and Automation, Barcelona, Spain (April 18–22, 2005)

[7] Stark, L., Bowyer, K.W.: Function-based recognition for multiple object categories. Image Understanding 59(10), 1–21

[8] Rivlin, E., Dickinson, S.J., Rosenfeld, A.: Recognition by functional parts. Computer Vision and Image Understanding 62, 64–176 (1995)

[9] Bogoni, L., Bajcsy, R.: Interactive Recognition and Representation of Functionality. Computer Vision and Image Understanding: CVIU 62(2), 194–214 (1995)

[10] Edwards, M.G., Humphreys, G.W., Castiello, U.: Motor facilitation following action observation: a behavioural study in prehensile action. Brain Cognition 53, 495–502 (2003)

[11] Lowe, D.: Distinctive image features from scale-invariant keypoints. International Journal of Computer Vision 60(2), 91–110 (2004)

[12] Quinlan, J.R.: C4.5 Programs for Machine Learning. Morgan Kaufmann, San Mateo, CA (1993)

[13] Cos-Aguilera, I., Cañamero, L., Hayes, G.M., Gillies, A.: Ecological integration of affordances and drives for behaviour selection. In: Bryson, J., et al. (eds.) Proc. Workshop on Modeling Natural Action Selection, pp. 225–228. AISB Press (2005)

[14] Fritz, G., Paletta, L., Kumar, M., Dorffner, G., Breithaupt, R., Rome, E.: Visual Learning of Affordance based Cues. In: Nolfi, S., Baldassarre, G., Calabretta, R., Hallam, J.C.T., Marocco, D., Meyer, J.-A., Miglino, O., Parisi, D. (eds.) SAB 2006. LNCS (LNAI), vol. 4095, Springer, Heidelberg (2006)

[15] Cos-Aguilera, I., Hayes, G.M., Canamero, L., Gillies, A.: Ecological Integration of Affordances and Drives for Behaviour Selection. In: Proc. Workshop on Modelling Natural Action Selection, SMNAS, Edinburgh, UK (2005)

[16] Puterman, M.: Markov decision processes: Discrete stochastic dynamic programming. John Wiley & Sons, New York (1994)

[17] Draper, B.A.: Modeling Object Recognition as a Markov Decision Process. In: Proc. 13th International Conference on Pattern Recognition, vol. 4, p. 95

[18] Paletta, L., Fritz, G., Seifert, C.: Q-Learning of Sequential Attention for Visual Object Recognition from Informative Local Descriptors. In: ICML 2005. Proc. 22nd International Conference on Machine Learning, Bonn, Germany, August 7-11, 2005, pp. 649–656 (2005)

[19] Watkins, C., Dayan, P.: Q-learning. Machine Learning 8, 279–292 (1992)

A Functional Model for Affordance-Based Agents

Martin Raubal[1] and Reinhard Moratz[2]

[1] Department of Geography, University of California at Santa Barbara
5713 Ellison Hall, Santa Barbara, CA 93106, U.S.A.
[2] Department of Mathematics and Informatics, University of Bremen
Bibliothekstr. 1, 28359 Bremen, Germany
raubal@geog.ucsb.edu, moratz@informatik.uni-bremen.de

Abstract. Today's mobile artificial agents, such as mobile robots, are based on an object-oriented paradigm. They partition their environment into various objects and act in relation to individual properties of these objects. Such perception and acting is insufficient for goal-directed behavior in dynamic environments, which requires action-relevant information in the form of affordances. Affordances describe action possibilities with respect to a specific agent. In this paper, we propose a functional model for affordance-based agents. This model integrates an adjusted version of the HIPE theory of function and an extended theory of affordances. We demonstrate the applicability of the functional model by relating it to two different cases of mobile robot interaction and outline an affordance-oriented robot architecture.

1 Introduction

Current mobile robot interaction with the environment is limited due to the wealth of dynamic and action-relevant information, which cannot be handled by today's architectures (Rome *et al.* 2006). Perception mechanisms are focused on the objects and their properties but do not directly concentrate on the available action possibilities. Detecting agent-specific action possibilities is a necessary process for the robot in order to evaluate whether certain tasks can be fulfilled or not. In this paper we propose a functional model for affordance-based agents. Affordances are action possibilities with regard to a specific user and allow for a distinction between such possibilities and the actual performance of actions. They are ideal candidates for focusing on the *agent-environment mutuality* (Gibson 1979).

The original affordance idea introduced by J. J. Gibson was grounded in the paradigm of direct perception. In order to compensate for the neglect of cognitive processes, we use an extended theory of affordances (Raubal 2001)—including cognition, situational aspects, and social constraints—for the affordance-based representation. This theory is integrated with the HIPE theory of function (Barsalou *et al.* 2005) and therefore makes a functional model for affordance-based agents possible. Such representation allows the robot to detect action-relevant properties of the environment tailored to its own spatio-temporal context, tasks, and capabilities. In addition, action possibilities for humans can be modeled in the same way, which supports the sharing of functionalities between human and robot, and facilitates communication. We apply this model to two different

E. Rome et al. (Eds.): Affordance-Based Robot Control, LNAI 4760, pp. 91–105, 2008.

scenarios for mobile robots and discuss the advantages of this approach also with regard to architectural issues.

Section 2 introduces Gibson's affordance theory, discusses its downsides, and presents an extended theory of affordances. In Section 3 we describe the functional framework of representing affordances, which is based on the HIPE theory of function. Two mobile robot systems (*Rolland* and *PEIS*) are briefly illustrated in Section 4. We then develop possible scenarios for these systems and represent them within the new functional affordance model. Section 5 proposes an integration of the model within a robot architecture. Finally, we give conclusions and present directions for future research.

2 Affordances

This section introduces the notion of affordance, discusses deficiencies of the original theory, and presents an extended affordance theory.

2.1 Gibson's Theory of Affordances

The term *affordance* was originally introduced by James J. Gibson who investigated how people visually perceive their environment (Gibson 1977). His theory is based on *ecological psychology*, which advocates that knowing is a direct process: The perceptual system extracts invariants embodying the ecologically significant properties of the perceiver's world. Gibson's theory is based on the tenet that animal and environment form an inseparable pair. This complementarity is implied by Gibson's use of *ecological physics*. Such physics considers functions of the environment at an ecological size level contrary to a description in terms of space, time, matter, etc., within classical physics.

Affordances have to be described relative to the person. For example, a chair's affordance 'to sit' results from a bundle of attributes, such as 'flat and hard surface' and 'height', many of which are relative to the size of an individual. Later work with affordances builds on this so-called *agent-environment mutuality* (Gibson 1979; Zaff 1995). According to Zaff (1995), affordances are measurable aspects of the environment, but only to be measured in relation to the individual. It is particularly important to understand the *action relevant* properties of the environment in terms of values intrinsic to the agent. Warren (1995) demonstrates that the 'climbability' affordance of stairs is more effectively specified as a ratio of riser height to leg length. Experimentally, subjects of different heights perceived stairs as climbable depending on their own leg length, as opposed to some extrinsically quantified value. Additionally, dynamic or task specific conditions must be considered.

Norman (1988) investigated affordances of everyday things, such as doors, telephones, and radios, and argued that they provide strong clues to their operation. He recast affordances as the results from the mental interpretation of things, based on people's past knowledge and experiences, which are applied to the perception of these things. Gaver (1991) stated that a person's culture, social setting, experience, and intentions also determine her perception of affordances. Affordances, therefore, play a key role in an *experiential* view of space (Lakoff 1988; Kuhn 1996), because they offer a user centered perspective. Similarly, Rasmussen and Pejtersen (1995) pointed out that modeling the physical aspects of the environment provides only a part of the picture. "The framework must serve to represent both the physical work environment and the 'situational' interpretation of this environment by the actors involved, depending on their skills and values." (Rasmussen and Pejtersen 1995, p. 122) This can be broken into three relevant parts, the mental strategies and capabilities of the agents, the tasks involved, and the material properties of the environment.

2.2 Extended Theory of Affordances

In this work we use an extended theory of affordances within a functional model for affordance-based agents. It supplements Gibson's theory of perception with elements of cognition, situational aspects, and social constraints. This extended theory of affordances suggests that affordances belong to three different realms: physical, social-institutional, and mental (Raubal 2001).

Physical affordances require bundles of physical substance properties that match the agent's capabilities and properties—and therefore its interaction possibilities. One can only place objects on stable and horizontal surfaces, one can only drink from objects that have a brim or orifice of an appropriate size, and can be manipulated, etc. Common interaction possibilities are grasping things of a certain size with one's hands, walking on different surfaces, and moving one's eyes to perceive things. Physical affordances such as the 'sittability' affordance of a chair depend on body-scaled ratios, doorways afford going through if the agent fits through the opening, and monitors afford viewing depending on lighting conditions, surface properties, and the agent's viewpoint.

Many times it is not sufficient to derive affordances from physical properties alone because people act in environments and contexts with social and institutional rules (Searle 1995; Smith 1999). The utilization of perceived affordances, although physically possible, is often socially unacceptable or even illegal. The physical properties of an open entrance to a subway station afford for a person to move through. In the context of public transportation regulations it affords moving through only when the person has a valid ticket. The physical properties of a highway afford for a person to drive her car as fast as possible. In the context of a specific traffic code it affords driving only as fast as allowed by the speed limit. Situations such as these include both physical constraints and social forces. Furthermore, the whole realm of social interaction between people is based on social-institutional affordances: Other people afford talking to, asking, and behaving in a certain way. Many of these affordances are not tied to particular locations, e.g., people can also talk to other people over the phone.

Physical and social-institutional affordances are the sources of *mental affordances*. During the performance of a task a person finds herself in different situations, where she perceives various physical and social-institutional affordances. For example, a public transportation terminal affords for a person to enter different buses and trains. It also affords to buy tickets or make a phone call. A path affords remembering and selecting, a decision point affords orienting and deciding, etc. In general, such situations offer for the person the mental affordance of deciding which of the perceived affordances to utilize according to her goal.

3 A Functional Affordance Model

The functional representation of affordance-based agents utilizes Barsalou's HIPE theory of function. We first describe this theory and then apply it to the construction of the functional affordance model.

3.1 HIPE Theory of Function

In an effort to analyze the detailed structure of *function* and how functional knowledge is represented and processed, Barsalou *et al.* (2005) developed the HIPE theory of function. This theory explains people's knowledge about function by integrating four types of conceptual knowledge: History, Intentional perspective, Physical environment, and Event sequences. Functional knowledge emerges during mental simulations of events based on these domains.

It is argued that agents believe that the *histories* of an artifact are central to its function. Furthermore, the physical structure of an object depends on its original design purpose. Barsalou et al. reason though that the physical structure alone is insufficient for knowing its function because context, such as knowledge of the setting, is necessary too[1]. This also leads to non-standard functions that obscure standard roles. For example, a hammer might also be used as a paper weight. When representing a function, the agent's *intentional perspective* determines the subset of functional knowledge, which gets retrieved. Such meta-cognitive perspective and point-of-view therefore determine the content of the functional simulation. The *physical environment* comprises not only the object whose function is to be determined and various aspects of the setting, but also external agents. Their physical structures are central to the function of an object[2]. Together, the object, the setting, and optional external agents constitute a physical system that is sufficient to produce a functional outcome, e.g., an affordance outcome. Finally, when this physical system is present, an *event sequence* is simulated. It includes the behaviors of all relevant objects and agents, and produces an outcome.

The HIPE theory explains function as a complex relational structure distributed across different modalities. It is a meta-framework that can distinguish different function theories at an abstract level, such as affordance theories and historical views. In addition, HIPE makes it possible to generate useful predictions depending on the represented theories.

3.2 Functional Representation of Affordances

The HIPE theory is well suited for the formalization of affordances because of their functional character. Similar to functions, affordances are complex relational constructs, which depend on the agent, its goal and personal history, and the setting. The HIPE theory allows for representing what causes an affordance and therefore

---

[1] S. Chaigneau and L. Barsalou (forthcoming) elaborate the fact that physical affordances in the sense of Gibson seem to be more important to understand functions, but history can become important under certain conditions.

[2] This is essentially a functional affordance, which emerges through the agent-environment mutuality.

supports reasoning about affordances. More specifically, it is possible to specify which components are necessary and sufficient to produce a specific affordance for a specific agent.

Figure 1 demonstrates the abstract functional representation of the relation between the three affordance categories presented in section 2.2 during the process of an agent performing a *task*. The agent is represented through its physical structure (*PS*), spatial and cognitive capabilities (*Cap*), and a goal (*G*). Physical affordances (*Paff*) for the agent result from invariant compounds (*Comp*)—unique combinations of physical, chemical, and geometrical properties, which together form a physical structure—and the physical structure of the agent. This corresponds to Gibson's original concept of affordance: a specific combination of (physical) properties of an environment taken with reference to an observer.

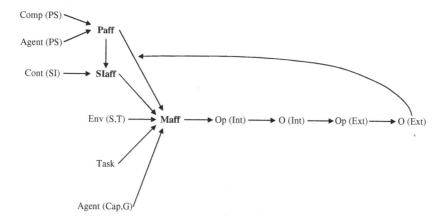

Fig. 1. Functional representation of affordances for an agent—from (Raubal *et al.* 2004)

Social-institutional affordances (*SIaff*) are created through the imposition of social and institutional constraints on physical affordances—when physical affordances are perceived in a social-institutional context *Cont (SI)*. While performing a task the agent perceives various physical and social-institutional affordances within a spatio-temporal environment represented through *Env (S,T)*. This corresponds to HIPE's notion of a physical system and allows for localizing the perception of affordances in space and time.

Mental affordances (*Maff*) arise for the agent when perceiving a set of physical and social-institutional affordances in an environment at a specific location and time. Affordances offer possibilities for action as well as possibilities for the agent to reason about them and decide whether to utilize them or not, i.e., mental affordances. The agent needs to perform an internal operation *Op (Int)* to utilize a mental affordance. Internal operations are carried out on the agent's beliefs (including its history and experiences) and lead to an internal outcome *O (Int)*. In order to transfer such outcome to the world, the agent has to perform an external operation *Op (Ext)*, which then leads to an external outcome *O (Ext)*, i.e., some change of the external world. This external change, in turn, leads to new physical affordances, situated in social-institutional and spatio-temporal contexts.

4 Application Scenarios for Linguistically Enabled Robots

In the following, we describe two real robotic systems, give scenarios for each of them, and present their semiformal representations within the new functional affordance framework.

4.1 Robotic System Descriptions

This section briefly introduces the two robotic systems considered for the proposed functional affordance model, namely the Bremen Autonomous Wheelchair *Rolland* and the *PEIS* (Physically Embedded Intelligent Systems) ecology.

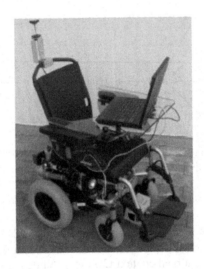

Fig. 2. Bremen Autonomous Wheelchair *Rolland*

4.1.1 Rolland

The Bremen Autonomous Wheelchair *Rolland* (figure 2) has a specific reactive layer, the so-called *safety layer* (Röfer and Lankenau 2000). Its purpose is to guarantee obstacle avoidance by a formally verified low-level module. More complex behaviors such as *wall following* send their commands to the safety layer, which checks their effects with regard to whether they would lead to collisions.

Rolland's linguistic module interprets route descriptions by a human instructor (driver) (Mandel *et al.* 2006). The mappings between linguistic constituents and internal qualitative spatial maps (route graphs) are based on ontological represent-ations (Ross *et al.* 2005).

4.1.2 PEIS Ecology

The *PEIS* (Physically Embedded Intelligent Systems) ecology is a network of heterogeneous smart devices that ranges from simple gadgets, such as refrigerators with sensors, to sophisticated mobile robots. These intelligent devices communicate on a high, abstract level to combine physical and virtual functionalities to perform complex tasks (Broxvall *et al.* 2006). In a typical application of the PEIS ecology a human inhabitant is supported in his flat (e.g., elderly care). Food supply checking, cleaning services, load carrying, and other support are provided by the PEIS network in this scenario. A detailed account of the PEIS ecology can be found in the present volume (Saffiotti this volume).

4.2 Affordance-Based Scenarios

This section shows exemplar interaction sequences for the robotic systems described in the previous section. These sequences focus on the involved affordances. Even if the examples are inspired by the capabilities of the real robotic systems we here refer to potential future versions of the systems with slightly enhanced features.

4.2.1 Scenario 1: Rolland

In this scenario a handicapped user of the Rolland system wants to make a tour starting at the rehabilitation centre with the goal of performing a transaction at the municipal authority. The first important affordance in this context is the social-institutional affordance created by the opening hours of the municipal authority. This affordance is represented as part of the background knowledge of the Rolland system, which shall also support users with cognitive deficits such as memory disorders. Taking into account this social-institutional affordance an adequate starting time for the journey is selected by the route planner of the Rolland system. Rolland's internal map of the city contains drivable sidewalks, possibilities for street crossing (lowered curbstones), suitable elevators in buildings, etc[3].

Based on the mental affordance of evaluating the possibility of performing the given task, the route planner of the Rolland system generates a route from the rehabilitation centre to the municipal authority. When the Rolland system follows the route, the physical affordances of the environment are perceived. In case of deviations, for example, due to road construction work, the system must replan based on the updated map. Additional mental affordances for the robotic system lead to high-level decisions (state/subgoal changes in the deliberative layer, see section 5) about the present location of the robot (self localization).

4.2.2 Scenario 2: PEIS Ecology

As reported above the PEIS ecology consists of multiple robots and smart devices that interact with a human user. In the presented scenario a small PEIS robot is blocked by an obstacle. The obstacle itself can be a simple PEIS entity. Then the necessary information about potential pushability would be communicated by this blocking

---

[3] Since these internal representations are not necessarily correct with respect to the corresponding true state of the physical world, they should not be confused with these real physical properties of the environment (physical affordances).

physical object itself. If the small robot were not able to push the obstacle, the PEIS network could offer a solution by shared functionalities. For example, the obstacle might offer different *physical affordances* to a bigger and stronger PEIS robot in the current network. This second robot could be capable of pushing the obstacle away. Then the smaller robot could send a message (i.e., communicate, which is a *social-institutional affordance*) to the bigger robot, asking it to move the obstacle away. In this scenario the *mental affordances* result from the offered functionalities of the different PEIS entities in the distributed PEIS network configuration memory (Broxvall *et al.* 2006). A planner on a local PEIS entity can then access these functionalities offered by other PEIS entities. Another example of *social-institutional affordances* in this scenario is the constraint for the mobile robots not to drive around too fast making noise at night and therefore wake up the human inhabitants of the flat.

4.3 Representation within Functional Affordance Model

In the following we represent both scenarios within the functional affordance model and discuss the proposed representations.

4.3.1 Representation of Scenario 1

It is important to notice that there are different hierarchical levels for the task of performing a transaction at the municipal authority. The most generic representation is at the top level and the further one goes down in the hierarchy the more specific the affordances become. For our scenario, one top-level action (resulting from a physical affordance) is navigating from the rehabilitation centre to the municipal authority office. Examples for actions on lower levels are street crossing, turning left/right, or halting in front of a red light. Figure 3 shows the representation at the top level. The compound affording something is marked through outgoing dotted arrows.

On the top level, the municipal authority building affords Rolland to enter the building. Entering is constrained by the opening hours of the municipal authority, which create a *Slaff* on top of the *Paff*. The environment for perceiving affordances consists here of two parts: first, the *physical environment*, where Rolland is spatio-temporally located, i.e., the rehabilitation centre at 9am; and second, Rolland's *internal map* of the city, which offers synthetic affordances in the sense that they might be different from the real-world affordances. Rolland's task is to perform a transaction at the municipal authority. Its capabilities comprise the safety layer and also various complex behaviors. The goal is imposed (through communication) by its handicapped user. All of these functions result in the top-level *Maff* for Rolland, namely to evaluate whether this task can be fulfilled with the given constraints represented through the functions. More formally, the (interconnected) sets of physical and social-institutional affordances at a given point in space and time result in a set of mental affordances for the agent: $\{Paff, Slaff\}_{Env(S,T)} \Rightarrow \{Maff\}$. *Maffs* are therefore higher-order functions because *Paffs* and *Slaffs* are functions themselves.

The second part of the top-level process is represented in Figure 4. Rolland performs internal operations (within a planning process), deciding whether the task can be performed based on the given functions. The outcome of this operation is a specific route (under temporal constraints) to the municipal authority building. Navigating

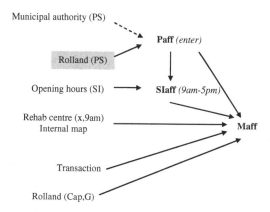

Fig. 3. Top level for Rolland's task

to this building is an external operation and after some time Rolland can reach the building. The external outcome is then reaching and finally entering the building (and subsequently performing the transaction). Again, during the actual process of navigating, Rolland perceives physical affordances in the actual environment and must react and replan if needed.

Fig. 4. Functional activity process for Rolland

4.3.2 Representation of Scenario 2

This representation is more complex because it involves two robots, which are also able to communicate with each other (figure 5). The obstacle is too heavy and therefore affords the small robot (Robot1) *not* to push it away, which is a *negative* affordance (Gibson 1977). On the other hand it affords a bigger robot (Robot2) to push it away due to the different physical structure and capabilities of this robot. An important point demonstrated in the PEIS scenario is the possibility of *affordance transfer*, i.e., affordances can be utilized indirectly via other agents[4]. Here, this is made possible by the physical network infrastructure, which affords communication (in the technical sense), and the *SIaff* for Robot1, i.e., that Robot2 affords asking to push the obstacle away. Robot1 is located in the flat at position x and time 10pm. The floor of the flat affords driving around (*Paff*) and the time of the day imposes a *SIaff*—drive slowly without making noise (not represented in the figure to keep it simple). The task of Robot1 is to move the obstacle, which is blocking the robot's way. Its capabilities comprise various behaviors and the overall goal might be driving into the kitchen. Again, all of these functions result in the *Maff* for Robot1, namely to determine the best way for moving the obstacle.

---

[4] This is crucial when considering computational complexity because often a large number of possibilities for affordance transfer exists in reality.

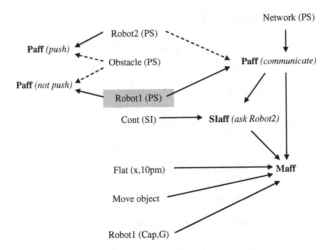

Fig. 5. Top level for PEIS scenario

Figure 6 represents the second part of the decision process for Robot1. The robot performs an internal planning operation with regard to its task of moving the obstacle. Based on the available functions and information from the distributed PEIS network configuration memory, the robot makes a decision to ask Robot2 for help, i.e., to utilize the *SIaff*. It then performs the corresponding external operation (sending a request over the network) and the resulting outcome of this process is a *Maff* for Robot2, namely to decide whether to help Robot1 or not. This also demonstrates the connectivity between various decision processes in the functional affordance model: The external outcome of one process offers another affordance for the same or other agents in the system. In this sense, all processes within spatio-temporal multi-agent environments can be represented as higher-order functions.

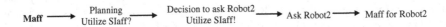

Fig. 6. Functional activity process for Robot1

5 Affordance-Based Architectures for Human-Robot Interaction

This section outlines an integration of the new functional affordance-based representation within a robot architecture. We also discuss the advantages of such an architecture compared to traditional approaches.

The proposed robot architecture is a modification of the standard three layer architecture (Gat 1998; Wasson *et al.* 1999). Three layer robot architectures typically consist of a *deliberative* layer, a *skill* layer, and a *reactive* layer. The deliberative layer takes a high-level goal (in our case typically an instructor command) and synthesizes it into a partially ordered list of operators. These operators correspond to skills/behaviors in the skill layer. The skill layer activates basic action and perception patterns in the reactive layer.

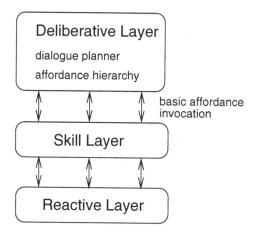

Fig. 7. Basic affordances as interface between deliberative and skill layer

Our proposed modification of this architecture (figure 7) aims at the nature of the skills/operators, and the interface between deliberative layer and skill layer. Similar to the architecture proposed by Arkin *et al.* (2003) we focus on a cognitive basis for defining the set of operators. Whereas Arkin et al. use motivation-oriented animal activities as blueprint for their design we pose the design constraint on our architecture that the operators have to represent relevant affordances of the shared interaction domain of human and robot (or robot and robot as in the PEIS scenario). Affordances are therefore 'first-class citizens'. Within this architecture, the robot's central focus is on functional compounds rather than properties in isolation.

The affordances in a scenario represent the relevant action possibilities for both robots and humans. Relevance of the robot action possibilities in this view does not only refer to the robot's planner but mainly to the user's mental model (Gentner and Stevens 1983) of the robot. In practice this results in the design principle to investigate the mental models of human users and to take them into account for the design of the interface between the deliberative layer of the robot and its lower levels.

Due to this design principle the robot can verbalize its currently planned sequence of high-level actions. The motivation for performing an action is to reach a subgoal. In our architecture the robot is then able to verbalize its subgoals. As humans expect their communication partners to be able to verbalize their subgoals our proposed architecture supports clarification dialogues. These clarification dialogues are crucial in situations where the human must support the robot with hints or even physical assistance. In general, the utility of dialogues in human-robot teams increases the trust of the human operator in the robots under command (Jones and Rock 2002).

This trust is crucial in situations were the robot (-team) supports a handicapped user. For example, the Rolland system could recognize that a lowered curbstone as part of its path is blocked by a halting car. Then Rolland could either autonomously replan the path or first communicate this blocked *physical affordance* to the user. If the driver of the car is present the user of Rolland could then ask the driver to remove

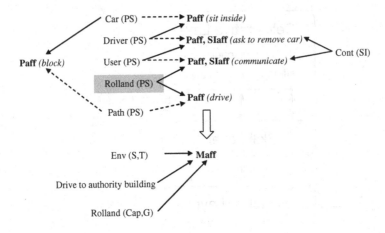

Fig. 8. Affordance-based representation of 'blocking situation'

the car. Figure 8 demonstrates the affordance-based representation of this situation. If we compare both alternatives it is obvious that the setting where Rolland would silently make a big detour to reach the goal would confuse the user and may destroy her trust in the system[5].

To sum up, the difference between our proposed architecture and more traditional ones is to represent the corresponding action possibilities for both humans and robots in a given scenario in a uniform manner. The presented functional theory offers such unifying framework, representing the whole process from sensing to acting in terms of physical, social-institutional, and mental affordances. This design principle makes it easier in joint efforts of humans and robots to flexibly share functions/operations within the heterogeneous human robot team. Especially important in our view is to assess the capabilities of the intended users and their mental models of the robots before designing the interface between high-level and lower-level layers of the robots involved.

The planning process itself would be performed by a planner capable of coordinating actions of several agents, e.g., human and robot in a typical scenario (Alami *et al.* 1998). A specific option relevant for our design methodology is using an interactive planner (Ambite *et al.* 2002). Another technology that fits well to the approach presented here, consists of a perception module for the robot, which is designed according to affordance-based criteria (Moratz and Tenbrink this volume).

6 Conclusions and Future Work

In this paper we presented first steps towards a framework for knowledge representation for human-robot interaction. The key elements of this knowledge representation are three classes of affordances: physical, social-institutional, and mental affordances. In such representation action-relevant properties of the environment, spatio-temporal context, tasks, and capabilities of the spatial agents are modeled. Affordances become 'first-class

---

[5] Generally, a handicapped person wants to be supported only in functionalities that she cannot perform on her own. Nobody would like to be carried by a robot like a passive payload.

citizens'—to be seen as functional compounds—and allow for separating the perception and cognition of action possibilities from action performance.

We propose a robot architecture that uses a hierarchical affordance-based representation in the deliberative layer of the robot control system. The interface of this deliberative layer to lower layers consists of invocation of action possibilities, which correspond to basic physical affordances. The benefit of this new architecture variant compared to more traditional ones that focus on physical constraints of the robots is that also action possibilities of human users can be modeled in the same way. Then a uniform affordance-oriented representation supports flexible sharing of functionalities between robots and humans.

The next step regarding our approach will be building a simple dialogue system and simulated robots as in the system of Jones and Rock (2002). With this system we will focus on the extraction of affordances from the environment to be simulated and from human subjects who serve as test users. Another important direction for future work is the theoretical foundation of affordance hierarchies. These hierarchies span several levels, which are scale-dependent. For example, agents perceive and consider different affordances when planning a trip than when actually moving along crosswalks. In order to make it possible for agents to evaluate the utility of different affordances it will also be necessary to establish a theory of similarity measurement for affordances. Often, agents cannot utilize the best affordance for a given task due to various constraints but have to search for the second-best. Similarity measures will support this search because their outcomes are based on a continuous matching scale (Hahn and Chater 1998). Finally, it will be important to investigate how agents can learn different types of affordances based on previous interactions in spatio-temporal environments, and how these learned affordances influence future behavior.

Acknowledgments

The major part of this work was done when the first author was at the Institute for Geoinformatics at the University of Münster, Germany. The comments from two reviewers provided useful suggestions to improve the content of the paper. We thank the organizers of the Dagstuhl Seminar on Affordance-Based Robot Control for creating a stimulating environment leading to fruitful and interdisciplinary discussions.

References

Alami, R., Ingrand, F., Qutub, S.: A Scheme for Coordinating Multi-robot Planning Activities and Plans Execution. In: Prade, H. (ed.) ECAI 1998 - 13th European Conference on Artifcial Intelligence, pp. 617–621 (1998)

Ambite, J., Barish, G., Knoblock, C., Muslea, M., Oh, J., Minton, S.: Getting from Here to There: Interactive Planning and Agent Execution for Optimizing Travel. In: AAAI/IAAI 2002. Eighteenth National Conference on Artificial Intelligence and Fourteenth Conference on Innovative Applications of Artificial Intelligence, Edmonton, Alberta, Canada, pp. 862–869 (2002)

Arkin, R., Fujita, M., Takagi, T., Hasegawa, R.: An ethological and emotional basis for human-robot interaction. Robotics and Autonomous Systems 42(3-4), 191–201 (2003)

Barsalou, L., Sloman, S., Chaigneau, S.: The HIPE Theory of Function. In: Carlson, L., van der Zee, E. (eds.) Representing functional features for language and space: Insights from perception, categorization and development, pp. 131–147. Oxford University Press, New York (2005)

Broxvall, M., Gritti, M., Saffiotti, A., Seo, B.-S., Cho, Y.-J.: PEIS Ecology: Integrating Robots into Smart Environments. In: ICRA. IEEE International Conference on Robotics and Automation, Orlando, Florida (2006)

Chaigneau, S., Barsalou, L.: The Role of Function in Categories. Theoria et Historia Scientiarum (forthcoming)

Gat, E.: On Three-Layer Architectures. In: Kortenkamp, D., Bonnasso, P., Murphy, R. (eds.) Artificial Intelligence and Mobile Robots, AAAI Press, Cambridge, MA (1998)

Gaver, W.: Technology Affordances. In: Human Factors in Computing Systems, CHI 1991 Conference Proceedings, pp. 79–84. ACM Press, New York (1991)

Gentner, D., Stevens, A. (eds.): Mental Models. Lawrence Erlbaum Associates, Mahwah (1983)

Gibson, J.: The Theory of Affordances. In: Shaw, R., Bransford, J. (eds.) Perceiving, Acting, and Knowing - Toward an Ecological Psychology, pp. 67–82. Lawrence Erlbaum Ass., Hillsdale, New Jersey (1977)

Gibson, J.: The Ecological Approach to Visual Perception. Houghton Mifflin Company, Boston (1979)

Hahn, U., Chater, N.: Understanding Similarity: A Joint Project for Psychology, Case-Based Reasoning, and Law. Artificial Intelligence Review 12, 393–427 (1998)

Jones, H., Rock, S.: Dialogue-based human-robot interaction for space construction teams. In: Aerospace Conference (2002)

Kuhn, W.: Handling Data Spatially: Spatializing User Interfaces. In: Kraak, M., Molenaar, M., (eds.), SDH 1996, Advances in GIS Research II, Proceedings 2, pp. 13B.1–13B.23, International Geographical Union, Delft (1996)

Lakoff, G.: Cognitive Semantics. In: Eco, U., Santambrogio, M., Violi, P. (eds.) Meaning and Mental Representations, pp. 119–154. Indiana University Press, Bloomington (1988)

Mandel, C., Frese, U., Röfer, T.: Robot Navigation based on the Mapping of Coarse Qualitative Route Descriptions to Route Graphs. In: IROS 2006. IEEE/RSJ International Conference on Intelligent Robots and Systems (2006)

Norman, D.: The Design of Everyday Things. Doubleday, New York (1988)

Rasmussen, J., Pejtersen, A.: Virtual Ecology of Work. In: Flack, J., Hancock, P., Caird, J., Vicente, K. (eds.) Global Perspectives on the Ecology of Human-Machine Systems, vol. 1, pp. 121–156. Lawrence Erlbaum Associates, Hillsdale, New Jersey (1995)

Raubal, M.: Ontology and epistemology for agent-based wayfinding simulation. International Journal of Geographical Information Science 15(7), 653–665 (2001)

Raubal, M., Miller, H., Bridwell, S.: User-Centred Time Geography For Location-Based Services. Geografiska Annaler B 86(4), 245–265 (2004)

Röfer, T., Lankenau, A.: Architecture and applications of the Bremen Autonomous Wheelchair. Information Sciences 126(1-4), 1–20 (2000)

Rome, E., Hertzberg, J., Dorffner, G., Doherty, P.: Towards Affordance-based Robot Control. In: Dagstuhl Seminar 06231 Affordance-based Robot Control, Dagstuhl Castle, Germany, (June 5-9, 2006) (2006)

Ross, R., Shi, H., Vierhuff, T., Krieg-Brückner, B., Bateman, J.: Towards Dialogue Based Shared Control of Navigating Robots. In: Freksa, C., Knauff, M., Krieg-Brückner, B., Nebel, B., Barkowsky, T. (eds.) Spatial Cognition IV. LNCS (LNAI), vol. 3343, pp. 478–499. Springer, Heidelberg (2005)

Searle, J.: The Construction of Social Reality. The Free Press, New York (1995)

Smith, B.: Les objets sociaux. Philosophiques 26(2), 315–347 (1999)

Warren, W.: Constructing an Econiche. In: Flack, J., Hancock, P., Caird, J., Vicente, K. (eds.) Global Perspectives on the Ecology of Human-Machine Systems, vol. 1, pp. 121–156. Lawrence Erlbaum Associates, Hillsdale, New Jersey (1995)

Wasson, G., Kortenkamp, D., Huber, E.: Integrating active perception with an autonomous robot architecture. Robotics and Autonomous Systems 29(2), 175–186 (1999)

Zaff, B.: Designing with Affordances in Mind. In: Flack, J., Hancock, P., Caird, J., Vicente, K. (eds.) Global Perspectives on the Ecology of Human-Machine Systems, vol. 1, pp. 121–156. Lawrence Erlbaum Associates, Hillsdale, New Jersey (1995)

Affordances in an Ecology of Physically Embedded Intelligent Systems

Alessandro Saffiotti and Mathias Broxvall

AASS Mobile Robotics Laboratory
Dept. of Technology, Örebro University
S-70182 Örebro, Sweden
{alessandro.saffiotti,mathias.broxvall}@aass.oru.se
http://www.aass.oru.se

Abstract. The concept of Ecology of Physically Embedded Intelligent Systems, or PEIS-Ecology, combines insights from the fields of autonomous robotics and ambient intelligence to provide a new solution to building intelligent robotic systems in the service of people. The concept of PEIS-Ecology also offers an interesting setting to study the applicability of Gibson's notion of affordances to an ecology of robots. In this paper we introduce this concept, and discuss its potential and implications both from an application point of view and from an ecological (Gibsonian) point of view. We also discuss some new scientific challenges introduced by a PEIS-Ecology, present our current steps toward its realization, and point at a few experimental results that show the viability of this concept.

1 Introduction

In the classical view of autonomous robotics, the robot and the environment are seen as two distinct entities. The environment is usually assumed to be non-deterministic and only partially observable, and the robot can only interact with it through its noisy sensors and unreliable actuators. This view is often assimilated to a two-player antagonistic game, in which the robot has to find a strategy to achieve its goal in spite of the "actions" taken by the environment.

In this paper, we take an ecological view of the robot-environment relationship [2,11,10]. We see the robot and the environment as parts of the same system, which are engaged in a symbiotic relationship. We assume that robotic devices are pervasively distributed throughout the environment in the form of sensors, actuators, smart appliances, RFID-tagged objects, or more traditional mobile robots. We further assume that these devices can communicate and collaborate with each-other by providing information and by performing actions. We call a system of this type an *Ecology of Physically Embedded Intelligent Systems*, or PEIS-Ecology.

As an example, consider a robot trying to grasp a milk bottle. In a PEIS-Ecology, this robot would not need to use its camera to acquire the properties of the bottle (shape, weight, etc.) in order to compute the grasping parameters — a task which has proved elusive in decades of robotic research. Instead, the bottle

E. Rome et al. (Eds.): Affordance-Based Robot Control, LNAI 4760, pp. 106–121, 2008.

itself, enriched with a radio-tag, would hold this information and communicate it to the robot.

The PEIS-Ecology approach offers a new paradigm to develop pervasive robotic applications. As we shall discuss below, this paradigm has a great potential to bring robotic technologies inside our homes and working places in the service of humans. However, the development of PEIS-Ecology entails a number of new research challenges that need to be solved before this potential can be fully exploited. Some of these challenges involve issues similar to what Gibson [11] refers to as the problem of perceiving and exploiting the "affordances" of the environment. The purpose of this paper is to introduce these research challenges, and to discuss how these relate to Gibson's notion of affordance. We then present some initial solutions to these challenges, which have been developed in the context of a collaborative project between Sweden and Korea.

In the next section, we briefly recall the concept of PEIS-Ecology, and discuss its potential and implications from an application point of view and from an ecological (Gibsonian) point of view. In the following sections, we discuss the research challenges that this concept entails, and we summarize the current progress in our realization of a PEIS-Ecology. In the interest of space, we do not give technical details or show full experiments in this paper, but we shall refer the reader to the relevant papers in which these details and experiments are reported. More information can also be found at the project web site [25].

2   The Concept of PEIS-Ecology

The concept of PEIS-Ecology, originally introduced by Saffiotti and Broxvall [28], combines insights from the fields of ambient intelligence and autonomous robotics to generate a radically new approach toward the inclusion of robotic technologies into everyday environments. In this approach, advanced robotic functionalities are not achieved through the development of extremely advanced stand-alone robots, but rather through the cooperation of many simple robotic components pervasively distributed in the environment.

2.1   Definitions

The concept of PEIS-Ecology builds upon the following ingredients.

First, any robot in the environment is abstracted by the *uniform notion* of PEIS[1] (Physically Embedded Intelligent System). The term "robot" is taken here in its most general interpretation: any device incorporating some computational and communication resources, and able to interact with the environment via sensors and/or actuators. A PEIS can be as simple as a toaster or as complex as a humanoid robot. In general, we define a PEIS to be a set of inter-connected software *components* residing in one physical entity. Each component can be connected to sensors and actuators in that physical entity, as well as to other components in the same PEIS or in other PEIS.

---

[1] PEIS is pronounced /peɪs/ like in 'pace'.

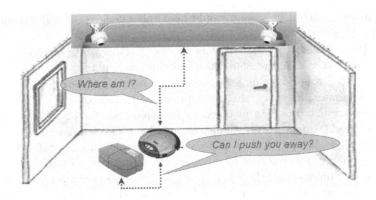

Fig. 1. A simple example of PEIS-Ecology

Second, all PEIS are connected by a *uniform communication model*, which allows the exchange of information among the individual PEIS-components, while hiding the heterogeneity of the PEIS and of the physical communication layers. In practice, we use a distributed communication model that combines a tuple-space with an event mechanism (see Section 4.1 below).

Third, all PEIS in an ecology can cooperate by a *uniform cooperation model*, based on the notion of linking functional components: each participating PEIS can use functionalities from other PEIS in the ecology to complement its own. Functionalities here are meant to be modules that produce and consume information, and may interact with the physical environment by means of sensors and actuators. Typically, functionalities are in one-to-one correspondence to the software components in a PEIS.

Finally, we define a *PEIS-Ecology* to be a collection of inter-connected PEIS, all embedded in the same physical environment.

As an illustration of these concepts, consider an autonomous vacuum cleaner in a home. (See Figure 1.) By itself, this simple PEIS does not have enough sensing and reasoning resources to assess its own position in the home. But suppose that the home is equipped with an overhead tracking system, itself another PEIS. Then, we can combine these two PEIS into a simple PEIS-Ecology, in which the tracking system provides a global localization functionality to the navigation component of the cleaning robot, which can thus realize smarter cleaning strategies. Suppose further that the cleaner encounters an unexpected parcel on the floor. It could push it away and clean under it, but its navigation component needs to know the weight of the parcel in order to decide this. This information is difficult to obtain using the on-board sensors. If, however, the parcel is equipped with a small device able to store and transmit information (e.g., an RFID tag), then it can act as a PEIS and communicate its weight directly to the cleaner.

Given a PEIS-Ecology, we call a set of connections between components within and across the ecology a *configuration* of that PEIS-Ecology. Figure 2 shows the configuration of the ecology in our example. Note that all the connections

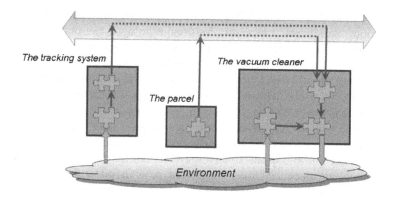

Fig. 2. Functional view of the same PEIS-Ecology

are mediated by a shared middleware (see Section 4.1). Importantly, the same ecology can be configured in many different ways depending on the context — e.g., depending on the current task, the environmental situation, and available resources. In the above example, if the vacuum cleaner exits the field of view of the cameras, then the ecology may be reconfigured to let it use its own odometric component for localization.

2.2   PEIS-Ecology from a Robotic Point of View

A PEIS-Ecology redefines the very notion of a *robot* to encompass the entire environment: a PEIS-Ecology may be seen as a "cognitive robotic environment" in which perception, actuation, memory, and processing are pervasively distributed in the environment. The complex functionalities of this environment are not determined in a centralized way, but they emerge from the co-operation of many simpler, specialized, ubiquitous PEIS devices. The number and capabilities of these devices do not need to be known *a priori*: new PEIS can join or leave the ecology at any moment, and their existence and capabilities should be automatically detected by the other PEIS.

The PEIS-Ecology approach simplifies many of the difficult problems of current autonomous robotics by replacing complex on-board functionalities with simple off-board functionalities plus communication. In the vacuum cleaner example above, the global localization of the robot is easily achieved by the static cameras; and the best way to access the properties of the parcel is to store those properties in the parcel itself.

The PEIS-Ecology approach can also help us to address problems which are beyond the capabilities of current robotic systems. As an example, consider a mobile robot who should monitor a large home using an electronic nose (e-nose), e.g., to spot degrading food, gas leakages, or other problems. The robot would have to detect any anomalous odor, navigate to its source, and classify it. This solution is not possible today due the current limitations of mobile olfaction. First, the e-nose must be brought near the odor source in order to classify it, but locating an odor source by following the odor plume is still an unsolved problem. Second, odor classification can only be done reliably if the number of possible classes is small, but a realistic scenario may involve hundreds of objects (e.g., food types) each with its own range of possible odors. A PEIS-Ecology solution to this problem would be as follows. The environment is equipped with a number of very simple (and cheap) e-noses placed at critical locations, e.g., inside the refrigerator or near the cooker. These simple devices can detect an abnormal gas concentration, but are unable to classify the type of odor. Relevant objects in the environment (e.g., goods in the refrigerator) have RFID tags attached, which contain information about the object itself, including its type. When a simple e-nose detects an alarm, its location is sent to a mobile robot equipped with a sophisticated (and expensive) e-nose. The robot navigates to that place, and smells the different objects there. The information stored in the object's tags is communicated to the robot, and it provides a context to restrict the classification problem. This solution has been explored and experimentally validated in a small scenario [3].

In addition to simplifying technical problems, the PEIS-Ecology approach can also bring a number of pragmatic benefits. A PEIS-Ecology is intrinsically modular, flexible and customizable. Users would only need to acquire new robotic components as needed, e.g., starting with just a simple robotic vacuum cleaner and adding new PEIS devices according to their changing needs and desires. Thus, the PEIS-Ecology approach is likely to provide an affordable and acceptable road to include robotic technologies in everyday environments. Since each new PEIS can combine its functionalities with those of the already exiting ones, the value of the whole PEIS-Ecology can increase more than linearly with its cost.

The PEIS-Ecology approach recognizes the fact that our environments are increasingly populated by embedded devices and tagged objects. For instance, Wal-Mart already requires that all commercial goods are equipped with an RFID tag. These tags can carry a large amount of information about the objects in the environment. In future, they may also be writable or may be able to transmit sensor-based information. We claim that robots should exploit, rather than ignore, the richness of this environment.

2.3   PEIS-Ecology from an Ecological Point of View

Ecology is usually defined as the study of biological species in their relations to each other and to their environment. Essential to an ecological perspective is the fact that the relation between the animal and its environment is characterized as a mutuality and a reciprocity [13]. We can conceive PEIS-Ecology in similar terms. A PEIS-Ecology includes "animate" entities (PEIS) embedded in an "inanimate" environment (the non-PEIS objects). Animate entities interact with the inanimate environment using sensors and actuators. In addition, they interact among them both using their sensors and actuators, and using direct (digital) communication. A PEIS-Ecology is heterogeneous, that is, it includes different *species* of animate entities. In the PEIS-Ecology vision, humans constitute one of the species that can participate in the ecology, and interact with the other PEIS.

Different species in a PEIS-Ecology may entertain different types of *symbiotic* relations via the above cooperation model, that is, using each-other's functionalities. These relations include mutualism, in which the relation is advantageous to both PEIS; and commensalism, in which one PEIS benefits while the other is not affected.[2] By exploiting the right symbiotic relations, a PEIS-Ecology may exhibit an *emergent behavior* that allows it to achieve tasks beyond those that could be performed by any individual PEIS in the ecology. A PEIS-Ecology could provide a good illustration of the famous quote by Margulis and Sagan [20] "Life did not take over the globe by combat, but by networking".

This ecological viewpoint is useful to understand the potential role of affordances in a PEIS-Ecology. The notion of affordance was introduced by James J. Gibson as part of his *ecological* approach to perception [11]. What makes Gibson's approach ecological is the fact that perception is studied as a phenomenon which originates in the relation between the animal and its environment, as opposed to the many studies which look at perception as a process originating only in the neuro-biology of the animal.

In Gibson's terms, "the affordances of the environment are what it offers the animal, what it provides or furnishes, either for good or ill" [11, p. 127]. Typical examples include: a nearly flat solid surface (e.g., floor) affords support and walking; a graspable rigid object of moderate size and weight (e.g., a stone) affords throwing; and a rigid object with a sharp edge (e.g., a knife) affords cutting. A naive application of the notion of affordance to a PEIS-Ecology, then, could identify the affordances of a PEIS with the functionalities that this PEIS makes available to the rest of the PEIS-Ecology. For instance, the ceiling tracking system in the example above would afford "position tracking" to any PEIS in the environment. In order to allow other PEIS to use its tracking functionality, the tracking system should advertise this functionality in some way. As we shall see in Section 4 below, this could be done using mechanisms similar to the ones developed by the semantic web community. By receiving the advertisement, a PEIS would perceive the corresponding affordance. This is in accordance with Gibson's claim that affordances are not attributes that minds impose on the world, but perceivable properties of the world.

The reason why the above solution is naive is that affordances are not objective functional properties of objects, but they are always relative to a given agent. For example, a leaf floating on a lake affords support and walking to an insect but not to a human; and a stone affords throwing to a human but it may afford hiding to a mouse. An affordance is an *action possibility*, and as such it depends on the action capabilities of the actor. Therefore, an affordance should not be seen as a property of an object in the environment, but as a relation between an agent and that object.

---

[2] Parasitism, which is advantageous to one PEIS but detrimental to the other, might also be needed in some case, e.g., if the goal of the first PEIS is of primary importance to the entire ecology.

Correspondingly, a better view of an affordance in a PEIS-Ecology is as a relation between two PEIS. Consider again the tracking system example. The tracking PEIS cannot advertise the general affordance "position-tracking" since it cannot track any arbitrary object — e.g., it would be unable to track an object which is too small, which is outside the field of view of the cameras, or whose color cannot be distinguished from the floor. So, a more realistic advertisement for this PEIS would be: "I can afford position tracking to x, provided that x is in my field of view, I am given its color and size signature, and these signatures satisfy certain constraints".

In some cases, an affordance is not provided by an individual PEIS in the PEIS-Ecology, but by a set of PEIS configured in a given way. In the above example, the tracking system can be connected to a PEIS-camera mounted on the ceiling of another room: the combined system would then afford position-tracking to a vacuum cleaner in that room. Often, we are mainly interested in what the whole PEIS-Ecology can afford to any given PEIS. The question of which specific PEIS participates in providing a specific affordance is irrelevant to the PEIS who uses this affordance, and it only matters for the mechanisms that must configure the PEIS-Ecology by connecting PEIS in the proper way.

This point of view is in line with Gibson's in emphasizing that affordances are possibilities which are in the environment, without necessarily being bound to a specific object [11]. However, while for Gibson the presence of affordances is independent of the ability of an individual to recognize them [22], in our case it is important that each PEIS in a PEIS-Ecology is aware of what affordances are present in the ecology. In practice, the PEIS-Ecology should be equipped with mechanisms that allow each PEIS to dynamically discover what the ecology can afford to it, and to exploit those affordances. (See Section 4.3.) In this sense, the view of affordances adopted here is somehow closer to the one put forward by Donald Norman [23] in the field human machine interaction. Norman's definition of an affordance also takes into account the actor's ability to perceive it, as well as the needs and goals of the actor [21].

3   Challenges of PEIS-Ecology

The above discussion suggests that the PEIS-Ecology approach has a great potential to bring robotic technologies inside our homes and working places. Before this potential can be fully exploited, however, there are several fundamental research challenges that need to be addressed. In this section, we focus on those challenges that are more directly related to the notion of affordance.

3.1   Integrating the Physical and the Digital World

In a classical robotic system, the robot's interaction with the environment and its objects is physically mediated: properties of the objects are estimated using sensors, and their state can be modified using actuators. In a PEIS-Ecology, a robot (PEIS) can interact with an object (another PEIS) both physically and digitally: the robot can directly query properties from the object, and it can ask it to perform an action. How to coordinate and integrate these two forms of interaction is a new research problem.

The above problem also applies to the perception and use of affordances. In a standard robotic setting, the robot would perceive affordances based solely on its sensor input. (Actually, in Gibson's view affordances are the first thing which is perceived about an object, even before its qualities [11, p. 127].) By contrast, in a PEIS-Ecology both the qualities of a PEIS and its affordances can be acquired through physical sensing, through digital communication, or both.

Consider a robot in a PEIS-Ecology, which is facing a closed door. The robot would need to know if this door affords the action of being opened. Suppose that the robot is aware that there is a PEIS in the PEIS-Ecology, with ID = Peis-301, which offers the affordance to 'open'. If the robot can establish that the door in front of it is the same physical object as Peis-301, then the robot will also know that the door in front of it affords opening, by linking the (digital) affordance 'open' of Peis-301 with the (physical) affordance 'open' of that door. Furthermore, it will know that in order to open that door it needs to send the request <open> to the PEIS with ID = Peis-301.

3.2   Self-configuration

Perhaps the strongest added value of a PEIS-Ecology comes from the ability to integrate the functionalities available in the different PEIS according to a given configuration, and to automatically create and modify this configuration depending on the current context. Here, the relevant contextual conditions include the current task(s), the state of the environment, and the resources and affordances available in the ecology. Self-configuration is the key to flexibility, adaptability and robustness of the system — in one word, to its *autonomy*. Although much work has been done in several fields on the principles of self-configuration (e.g., ambient intelligence [14], web service composition [26], distributed middleware [6], autonomic computing [31]), no satisfactory solution exists.

An essential requirement for self-configuration is that the PEIS-Ecology as a whole should have the capability to *reflect* on its own status, e.g., to be aware of the functionalities and affordances in it, and of their current availability. In the scenario in Figure 1, the PEIS-Ecology should determine, at the system-level, that there is a PEIS (the camera system) which can afford position tracking to the vacuum cleaner, in order to decide to connect that system to the cleaner. This requires that the PEIS-Ecology incorporates mechanisms to discovery the affordances present in it, to decide which affordances should be exploited, and to create a corresponding configuration.

As an important part of self-configuration, a PEIS-Ecology should incorporate mechanisms to dynamically adapt to a changing environment and new situations. These mechanisms should be able to discover and exploit new affordances when they become available, and to compensate for affordances that are no longer available.

3.3   The Human Dimension

A Peis-Ecology is meant to operate in the presence of, and in the service of, humans. It is therefore essential that the development of a Peis-Ecology take into careful consideration the place of the humans in it.

The way in which a Peis-Ecology interfaces with the human inhabitants is critical to its usability and acceptability. Humans should perceive the Peis-Ecology either as one entity, or as a set of individual Peis, depending on the context. In either case, they should use similar interaction modalities, and experience a natural interaction in compliance with social rules. The humans should also be made aware of what the Peis-Ecology can afford to them, with special emphasis on those affordances which are most relevant given the current context.

In the reverse direction, a Peis-Ecology should be able to incorporate humans among its parts, and to operate in symbiosis with them [8]. It should be able to infer the status and intentions of humans from observations, and adapt its behavior to that. For instance, if a human shows the intention to relax, the vacuum cleaner should move to a different room. A Peis-Ecology should also be able to infer what the humans can afford to it: for instance, the vacuum cleaner could ask the human to empty its dust-bag if it knows that the human can afford that. Ideally, it should also be able to smoothly update its model of what a human user can afford to adapt to changes in this user, e.g., growing older.

4   Progress Toward a Peis-Ecology

The above challenges involve hard long-term research problems, and even relatively small steps are crucial to the realization of the Peis-Ecology vision. In this section, we hint at the initial solutions to these challenges that have developed in the framework of our project [25], and we discuss the role of affordances in these solutions. Detailed descriptions of the proposed methods and of the results achieved are omitted, but can be found in the referenced papers.

4.1   The Peis-Ecology Middleware

As a prerequisite to develop practical Peis-Ecology systems, we need to establish mechanisms that allow different Peis to communicate and cooperate, by implementing the models discussed in Section 2.1 above. These mechanisms should account for the inherent heterogeneity of a Peis-Ecology, which may include devices that rely on different hardware and software platforms and use different communication media; and for its inherent dynamics, in that Peis may join and leave the ecology at any time.

In our work, the above mechanisms are implemented in a middleware called the Peis-kernel [4]. This provides uniform communication primitives, and performs services like network discovery and routing of messages between Peis on a P2P network. The Peis-kernel also implements a communication model based on a distributed tuple-space, endowed with the usual `insert` and `read` operations.

In addition, it provides event-based primitives `subscribe` and `unsubscribe`, by which a PEIS-component can signal its interest in a given tuple key. When an insert operation is performed, all subscribers are notified. Subscription, notification, and distribution of tuples are managed by the PEIS-kernel in a way which is transparent to the PEIS-component. Hybrid tuple/events approaches of this type are increasingly used in ubiquitous computing and in ambient intelligence [1,30].

The PEIS-kernel can cope with the fact that PEIS may dynamically join and leave the ecology. At any moment, each PEIS-component can detect the presence of other components and trade with them the use of functionalities. For instance, if the navigation component in the vacuum cleaner in Figure 2 above requires a localization functionality, it simply looks for a tuple announcing a *compatible* functionality in any PEIS-component: if one is found, then that component is booked and a subscription to it is created. Compatibility is decided using a shared PEIS-Ontology, as described in Section 4.3 below.

The PEIS-Ecology middleware has been released as open-source under a set of GNU licenses, and it is available from the project website [25].

4.2   Integrating the Physical and the Digital World

Our approach to cope with this challenge is based on an extension of the concept of *perceptual anchoring* [7]. Anchoring is the process of connecting, inside an intelligent system, the symbols used to denote an object (e.g., `box-4`) and the percepts originating from the same objects (e.g., a green blob in the camera image).

In a PEIS-Ecology, anchoring must connect the perceptually acquired information about the properties of an object, and the information about that object which is provided by the object itself. Consider for instance the situation shown in Figure 3. The robot is seeing a green PEIS-box, which it has internally labeled as `box-4`. The box could afford pushing to the robot, provided that its weight is low enough. How can the robot decide that, in order to know the weight of that box it has to read the `weight` property from the PEIS with ID = `Peis22`?

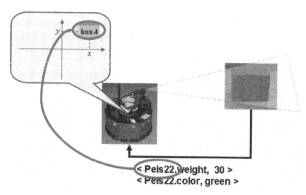

Fig. 3. Linking perceptual information and digital information in a PEIS-Ecology

We use a mechanism similar to the `Find` primitive used in the anchoring framework [7]. The robot queries the tuple-space for all `PhysicalRepresentation` tuples of each PEIS in the ecology (each PEIS must publish this tuple by convention). It then tries to match these tuples to the perceived properties of the box in front of it, e.g., being box-shaped, green, and of a certain size. The matching succeeds for the PEIS with ID = `Peis22`. Once this is done, the robot can ask additional properties to `Peis22` (e.g., its weight) and combine these properties with the observed ones, e.g., to decide if the box can afford pushing. (See [27] for an interesting variation of this scenario.)

The above scenario was tested in a concrete experiment, reported in [4]. Figure 4 shows two snapshots from the execution of that experiment. More in general, the above mechanism can be used to combine perceptual and symbolic information about the same object coming from several different PEIS. More details about the use of perceptual anchoring in a PEIS-Ecology setting are provided in [16].

4.3   Self-configuration

The problem of self-configuration is a hard open problem for autonomous systems in general, and for distributed robotic systems in particular. In a PEIS-Ecology, this problem is exacerbated by the fact that a PEIS-Ecology is highly heterogeneous and intrinsically dynamic.

Our current approach to self-configuration is partly inspired by work in the field of web service composition [26]. It is based on the following ingredients (see [12] for a more detailed description).

- An *advertising mechanism* that allows any PEIS to dynamically join the ecology and let all the other PEIS know about the functionalities it can provide.
- A *discovery mechanism* that allows each PEIS to find which other PEIS can provide a functionality compatible with its needs.
- A *configuration mechanism* able to create a configuration for a given task by composing functionalities from different PEIS.

Fig. 4. A robot querying and then pushing a PEIS-box through a doorway

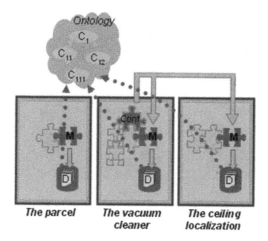

The parcel   The vacuum   The ceiling
                 cleaner   localization

Fig. 5. Outline of our self-configuration framework

- A *monitoring mechanism* able to change the configuration if these functionalities become unavailable.

The above mechanisms help to cope with the dynamic aspect. To help coping with the heterogeneity aspect, we also need an *ontology*, which allows us to describe in a uniform way the functionalities provided by each PEIS in the ecology and the data on which they operate, and to define the notion of compatibility used by the discovery mechanism.

Figure 5 illustrates our approach. Every PEIS is provided with a local directory of descriptions D and with a special component M that can access the descriptions and advertise them to the rest of the ecology. Some PEIS can be equipped with a special *configurator* component, denoted by Conf, that is capable of retrieving the descriptions and computing a meaningful configuration based upon the information stored in them. The configurator also takes care of deploying and monitoring the generated configuration. For the monitoring part, the configurator subscribes to fail signals from the connected PEIS, and re-triggers the configuration algorithm if any PEIS drops from the configuration for any reason.

Note that not all PEIS need to include a configurator, and that multiple configurator components can exist in the ecology. Whenever a PEIS needs to generate a configuration to perform a task, it asks the service of an available configurator component. In terms of affordances, the role of the Conf component is to discover the relevant affordances for the task by (1) asking the right queries, and (2) selecting the right descriptions. Note that the found affordances can be either provided by a single PEIS, or by a suitable configuration of a set of PEIS: this is irrelevant to the querying PEIS, for which the found affordances are simply provided by the PEIS-Ecology as a whole.

The configurator component can be implemented using different approaches. In our project, we are exploring two complementary approaches for that. The

Fig. 6. Two views of the PEIS-Ecology testbed

first is a *plan-based*, centralized approach [19]. In this approach, we use a global hierarchical planner to generate the (minimum cost) configuration for a given task. The second is a *reactive*, distributed approach [12]. In this approach, the configurator creates a local configuration, and assumes that the connected PEIS are able to recursively extend this configuration if needed. If they are not, the configurator receives a `fail` signal and tries a different local configuration. Both approaches provide some simple form of self-repair: if a PEIS signals that a functionality used in the current configuration is not available any more, the configurator tries to generate an alternative configuration.

The two approaches have the typical complementary strengths and weaknesses of plan-based and reactive approaches. The plan-based approach is guaranteed to find the optimal configuration if it exists, but it has problems to scale up and it cannot easily cope with changes in the ecology. The reactive approach scales up smoothly and it can quickly adapt to changes in the state of the ecology, but it might generate non-optimal configurations and it might fail to find a configuration even if one exists. Eventually, we hope to be able to combine these two approaches into a hybrid configurator.

4.4   The Human Dimension

In order to validate the utility and acceptability of a PEIS-Ecology for humans, we have built a physical testbed facility, called the PEIS-Home, which looks like a typical Swedish bachelor apartment (Figure 6). The PEIS-Home is equipped with a communication infrastructure and with a number of PEIS, including static cameras, mobile robots, multi-media devices, sensor nodes (motes), a refrigerator equipped with gas sensors and an RFID reader, and many more. We have used this testbed to run several experiments, including some involving perceptual anchoring [4] and some reproducing the olfaction scenario discussed in Section 2.2 above [3].

Work more directly concerned with the inclusion of humans into a PEIS-Ecology has just started at the time of this writing. Our approach is to see humans as just another species of PEIS in the ecology, which may use the affordances provided by the rest of the PEIS-Ecology, and may provide affordances to it. What makes humans a peculiar type of PEIS is that their goals and desires have a high priority status, and that they need to use dedicated human interface components to communicate with the rest of the ecology. Currently, we are exploring the use of template-based interface components to select, and make visible to the users, the affordances of the PEIS-Ecology which are relevant to the current context [5]. For instance, when a human sits on the sofa after dinner, the affordances of bringing a drink, bringing the phone, or playing music, are made available to her. When the same human leaves the house, the affordances of patrolling the house or keeping the house warm are offered instead.

5 Conclusions

The idea to integrate robots and smart environments is starting to pop up at several places and under several names, including network robot systems [24], intelligent space [17], sensor-actuator networks [9], ubiquitous robotics [15], artificial ecosystems [29], and still others. A few projects were recently started with the aim to explore the scientific, technological and practical implications of this integration. Currently the largest efforts are probably the Network Robot Forum [24], the U-RT project at AIST [18], and the Korean Ubiquitous Robot Companion program [15]. The PEIS-Ecology project presented in this paper is part of the latter effort. This project is distinct in its emphasis on the study of the fundamental scientific principles that underlie the design and operation of an ubiquitous robotic system.

In this paper, we have discussed the strong potential of the PEIS-Ecology approach, as well as the main research challenges that it entails. We have also discussed how Gibson's notion of affordances enters in a PEIS-Ecology. Although the PEIS-Ecology approach was developed independently, the notion of affordances provides some interesting insights on the mechanisms by which a PEIS-Ecology may gain awareness of the opportunities which are available in it, and use this awareness to self-configure and to interact with a human user. These are important open issues in the development of a PEIS-Ecology, and we plan to use these insights in our future work to address those issues. While this paper has focused on the PEIS-Ecology approach, we believe that many of these insights can also apply to other approaches to ubiquitous robotic systems, like the ones listed above.

Acknowledgments

This work is supported by the Swedish Research Council (Vetenskapsrådet), and by ETRI (Electronics and Telecommunications Research Institute, Korea) through the project "Embedded Component Technology and Standardization for URC (2004-2008)". Many thanks to Marco Gritti, Donatella Guarino, Kevin LeBlanc, Amy Loutfi, Robert Lundh and Beom-Su Seo for their invaluable help.

References

1. Arregui, D., Fernstrom, C., Pacull, F., Gilbert, J.: STITCH: Middleware for ubiquitous applications. In: Proc. of the Smart Object Conf., Grenoble, France (2003)
2. Barker, R.G.: Ecological psychology. Stanford University Press, Stanford, CA (1968)
3. Broxvall, M., Coradeschi, S., Loutfi, A., Saffiotti, A.: An ecological approach to odour recognition in intelligent environments. In: Proc. of the IEEE Int. Conf. on Robotics and Automation, Orlando, FL, pp. 2066–2071 (2006)
4. Broxvall, M., Gritti, M., Saffiotti, A., Seo, B.S., Cho, Y.J.: Peis ecology: Integrating robots into smart environments. In: Proc. of the IEEE Int. Conf. on Robotics and Automation, Orlando, FL, pp. 212–218 (2006)
5. Broxvall, M., Loutfi, A., Saffiotti, A.: Interacting with a robot ecology using task templates. In: Ro-Man. Proc. of the IEEE Int. Symp. on Robot and Human Interactive Communcation Jeju island, Korea (2007)
6. The JXTA community. The project JXTA web site, http://www.jxta.org
7. Coradeschi, S., Saffiotti, A.: An introduction to the anchoring problem. Robotics and Autonomous Systems 43(2-3), 85–96 (2003)
8. Coradeschi, S., Saffiotti, A.: Symbiotic robotic systems: Humans, robots, and smart environments. IEEE Intelligent Systems 21(3), 82–84 (2006)
9. Dressler, F.: Self-organization in autonomous sensor/actuator networks. In: Proc. of the 19th IEEE Int. Conf. on Architecture of Computing Systems (2006)
10. Duchon, A.P., Warren, W.H., Kaelbling, L.P.: Ecological robotics. Adaptive Behavior 6(3), 473–507 (1998)
11. Gibson, J.J.: An ecological approach to visual perception. Houghton Mifflin, Boston, MA (1979)
12. Gritti, M., Broxvall, M., Saffiotti, A.: Reactive self-configuration of an ecology of robots. In: Proc. of the ICRA Workshop on Networked Robot Systems, Rome, Italy (2007)
13. Heft, H.: Ecological Psychology in Context. Lawrence Erlbaum Associates, Mahwah (2001)
14. Kaminsky, A.: Infrastructure for distributed applications in ad hoc networks of small mobile wireless devices. Technical report, Rochester Institute of Technology, IT Lab, (May 2001)
15. Kim, J.H., Kim, Y.D., Lee, K.H.: The third generation of robotics: Ubiquitous robot. In: Proc. of the 2nd Int. Conf. on Autonomous Robots and Agents, Palmerston North, New Zealand (2004)
16. LeBlanc, K., Saffiotti, A.: Issues of perceptual anchoring in ubiquitous robotic systems. In: Proc. of the ICRA Workshop on Omniscent Space, Rome, Italy (2007)
17. Lee, J.H., Hashimoto, H.: Intelligent space – concept and contents. Advanced Robotics 16(3), 265–280 (2002)
18. Lemaire, O., Ohba, K., Hirai, S.: Dynamic integration of ubiquitous robotic systems using ontologies and the rt middleware. In: Proc. of the 3rd Int. Conf. on Ubiquitous Robots and Ambient Intelligence, Seoul, Korea (2006)
19. Lundh, R., Karlsson, L., Saffiotti, A.: Plan-based configuration of an ecology of robots. In: Proc. of the IEEE Int. Conf. on Robotics and Automation, Rome, Italy, pp. 64–70 (2007)
20. Margulis, L., Sagan, D.: Microcosmos. Summit Books, New York (1986)
21. McGrenere, J., Ho, W.: Affordances: Clarifying and evolving a concept. In: Proc. of the Graphcis Interface Conf., Toronto, pp. 179–186 (2000)

22. Michaels, C.F: Affordances: Four points of debate. Ecological Psychology 15(2), 135–148 (2003)
23. Norman, D.: The Design of Everyday Things. Basic Books (1988)
24. Network Robot Forum. www.scat.or.jp/nrf/English/
25. The PEIS ecology project. Official web site, www.aass.oru.se/~peis/
26. Rao, J., Su, X.: A survey of automated web service composition methods. In: Proc. of the 1st Int. Workshop on Semantic Web Services and Web Process Composition, San Diego, California, USA (2004)
27. Raubal, M., Moratz, R.: A functional model for affordance-based agents. In: Rome, E., Doherty, P., Dorffner, G., Hertzberg, J. (eds.) Towards Affordance-Based Robot Control. LNCS, vol. 4760, pp. 106–121. Springer, Heidelberg (2007)
28. Saffiotti, A., Broxvall, M.: PEIS ecologies: Ambient intelligence meets autonomous robotics. In: sOc-EUSAI. Proc. of the Int. Conf. on Smart Objects and Ambient Intelligence, Grenoble, France, pp. 275–280 (2005)
29. Sgorbissa, A., Zaccaria, R.: The artificial ecosystem: a distributed approach to service robotics. In: Proc. of the IEEE Int. Conf. on Robotics and Automation, pp. 3531–3536 (2004)
30. Siegemund, F.: A context-aware communication platform for smart objects. In: Proc. of the Int. Conf. on Pervasive Computing (2004)
31. Tesauro, G., Chess, D.M., Walsh, W.E., Das, R., Segal, A., Whalley, I., Kephart, J.O., White, S.R.: A multi-agent systems approach to autonomic computing. In: Proc. of the Int. Conf. on Autonomous Agents and Multiagent Systems, pp. 464–471 (2004)

Use of Affordances in Geospatial Ontologies

Sumit Sen

University of Münster, Robert-Koch Str. 26, 48149 Münster, Germany
sumitsen@uni-muenster.de

Abstract. Affordances are important constituents of our knowledge about geospatial artifacts. They should be seen as complementary to the knowledge of functions of various agents in respect to the geospatial artifacts. While functions combine to form complex activities in which agents can participate, affordances can be nested, or sequential in nature. We extract nested and sequential affordances based on statistical analysis of formal texts to construct hierarchies. Our approach considers affordances of classes of artifacts and thus is relevant to specifications of ontologies. The use of such affordances in function based ontologies is demonstrated using a Road ontology example. The implication of this work can be seen in the building of ontologies used by a robotic vehicle for autonomous driving.

Keywords: Affordances, geospatial ontologies, text analysis.

1 Introduction

The term affordance refers to those uses of an object which can be readily perceived. In the context of a human agent, such uses are closely related to the experiences of the objects. This notion of experience of any object has strong relevance to the meaning of "places". "Places" are reported to be a combination of the concept of a "space" along with the "meaning" implied by that "space". The "meaning" of "places" is expressed by a combination of factors but which are primarily related to the perception related to uses and experiences of a human in that "place".

Simply put, affordances[1] are core constituents of what defines a place. Geospatial ontologies which seek to provide semantic interoperability among users of geospatial information from different domains [1] need to include such information and such a need has been discussed by [2]

The notion of affordance was first suggested by Gibson [3] in his theory of perception and was later re-articulated by Norman [4] in the field of interface design. For Gibson, affordances are objective, actionable properties of objects in the world. For an animal to make use of the affordance, it must of course perceive it in some

---

[1] The term 'affordance' is used in a broader sense which encompasses the notion of functions and perceived affordances of entities. Normally, 'functions' are used to represent designed behavior of entities and 'affordances' to represent perceived uses or functions of the same. In this paper we shall use the term 'affordance' to accommodate both based on the assumption that designed behaviors or 'functions' are usually a part of the perception. We provide some further discussion in section 4.

E. Rome et al. (Eds.): Affordance-Based Robot Control, LNAI 4760, pp. 122–139, 2008.

way, but for Gibson, the affordance is there whether the animal perceives it or not; an unperceived affordance is waiting to be discovered. For Norman, affordances become perceived and culturally dependent. That is, rather than viewing the relationship between sensory object and action as an independent property of the object + animal system, this relationship is contingent, dependent on the experiences of the perceiver within some cultural framework. For example, for a person who has spent the last 10 years driving on *expressways* in the US, *expressways* afford the action of driving up to 65 mph. It would not be possible for such a person to perceive a road where the maximum speed limit is 40 km/h as an expressway.

Extracting knowledge about affordances is a difficult process and the first challenge is to understand that such knowledge is probabilistic in nature and differs from person to person. The affordances are perceived at a certain point in time and are amenable to revision. Some affordances are not yet learnt and some are "unlearnt" over time (and also the learning of 'non-affordances'). At the same time it is important that communities have common notions about publicly shared entities. Public places and affordances of such places have such shared notions. Formal texts such as traffic code texts are important sources of such shared knowledge. Traffic code texts have both legal binding as well as well as an instructive sense which defines what actions should be done (or not be done) in relation to elements of the road network.

The notion of affordances allows two possibilities in the process of identifying objects in a given environment with respect to a human agent. The first option concurs with conventional categorization principles which identify objects as members of certain categories based on their physical structures such as boundaries and features. Such categorization results in classes such as Footpaths, Motorways, etc. According to this first option human agents visualize the environment as objects and attach affordances as we learn them.

Contrastingly a second option is to see the environment in terms of the affordances (and non-affordances) and identify objects based on them. The distinction of categories could be based on a single affordance notion (for example we can categorize walkable and non-walkable areas on a road network as opposed to Footpaths and Roads) and also bundles of affordances in the form of multiple affordances which could also be nested in one another (for example 'non parkable areas'. Parking entails 'stopping the car' and 'walking' and hence is an example of nested affordance).

In this paper we present a case study of extracting knowledge about affordances of road network entities, which includes notions of nested and sequential affordances. We conduct analysis of two traffic code texts based on a word co-occurrence model and discuss the possible options to integrate such information in geospatial ontologies. The work of Kuhn [2] serves as an inspiration of this work but has several extensions to the original approach including automated text analysis and quantitative values for affordances discussed later in the paper.

The remaining of this paper is arranged as follows. In this § we provide further introduction to the motivation of this work and some background of previous work in this area. § 2 describes concepts of text analysis useful for extraction of affordances. The case study involving extraction of entity terms and the functional terms from two traffic code texts is described in § 3. We discuss the results of the case study and difficulties to integrate the different levels of affordance in the subsequent section. Finally we present some conclusions and outlook for future work in this area.

1.1 Motivation

Geospatial ontologies have evolved as the knowledge sharing tool to ensure semantic interoperability among Geographic information systems. Web based geospatial services which provide data as well as processing to potential user communities have become popular with the introduction of standards such as Web Mapping Services (WMS) and Web Feature Services (WFS) [5]. The explosion of such services has increased the availability of geospatial data from a variety of sources ranging from geo-sensors [6] and spatial data infrastructures [7]. The need to address semantic interoperability issues in such increased sharing of geospatial information has led to numerous attempts of developing geospatial ontologies. Agarwal [1] surveys various approaches towards geospatial ontologies and concludes that currently no consensual shareable ontology exists.

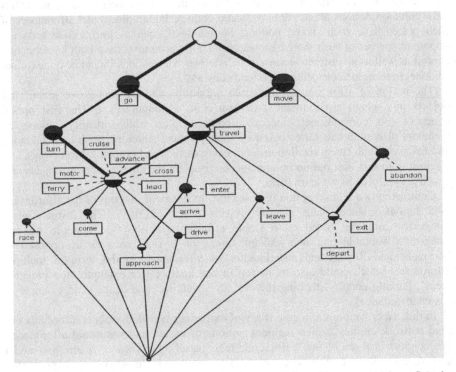

Fig. 1. Hierarchy of action concepts based on entailment relations. The concepts also reflect the hierarchy of affordances and thus the topmost concepts like go and move are afforded by most elements of the road network [8].

One of the important distinctions that can be found in the approaches towards geospatial ontologies is that of the precedence given to affordance concepts as opposed to the entity concepts expressed in the ontology. Hierarchies of action concepts have been reported independently of the hierarchies of entities concepts [2] as shown in the figure 1 below. It is important to note that the action concepts assume a human agent in a road network environment.

The information about what you can do on a certain road is closely related to providing meaning to the given physical space. Such arguments are supported by theories in human geography which suggest that human actions provide meanings to 'Places' as opposed to 'spaces' where they are located[10].

The overall motivation of this case study is to extract such meanings and support the hypothesis that, the inclusion of knowledge of affordances in geospatial ontologies improves precision and recall for queries, within the ontology. For this paper, however, we shall concentrate on the aspect of extraction of affordance concepts and their values, in respect to entities in a road network.

1.2 Background

The term 'Action-driven ontologies' was first coined by Gilberto Camera *et al* [10] to address the intentionality perspective in categorizing the *fiat* and *bona-fide* objects in geospatial ontologies. The view of affordances of geospatial entities should be considered complimentary to that of actions, and is taken in a broader sense as it appears in ontology literature. Affordances are those properties by virtue of which *entities afford* certain *actions*.

Cai [11] has shown that meaning of geospatial data and processing is dependent on the problem solving activities. Timpf [12] maintains that geography activity models help to disambiguate semantics of data in a particular domain. Kuhn [2] postulates that geospatial ontologies need to be designed with a focus on human actions and activities in geographical spaces. The assumption underlying this approach is that increasingly complex activities are a precursor to increasingly complex conceptualizations of the environment and that such a paradigm ensures that ontologies are both concise and related to human activities. Thus as thumb rule concepts of functions are less in number than concepts of entities.

Knowledge sharing about the functionality of engineering artifacts in the manufacturing domain has been discussed by Kitamura *et al* [13]. It shown that an ontological framework for functional knowledge helps interoperability of design data in the form CAD/CAM diagrams. In the context of this discussion two aspects of the use of term *function* can be seen.

- Function as the intended behavior of an artifact
- Function as the Role played by the artifact in a given context

The main point of distinction about these two is the contention that function could be available to an artifact by design or it might be based on its ability to play a certain role. The later is parallel to the notion of affordances [3]. Although it is beyond the scope of this paper to consider the complex relation between design and affordance [14] it is necessary to state that our view on affordances considers both aspects. We assume that our perception of affordances does include the notion of designed functions as well. A far more serious assumption that concerns this paper is related to the absoluteness of affordances. Affordances cannot be said to be absolute and they change based on the physical state and constraints of the human agent. However it is equally true that certain aspects are more salient in respect to the 'concept' of a certain entity and therefore in the context of a Road, the affordance of driving a car is more significant in most situations than other ones such as the affordance of an aircraft landing.

As already discussed, actions are described to have entailment relations between themselves, which tends to lead us to action hierarchies as described in figure 1. A similar hierarchy, in relation to the German Traffic Code is shown by Kuhn [2]. The fundamental aspect here is to recognize the hierarchical structure of actions as described in activity theory [15] and recognize the related notion of nested and sequential affordances. This is particularly important while considering that such information is not integrated in conventional ontologies which treat functional properties or affordances as yet another property of an entity.

Finally, we have also to consider the separation of the notions of affordances into those which are strictly physical (constrained by physical laws) and those governed by socio-legal frameworks. Raubal [16] distinguishes affordances into physical, social and mental categories which are regulated by respective constraints. Zhang and Patel [17] discuss another mechanism to segregate affordances into Biological, Physical, Perceptual, Cognitive and mixed ones[2]. In the legal-instructive framework of traffic codes, it is imperative that our affordances are mixed and are bound by both physical and social constraints. They are also partly cognitive and also perceptual. It is often that physical affordances and social affordances are involved in a nested or a sequential relation.

Sequential affordances are defined as affordances that are revealed over time after a previous action has been afforded. Similarly 'nested affordances' are grouped in space [18]. Such affordances are critical in the context of complex actions and their affordance by entities. We shall use these concepts to encode the hierarchies of affordances in our case study.

1.3 Traffic Codes as Knowledge Sources for Affordances

Analysis of formal documents relevant to the domain are important in this aspect. Traffic code texts are a good source to develop hierarchies of activities in geographical space [19], [2]. Such texts are important sources to develop the theory of how activities are structured in the context of a particular domain. Kuhn [2] analyses one particular traffic code (namely the German traffic code text) and provides a stepwise methodology to design ontologies in support of activities. These steps include

- ♦ Part of Speech tagging of the given text[3].
- ♦ Frequency analysis of verbs and related occurrences such as gerunds etc to generate a first list of action terms.
- ♦ Merging synonymous cases including those with different words but a similar sense of use.
- ♦ Searching for entities which afford these actions. These are typically nouns and noun forms.
- ♦ Cross tabulation of entities and affordances based on their co-occurrence in the text and based on manual inspection.
- ♦ Generation of action hierarchies based on entailment relations.

---

[2] Note that such categorization of affordances not only helps to organize the affordances but also recognize the lack of affordances in a certain category.

[3] In the event of using manual analysis, this may be still serve as an important to guide the person analyzing the text.

Although these steps appear simple and straightforward, there are many challenges to automate such steps. We discuss these details, along with our adaptations of these steps in our case study in section 3.2.

2 Text Analysis for Affordance Extraction

We have introduced the steps suggested by Kuhn [2] for text analysis above. In this section we discuss some of the important aspects of such analysis in terms of natural language processing techniques that are used in our case study.

It is important to note that affordances are usually learnt by agents while interacting with its environment and the same object loses some of its affordances when it is located in the vicinity of another object with different affordance properties[4]. Thus it is intrinsically difficult to assign an affordance to an object at the class level. We therefore borrow from the idea of mental affordances and assume that traffic codes describe the actions that can be afforded on the road network. The information is therefore related to the society as such and is also complete and consistent. This means that unlike the perceptions of individuals in a society the traffic code does not contain contradictory perceptions.

Traffic code texts are important sources of learning traffic rules (besides others such as peer advice, driving schools, etc) for any individual not familiar with them. They play both roles of legal and instructive texts. Unlike documentation about various types of roads based on their width and surface, it provides information about the actions that can take place on them.

2.1 Part of Speech Tagging

Verbs and verb forms have special relevance in comprehension of affordances from the formal texts. Gibson's definition of the term affordance provides a clear link between verbal phrases and affordances.

> "The affordances of the environment are what it offers the animal, what it provides or furnishes, either for good or ill. The verb to afford is found in the dictionary, but the noun affordance is not. I have made it up..." [3].

The close relation between verbs and verb forms are also shown by Kaschak and Glenberg [20]. It is therefore useful to probe the syntactic structure of the traffic code before proceeding to the semantic aspect. We use an online part of speech (POS) tagger based on genetic algorithms in order to distinguish the verbs and verb forms. The GAMBL [21] POS tagger also provides Word Sense Disambiguation (WSD) in order to isolate different senses of the words used. The tool uses the WordNet electronic lexicon [22] to report the different types of senses.

Sample output of the tagged text is shown in table 1 shown below. Part of speech tags based on the Penn Treebank Set [23], the sense of the word and the relation to other words in the sentence are provided in the table. The relevant verb and verb forms to be analyzed are: VB (Verb, base form), VBD (Verb, past tense), VBG (Verb, gerund or present participle), VBN (Verb, past participle), VBP (Verb, non-3rd person singular present), VBZ (Verb, 3rd person singular present).

---

[4] See discussion on ad-hoc categories[38].

Table 1. Part of tagged output text from GAMBL for NYDM (token 179-189)

#	Token	Lemma	POS	Chunk	Relation	Sense	Sense Definition
179	You	you	PRP	NP-B	NPSBJ-B	no-sense	
180	must	must	MD	VP-B	VP-B	no-sense	
181	come	come	VB	VP-I	VP-I	come%2:38:04::	reach a "destination " arrive by movement or by making "progress " "She arrived home at 7 o'clock " "He got into college " She didn't get to Chicago until after midnight
182	to	to	TO	PP-B	PNP-B	no-sense	
183	a	a	DT	NP-B	PNP-I	no-sense	
184	stop	stop	NN	NP-I	PNP-I	stop%1:11:00::	the event of something "ending " it came to a stop at the bottom of the hill
185	before	before	IN	PP-B	PNP-B	no-sense	
186	the	the	DT	NP-B	PNP-I	no-sense	
187	stop	stop	NN	NP-I	PNP-I	stop%1:11:00::	the event of something "ending " it came to a stop at the bottom of the hill
188	line	line	NN	NP-I	PNP-I	line%1:06:00::	something (as a cord or rope) that is long and thin and "flexible " a washing line
189	,	,	,	,	,	no-sense	

The challenge in the next step is to find the affordances related to these verbs and hence identify the objects which afford them.

2.2 Identification of Actions and Entities

Frequency analysis of nouns and verbs results in a list of most significant entity and action terms in the traffic code text. This is combined with manual inspection of such occurrences for the less frequent ones.

Since our overall objective is to inspect affordances of road network artifacts and their affordances in the context of action concepts in relation to humans, we concentrate on

(i)   high frequency road network entity terms (noun forms)
(ii)   high frequency action terms (verb forms) related to the entity terms of item(i)

A cut off frequency is used in both cases. The evidence of affordance of an action by an entity in a formal text is based on their co-occurrence of noun-verb pairs (or co-occurrence of a pronoun representing the entity).

2.3 Noun-Verb Co-occurrences

Phrasal document analysis for Object Oriented requirement modeling commonly uses noun phrase – verb phrase linkage analysis [24, 25]. Similar techniques, based on an ratio of co-occurrence of a noun phrase with a verb phrase with respect to total occurrences of the noun phrase alone, provides a quantitative estimate of the belief about a linkage between a given entity and affordance.

Since the text is assumed to be consistent and complete it is safe to assume that occurrence of a negation statement about an action and an entity such as "Do not walk on Motorways", constitute proof for a 'non-affordance'. Since there are many nouns which do not co-occur with many of the nouns, it is imperative that much of the affordances are not known. These are to be dealt differently from non-affordances.

3   Case Studies on Traffic Codes

We conducted case studies involving two different traffic codes but in the same language [5]. These traffic codes are the highway code of the UK (http://www. highwaycode.gov.uk/), and NY state driver's manual (http://www.nydmv.state.ny.us/ dmanual/default.html). Both are available online and are comparable. However, the New York Driver's Manual (NYDM) is more relevant for automobile drivers; the Highway Code (HWC) is rather general and applicable to all kinds of users including pedestrians, horse riders or automobile drivers as such.

We applied the Text analysis techniques described in section 2 to extract Entity and their affordance related information.

3.1 The Highway Code

The Highway Code consists of Natural Language Texts in about 278 sections which serve as guidelines for all road users in the UK. It includes texts as well as figures to illustrate the proper usage of road network entities in the country. Thus it provides a socio-legal view on the affordances of such road network entities.

Table 2. Most frequent Road network entities from Highway Code

Term	Sense%senseID	Sense definition
Motorway	motorway%1:06:00::	a broad highway designed for high-speed traffic
Road	road%1:06:00::	an open way (generally public) for travel or transportation
Carriageway	carriageway%1:06:0(	(British) one of the two sides of a motorway where traffic travels in one direction only usually in two or three lanes
Footpath	footpath%1:06:00::	a trodden path
Street	street%1:06:00::	a thoroughfare (usually including sidewalks) that is lined with buildings; they walked the streets of the small town; he lives on Nassau Street
Pavement	pavement%1:06:00::	the paved surface of a thoroughfare
Footbridge	footbridge%1:06:00::	a bridge designed for pedestrians
Kerb	kerb%1:06:00::	an edge between a sidewalk and a roadway consisting of a line of curbstones (usually forming part of a gutter)
Path	path%1:04:00::	a course of conduct; the path of virtue; we went our separate ways; our paths in life led us apart; genius usually follows a revolutionary path
Lane	lane%1:06:00::-(defa	a narrow way or road

---

[5] Modern UK English and US English have been reported to be slightly different in two particular aspects, spellings and grammatical usage. However in our case study we use the WordNet lexicon which includes words from both and grammatical differences can be ignored.

The most frequent noun terms available from text analysis of the Highway Code are presented in table 2.

3.2 The New York Driver's Manual

Similar analysis of the New York Driver's Manual was carried out. Although this text was longer and mostly applicable to Drivers rather than Pedestrians or horse riders, it contained explicit instructions within 12 chapters about what drivers on the New York Roads should do.

The most frequent entity list for the NYDM is shown in table 3 below. This list shows certain new entities such as *Expressway*, *Crosswalk* etc which do not occur in the HWC.

3.3 Actions and Affordances

The verb forms extracted from both the text were common to both the texts[6]. However the relative frequencies were different in the two cases. It is important to note that all the different verb forms discussed in section 2.3 were analyzed. Similar to the results presented in the extraction of most frequent entities, the different senses of the words were grouped separately. Senses are taken from WordNet and represented as sense identities (senseID) in table 2 & 3.

Table 3. Most frequent Road network entities from the New York Driver's manual

Term	Sense%senseID	Sense definition
Driveway	driveway%1:06:00::	a road leading up to a private "house " they parked in the driveway
Road	road%1:06:00::	an open way (generally public) for travel or transportation
Lane	lane%1:06:00::- (default)	a narrow way or road
Way	way%1:04:01::	how a result is obtained or an end is "achieved " "a means of control " "an example is the best agency of instruction " the true way to success
Crosswalk	crosswalk%1:06:00::	a path (often marked) where a street or railroad can be crossed
Two-way(road)	two-way%5:00:00:bidirectional:00-(default)	operating or permitting operation in either of two opposite "directions " "a two-way valve " "two-way traffic " "two-way streets
Street	street%1:06:00::	a thoroughfare (usually including sidewalks) that is lined with buildings; they walked the streets of the small town; he lives on Nassau Street
U-turn	u-turn%1:04:00::	complete reversal of direction of travel
Path	path%1:04:00::	a course of conduct; the path of virtue; we went our separate ways; our paths in life led us apart; genius usually follows a revolutionary path
Route	route%1:15:00::	an established line of travel or access
Incline	incline%1:06:00::- (default)	an inclined surface or roadway that moves traffic from one level to another or axle (as in vehicles or other machines)
Expressway	expressway%1:06:00::	a broad highway designed for high-speed traffic
Sidewalk	sidewalk%1:06:00::	walk consisting of a paved area for "pedestrians " usually beside a street or roadway

---

[6] The high frequency verbs occurring in the HWC relevant to the high frequency nouns of table 2 were all found to occur in the NYDM.

Table 4 below presents the list of such frequently occurring verb terms. The corresponding affordance terms are explained alongside. Note that the frequency ranks for the two different texts are different. The walkability affordance is different from the others because it is not relevant to a human agent who is in a car. However it is critical to understand that walking is an important action in relation to actions such as parking.

Table 4. Frequent Action &affordance concepts from HWC and NYDM with freq ranks

Term	NYDM	HWC	Sense definition	Affordance
go	1	1	move away from a place into another "direction " "Go away before I start to cry " The train departs at noon	Ability to go on that object
cross	2	3	travel across or pass "over " The caravan covered almost 100 miles each day	Abitlity to Cross the object
drive	3	2	operate or control a vehicle; drive a car or bus; Can you drive this four-wheel truck?	Ability to drive on the object
pass	4	1	go across or "through " "We passed the point where the police car had parked " A terrible thought went through his mind	Ability to (go) passed the object
approach	5	4	move "towards " "We were approaching our destination " "They are drawing near " The enemy army came nearer and nearer	Ability to approach the object
come	6	5	reach a "destination " arrive by movement or by making "progress " "She arrived home at 7 o'clock " "He got into college " She didn't get to Chicago until after midnight	Ability to come to an object
walk	8	4	use one's feet to "advance " advance by "steps " "Walk, don't run! " "We walked instead of driving " "She walks with a slight limp " "The patient cannot walk yet " Walk over to the cabinet	Ability to walk on an object

4   Affordances in Ontologies of Road Networks

Kuhn [2] has discussed why supporting human beings in geographic space requires ontologies that are developed paying attention to both, objects and activities. He argues that such an approach needs some theory of how activities are structured, before connecting them to objects through affordances.

Inclusion of affordance related information into ontologies of entities with in a road network ontology is important because

- Road network entities are spaces that have meaning. These are conveyed by affordances which are often physical as well as legal.
- Affordances express the meaning of a given entity for a particular domain, in terms of the activities associated with it. It is essential domain knowledge.
- The theory of affordances, along with categorization of different types of affordances allows us to structure such knowledge in a pragmatic way.

We now present some steps to use affordances in the geospatial ontologies for the road network entities.

4.1 Linking Affordances to Concepts

As discussed in section 2.3 we know that noun-verb co-occurrences are important sources for extraction of comprehension of the affordance of a road network entity. Thus a sentence from the NYDM which says:

You may never make a U-turn on a limited access expressway, even if paths connect your side of the expressway with the other side.

means, *limited access expressways* do not afford *U-turns*, although the physical affordance still exists. For our paper we shall not distinguish between physical and social/legal affordances but recognize that such distinctions can be made.

The co-occurrence analysis of the two texts gives us values as shown in table 5 below. These values indicate the affordance each of the entities listed have for the corresponding actions. The zero values in the table indicate non-affordances where as blanks indicate that no information was available to ascertain affordance or non-affordance.

Table 5. Affordances of road network entities based on co-occurrence analysis of the two traffic code texts

HWC	Street	Road	Footpath	Motorway	Lane	Way	Path	Crosswalk	Expresswa
move	0.015	0.049	-	0.012	0.107	0.035	-	-	-
walk	-	0.026	0.056	0.000	-	-	-	-	-
drive	0.057	0.062	0.000	0.069	0.000	-	-	-	-
enter	-	0.025	-	-	0.000	0.020	-	-	-
stop	0.010	0.075	-	0.000	0.000	0.051	-	-	-
be	0.014	0.215	0.006	0.028	0.061	0.033	0.014	-	-
cross	0.029	0.135	-	0.000	0.024	0.067	0.020	-	-
turn	0.038	0.059	-	-	0.042	0.041	-	-	-
wait	-	0.040	-	0.000	0.009	0.031	-	-	-
approach	0.022	0.052	-	0.016	0.065	0.045	0.023	-	-
go	-	0.021	-	-	0.063	-	-	-	-
pass	-	0.038	-	-	0.032	0.012	0.017	-	-
NYDM									
move	0.026	0.032	-	-	0.107	-	0.032	-	-
walk	-	0.010	-	-	-	-	-	-	-
drive	0.020	0.061	-	-	0.056	-	-	-	0.047
enter	0.025	0.048	-	-	0.077	0.041	-	0.053	0.064
stop	0.019	0.048	-	-	0.038	0.026	-	0.059	0.026
be	0.011	0.068	-	-	0.089	0.026	0.004	0.009	0.024
cross	0.061	0.033	-	-	0.017	0.071	-	0.030	
turn	0.037	0.080	-	-	0.094	0.051	0.029	0.018	0.008
wait	0.040	-	-	-	0.009	0.059	-	-	0.029
approach	0.015	0.060	-	-	0.034	-	-	-	0.026
go	0.020	0.029	-	-	0.030	0.051	-	-	0.017
pass	0.044	0.039	-	-	0.130	0.025	-	0.014	0.013

Kuhn [2] reports similar results about the German traffic code, although his results are rather deterministic (do not use a quantitative value to represent the affordance) and do not report non-affordances. We extend the work of Kuhn [2] by adding such information and propose to include such knowledge in the geospatial ontologies.

The level of automation in terms of machine based analysis of the affordance is greater in our case but is also accompanied with careful manual inspection. We confirm the observations of Kuhn [2] that manual extraction is tedious but at times most effective.

4.2 Nested and Sequential Affordances

Kuhn [2] has also reported hierarchies of actions in the German traffic code and this includes the notion of entailment of actions. Four notions of entailments commonly seen in verbs have been reported in linguistics [26]. These include:

- Troponymy, which express super-sub concept relationships among verbs and hence the actions.
- Inclusion, which expresses *part-of* relationships between two actions, implying that one action is a part of the other.
- Pre-requisiteness, where one action acts as a pre-requisite for the second but not necessarily causing the second action.
- Causality, when one action initiates (or is the cause) of the second action

These relations are very useful to probe nested and sequential affordances in correspondence with sequence of actions. For example the complex action *to overtake* is composed of the actions *drive, approach* and *pass*. The affordance of another vehicle to be *passed* on a road is only realized when the affordance of *approachability* has been utilized. Much more complex actions can be explored with the notion of such sequential affordances.

At the same time, by using *is-a* relations we can express hierarchies of action concepts. Figure 2 below shows such a hierarchy based on the action concepts extracted from both traffic code texts. The affordance of the lower concepts such as *walk, drive* etc. entails the affordance of *movement* and is nested inside the former.

4.3 Probabilistic Values and Levels of Affordances

There are several challenges to integrate information about actions and affordances in geospatial ontologies. Firstly, in the context of the hierarchies of actions as seen in figure 2 we know that affordances related to the actions can be arranged in a similar hierarchy. The levels of affordances briefly discussed in section 1.2. The core issue being that distinctions have to be made about the level of a given affordance [16]. As an extension of this notion, in Figure 3 we illustrate that affordances at each level is activated by a corresponding action of the same level. This representation also shows the close relation between actions and affordances. Nevertheless it should be noted that affordances are mere possibilities and hence require independent treatment in relation to actions themselves.

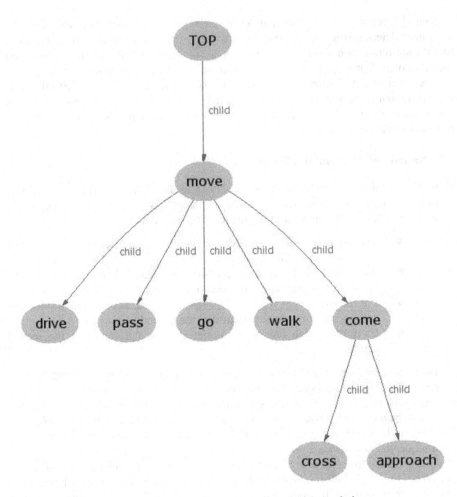

Fig. 2. Hierarchy of action concepts based on *is-a* relations

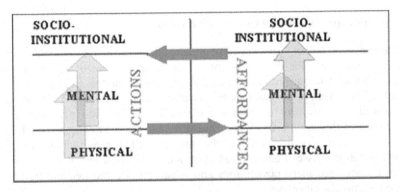

Fig. 3. Schematic representation of levels of functional knowledge about artifacts

Secondly, we are required to deal with probabilities such as the linkages between actions and entities. It is important to note that unlike actions affordances can be measured as shown by Raubal [27]. Such measurements are based on human subject testing but in our case this is done by text analysis. In both cases the separation of different levels as seen in figure 3 is important. As seen in table 5, such information is probabilistic rather than deterministic. It is rather difficult to obtain a Boolean value about the existence of an affordance. The link between an entity concept and affordances is a recorded as a value between 0 and 1. It is also true that such information is amenable to revision based on updated knowledge or revision of the formal text. It is therefore imperative to handle the links between entities and functions in a probabilistic framework such as a belief network .

Some probabilistic frameworks available in ontologies include that of Ding et al. [28] and that of Holi and Hyvönen [29]. Both the approaches are strikingly similar in their approaches of using Bayesian network to represent and ontology, BayesOWL [28] provides not only a framework to build the probabilistic ontologies but also build a reasoning framework around them. These approaches are distinctively different from other probabilistic extensions proposed such as P-CLASSIC [30], Fuzzy DL [31] besides others [32]. The Bayesian network based ontologies do not propose a new logic formalism for ontology representation but allows translation of existing DL based ontologies along with probabilistic knowledge [28].

5 Discussion

The main challenges of including knowledge of affordances in geospatial ontologies are

1 Affordances are difficult to quantify. At best it is possible to provide a relative value. This suggests that probability based values (which are amenable to revisions) are best suited for affordance specifications.

2 Since they are defined to be perceptions of individuals, a value for group of individuals cannot be verified without extensive human subject testing.

3 Formal texts are natural language texts and hence are still open to some level of interpretation. The values obtained by one individual may not be the same as that by another in spite of the level of automation achieved.

4 Hierarchies of actions are independent of the hierarchies of concepts which afford them. This means that inheritance of affordances is a complex affair and multiple inheritances which might capture some of such complex notions, are not advised by ontology engineering principles [33].

5 Lastly, we have already discussed that probabilistic extensions to ontology specification have only begun and the challenge to adapt such extensions for geospatial ontologies still exist.

Nevertheless this case study has also raised a few possibilities in terms of specification of road entities based on the actions that they can afford. Although there have been many different approaches in geospatial ontology specifications [1], it is important that this direction of work, which places primary significance to human actions in geographic space, is given its due importance.

The affordances expressed in table 5 are a vital to any translation or mapping of terms from the HWC to the NYDM and vice versa. Several terms such as *motorway* and *footpath* form the HWC which do not occur in the NYDM can be best expressed based on the similarity of their affordance to those of the NYDM. This is also applicable to terms such as *Expressway* and *Crosswalk* which do not appear on our list for the HWC.

5.1 Affordance Based Ontologies for Robot Control

Ontologies extracted from texts as described can have many uses such as task planning for robot vehicles for autonomous driving. The significance of using such affordance hierarchies as opposed to conventional taxonomies of entities can be explained as follows.

(1) affordance based ontologies are best suited for reasoning tasks which relate to activities and actions. Unlike conventional taxonomy based hierarchies they do not rely on structural properties of entities but their functional properties and hence are more useful.

(2) Since the affordance based ontologies are defined on the basis of a particular agent and its goal (context), it provides better opportunities for a cognitive agent to plan its tasks in a given environment. The translation of the same entities into another context requires a new set of affordance values as seen in table 5 (In this case the goal changes from "driving in UK" to "driving in NY").

(3) Since our system uses text analysis, collective knowledge of an expert group, in the form of documentation, is extractable. These ontologies can be acquired *a priori* by agents before beginning task planning [34]. Such a mechanism mimics the human practice of reading traffic code instructions before driving in a new country.

At the same time it is important to note that there is a need to integrate both views of the world in terms of functional properties as well as structure based conventional ontologies. Some approaches for integration of the two views can be seen in the work of Kozaki *et al* [35] and Sen [36].

6   Conclusions and Future Work

In this paper we have shown a mechanism to extract knowledge of affordances from formal texts and illustrated this with the help of two traffic code texts. Our case study highlights the utility of text analysis techniques and tools for such extraction. We have seen that the knowledge available from such analysis is complex and probabilistic in nature. Several challenges in order to incorporate such information in geospatial ontologies were presented.

This paper has extended some of the work presented by Kuhn [2] although much work remains. The following is a short list of the future work identified in this area

- Since our tool involved use of available tools for text analysis, the results were limited to a certain extent by the limitations of the tools themselves. For example the GAMBL POS tagger shows an efficiency of about 80%. The WordNet lexicon has its own limitations. Improvement in the automation process would help to reduce the manual interventions required.
- The automated analysis of verb-noun linkages currently ignores pronouns and these have to be analyzed manually. It is important to evaluate the machine processing of pronouns in such analysis by using anaphora resolution tools [37].
- A natural step forward from this case study would be to adopt a probabilistic framework for linking the two hierarchies (which in-turn represents the two different views of the geospatial domain). This includes evaluation of the available approaches discussed in 4.3. BayesOWL [27] is an ideal candidate for such experiments.

Acknowledgements

The author acknowledges the help from members of Institute of GeoInformatics and specially to Dr Werner Kuhn for ideas presented in this paper. Thanks are also due to the anonymous reviewer for the constructive comments. This work was completed with financial support from Ordnance Survey, UK.

References

1. Agarwal, P.: Ontological considerations in GIScience. International Journal of Geographical Information Science 19(5), 501–536 (2005)
2. Kuhn, W.: Ontologies in support of activities in geographical space. International Journal of Geographical Information Science 15, 613–631 (2001)
3. Gibson, J.J.: The Ecological Approach to Visual Perception. Houghton Mifflin, Boston (1979)
4. Norman, D.A.: Affordances, Conventions and Design. Interactions 6(3), 38–43 (1999)
5. OGC Web Services, Phase 2 (OWS-2) (2004), http://www.opengeospatial.org/initiatives/?iid=7
6. Schade, S.: Sensors on the Way to Semantic Interoperablity GeoSensornetwerke - von der Forschung zur praktischen. IfGI Prints, Münster, vol. 23 (2005)
7. Sen, S.: The α and β of SDI, Geospatial Today (July–August, 2005)
8. Sen, S., Janowicz, J.: Semantics of Motion verbs. In: WOSLAD. Proc. of Workshop on Spatial Language and Dialogue, Delmenhorst, Germany, pp. 23–25 (October 23–25, 2005)
9. Tuan, Y.-F.: Space and Place, The Perspective of Experience. Minneapolis: University of Minnesota Press (1977)
10. Câmara, G., Monteiro, A.M.V., Paiva, J.A., De Souza, R.C.M.: Action-Driven Ontologies of the Geographical Space. In: Egenhofer, M. (ed.) GIScience, Savanah, GA, USA (2000)
11. Cai, G.: Contextualization of geospatial database semantics for mediating human-GIS dialogues. Journal of Geoinformatica (accepted for publication 2006)
12. Timpf, S.: Geographic Task Models for geographic information processing. In: Duckham, M., Worboys, M.F. (eds.) Meeting on Fundamental Questions in Geographic Information Science, Palace Hotel, Manchester, UK, pp. 217–229 (2001)

13. Kitamura, Y., Koji, Y., Mizoguchi, R.: An Ontological Model of Device Function and Its Deployment for Engineering Knowledge Sharing. In: Proc. of the First Workshop FOMI 2005 - Formal Ontologies Meet Industry, Castelnuovo del Garda (VR), Italy (2005)

14. Barsalou, L.W., Sloman, S.A.: The HIPE theory of function. In: Carlson, L., van der Zee, E. (eds.) Representing functional features for language and space: Insights from perception, categorization and development, pp. 131–147. Oxford University Press, Oxford (2005)

15. Nardi, B. (ed.): Context and consciousness-activity theory and human-computer interaction. MIT Press, Cambridge, M.A (1996)

16. Raubal, M.: Ontology and epistemology for agent-based wayfinding simulation. International Journal of Geographical Information Science 15, 653–665 (2001)

17. Zhang, J., Patel, V.L.: Distributed cognition, representation, and affordance. Cognition & Pragmatics (in press, 2006)

18. Gaver, W.W.: Technology affordances. In: Proceedings of CHI 1991, pp. 79–84. ACM, New York (1991)

19. Kuhn, W.: Ontologies from Text. In: Egenhofer, M.J., Mark, D.M. (eds.) GIScience, AAG, Savannah, GA (2000)

20. Kaschak, M.P., Glenberg, A.M.: Constructing meaning: The role of affordances and grammatical constructions in sentence comprehension. Journal of Memory & Language 43(3), 508–529 (2000)

21. Decadt, B., Hoste, V., Daelemans, W., van den Bosch, A.: GAMBL, Genetic Algorithm Optimization of Memory-Based WSD. In: Mihalcea, R., Edmonds, P. (eds.) In Proc. of the Third International Workshop on the Evaluation of Systems for the Semantic Analysis of Text (Senseval-3), Barcelona, Spain, pp. 108–112 (2004)

22. Fellbaum, C. (ed.): WordNet - An Electronic Lexical Database. MIT Press, Cambridge (1999)

23. Marcus, M., Kim, G., Marcinkiewicz, M.A., MacIntyre, R., Bies, A., Ferguson, M., Katz, K., Schasberger, B.: The Penn Treebank: A Revised Corpus Design for Extracting Predicate Argument Structure. In: 1994 ARPA Human Language Technology Workshop, Princeton, NJ, Morgan-Kaufman (1994)

24. Sojitra, R.D.: Phrasal Document Analysis for Modeling, M.S. Desertation, available at (1998), http://scholar.lib.vt.edu/theses/available/etd-82398-164327/unrestricted/Thesis.pdf

25. Cyre, W.R.: Knowledge Extractor: A Tool for Extracting Knowledge from Text. In: Delugach, H.S., Keeler, M.A., Searle, L., Lukose, D., Sowa, J.F. (eds.) ICCS 1997. LNCS, vol. 1257, pp. 607–610. Springer, Heidelberg (1997)

26. Fellbaum, C.: On the Semantics of Troponymy. In: Green, R., Bean, C., Myaeng, S. (eds.) The Semantics of Relationships: An Interdisciplinary Perspective, Kluwer, Dordrecht, Holland, pp. 23–34 (2002)

27. Raubal, M.: Formalizing Conceptual Spaces. In: Varzi, A., Vieu, L. (eds.) FOIS 2004. Formal Ontology in Information Systems, Proceedings of the Third International Conference Frontiers in Artificial Intelligence and Applications, vol. 114, pp. 153–164. IOS Press, Amsterdam (2004)

28. Ding, Z., Peng, Y., Pan, R.: BayesOWL: Uncertainty Modelling in Semantic Web Ontologies. In: Soft Computing in Ontologies and Semantic Web, Springer, Heidelberg (2005)

29. Holi, M., Hyvönen, E.: Probabilistic Information Retrieval based on Conceptual Overlap in SemanticWeb Ontologies. In: Proceedings of the 11th Finnish AI Conference, Web Intelligence, vol. 2, Finnish AI Society, Finland (2004)

30. Koller, D., Levy, A., Pfeffer, A.: P-CLASSIC: A Tractable Probabilistic Description Logic. In: Proc. of AAAI-1997, pp. 390–397 (1997)
31. Straccia, U.: A fuzzy description logic. In: AAAI-98. Proc. of the 15th Nat.Conf. on Artificial Intelligence, Madison, USA, pp. 594–599 (1998)
32. Stuckenschmidt, H., Visser, U.: Semantic Translation based on Approximate Reclassification. In: KR 2000. Proc. of the Workshop Semantic Approximation, Granularity and Vagueness (2000)
33. Guarino, N., Welty, C.: An Overview of OntoClean. In: Staab, S., Studer, R. (eds.) Handbook on Ontologies, Springer, Heidelberg (2004)
34. Arkin, R.C., MacKenzie, D.: Planning to Behave: A Hybrid Deliberative/Reactive Robot Control Architecture for Mobile Manipulation. In: International Symposium on Robotics and Manufacturing, Maui, Hawaii, pp. 5–12 (1994)
35. Sen, S.: Linking hierarchies of entities and their functions in geospatial ontologies. Journal of Geomatics, vol. 1(1) (2007)
36. Kozaki, K., Kitamura, Y., Ikeda, M., Mizoguchi, R.: Hozo: An Environment for Building/Using Ontologies Based on a Fundamental Consideration of "Role" and "Relationship". In: Gómez-Pérez, A., Benjamins, V.R. (eds.) EKAW 2002. LNCS (LNAI), vol. 2473, pp. 213–218. Springer, Heidelberg (2002)
37. Mitkov, R., Evans, R., Orasan, C.: A new, fully automatic version of Mitkov's knowledge-poor pronoun resolution method. In: Gelbukh, A. (ed.) CICLing 2002. LNCS, vol. 2276, Springer, Heidelberg (2002)
38. Barsalou, L.: Ad hoc categories. Memory & Cognition 11, 211–227 (1983)

Learning the Affordances of Tools Using a Behavior-Grounded Approach

Alexander Stoytchev

Department of Electrical and Computer Engineering
Iowa State University, Ames IA 50011, USA
alexs@iastate.edu

Abstract. This paper introduces a behavior-grounded approach to representing and learning the affordances of tools by a robot. The affordance representation is learned during a behavioral babbling stage in which the robot randomly chooses different exploratory behaviors, applies them to the tool, and observes their effects on environmental objects. As a result of this exploratory procedure, the tool representation is *grounded* in the behavioral and perceptual repertoire of the robot. Furthermore, the representation is *autonomously* testable and verifiable by the robot as it is expressed in concrete terms (i.e., behaviors) that are directly available to the robot's controller. The tool representation described here can also be used to solve tool-using tasks by dynamically sequencing the exploratory behaviors which were used to explore the tool based on their expected outcomes. The quality of the learned representation was tested on extension-of-reach tasks with rigid tools.

1 Introduction

The ability to use tools is one of the hallmarks of intelligence. Tool use is fundamental to human life and has been for at least the last two million years. We use tools to extend our reach, to amplify our physical strength, to transfer objects and liquids, and to achieve many other everyday tasks. A large number of animals have also been observed to use tools [1]. Some birds, for example, use twigs or cactus pines to probe for larvae in crevices which they cannot reach with their beaks. Sea otters use stones to open hard-shelled mussels. Chimpanzees use stones to crack nuts open and sticks to reach food, dig holes, or attack predators. Orangutans fish for termites with twigs and grass blades. Horses and elephants use sticks to scratch their bodies. These examples suggest that the ability to use tools is an adaptation mechanism used by many organisms to overcome the limitations imposed on them by their anatomy.

Despite the widespread use of tools in the animal world, however, studies of *autonomous* robotic tool use are still rare. There are industrial robots that use tools for tasks such as welding, cutting, and painting, but these operations are carefully scripted by a human programmer. Robot hardware capabilities, however, continue to increase at a remarkable rate. Humanoid robots such as Honda's Asimo, Sony's Qrio, and NASA's Robonaut feature motor capabilities

E. Rome et al. (Eds.): Affordance-Based Robot Control, LNAI 4760, pp. 140–158, 2008.

similar to those of humans. In the near future similar robots will be working side by side with humans in homes, offices, hospitals, and in outer space. It is difficult to imagine how these robots that will look like us, act like us, and live in the same physical environment like us, will be very useful if they are not capable of something so innate to human culture as the ability to use tools. Because of their humanoid "anatomy" these robots undoubtedly will have to use external objects in a variety of tasks, for instance, to improve their reach or to increase their physical strength. These important problems, however, have not been well addressed by the robotics community.

Another motivation for studying robot tool behaviors is the hope that robotics can play a major role in answering some of the fundamental questions about tool-using abilities of animals and humans. After ninety years of tool-using experiments with animals (see next section) there is still no comprehensive theory attempting to explain the origins, development, and learning of tool behaviors in living organisms.

Progress along these two lines of research, however, is unlikely without initial experimental work which can be used as the foundation for a computational theory of tool use. Therefore, the purpose of this paper is to empirically evaluate one specific way of representing and learning the functional properties or affordances [2] of tools.

The tool representation described here uses a behavior-based approach [3] to *ground* the tool affordances in the existing behavioral repertoire of the robot. The representation is learned during a behavioral babbling stage in which the robot randomly chooses different exploratory behaviors, applies them to the tool, and observes their effects on environmental objects. The quality of the learned representation is tested on extension-of-reach tool tasks. The experiments were conducted using a mobile robot manipulator. As far as we know, this is one of the first studies of this kind in the Robotics and AI literature.

2   Related Work

2.1   Affordances and Exploratory Behaviors

A simple object like a stick can be used in numerous tasks that are quite different from one another. For example, a stick can be used to strike, poke, prop, scratch, pry, dig, etc. It is still a mystery how animals and humans learn these affordances [2] and what are the cognitive structures used to represent them.

James Gibson defined affordances as "perceptual invariants" that are directly perceived by an organism and enable it to perform tasks [2]. Gibson is not specific about the way in which affordances are learned but he suggests that some affordances are learned in infancy when the child experiments with objects. For example, an object affords throwing if it can be grasped and moved away from one's body with a swift action of the hand and then letting it go. The perceptual invariant in this case is the shrinking of the visual angle of the object as it is flying through the air. This highly interesting "zoom" effect will draw the attention of the child [2, p. 235].

Gibson defines tools as detached objects that are graspable, portable, manipulable, and usually rigid [2, p. 40]. A hammer, for example, is an elongated object that is graspable at one end, weighted at the other end, and affords hitting or hammering. A knife, on the other hand, is a graspable object with a sharp blade that affords cutting. A writing tool like a pencil leaves traces when applied to surfaces and thus affords trace-making [2, p. 134].

The related work on animal object exploration indicates that animals use stereotyped exploratory behaviors when faced with a new object [4,5]. This set of behaviors is species specific and may be genetically predetermined. For some species of animals these tests include almost their entire behavioral repertoire: "A young corvide bird, confronted with an object it has never seen, runs through practically all of its behavioral patterns, except social and sexual ones." [5, p. 44].

Recent studies with human subjects also suggest that the internal representation for a new tool used by the brain might be encoded in terms of specific past experiences [6]. Furthermore, these past experiences consist of brief feedforward movement segments used in the initial exploration of the tool [6]. A tool task is later solved by dynamically combining these sequences [6].

Thus, the properties of a tool that an animal is likely to learn are directly related to the behavioral and perceptual repertoire of the animal. Furthermore, the learning of these properties should be relatively easy since the only requirement is to perform a (small) set of exploratory behaviors and observe their effects. Based on the results of these "experiments" the animal builds an internal representation for the tool and the actions that it affords. Solving tool tasks in the future is based on dynamically combining the exploratory behaviors based on their expected results.

Section 3 formulates a behavior-grounded computational model of tool affordances based on these principles.

2.2   Experiments with Primates

According to Beck [1], whose taxonomy is widely adopted today, most animals use tools for four different functions: 1) to extend their reach; 2) to amplify the mechanical force that they can exert on the environment; 3) to enhance the effectiveness of antagonistic display behaviors; and 4) to control the flow of liquids. This paper focuses only on the extension of reach mode of tool use.

Extension of reach experiments have been used for the last 90 years to test the intelligence and tool-using abilities of primates [7,8,9]. In these experiments the animal is prevented from getting close to an incentive and thus it must use one of the available tools to bring the incentive within its sphere of reach.

Wolfgang Köhler was the first to systematically study the tool behaviors of chimpanzees. He performed a large number of experiments from 1913 to 1917. The experimental designs were quite elaborate and required use of a variety of tools: straight sticks, L-sticks, T-sticks, ladders, boxes, rocks, ribbons, ropes, and coils of wire. The incentive for the animal was a banana or a piece of apple which could not be reached without using one or more of the available tools. The experimental methodology was to let the animals freely experiment with the available tools for a limited time period. If the problem was not solved during that time, the experiment was terminated and repeated at some later time.

In more recent experimental work, Povinelli et al. [8] replicated many of the experiments performed by Köhler and used statistical techniques to analyze the results. The main conclusion was that chimpanzees solve these tasks using simple rules extracted from experience like "contact between objects is necessary and sufficient to establish covariation in movement" [8, p. 305]. Furthermore, it was concluded that chimpanzees do not reason about their own actions and tool tasks in terms of abstract unobservable phenomena such as force and gravity. Even the notion of contact that they have is that of "visual contact" and not "physical contact" or "support" [8, p. 260]. Similar results have been reported by Visalberghi and Trinca [9].

The conclusions of these studies were used to guide the design of the robot's perceptual routines (see Section 4).

2.3 Related Work in Robotics and AI

Krotkov [10] notes that relatively little robotics research has been geared towards discovering external objects' properties other than shape and position. Some of the exploration methods employed by the robot in Krotkov's work use tools coupled with sensory routines to discover object properties. For example, the "whack and watch" method uses a wooden pendulum to strike an object in order to estimate its mass and coefficient of sliding friction. The "hit and listen" method uses a blind person's cane to determine the acoustic properties of objects. Fitzpatrick et al. [11] used a similar approach to program a robot to poke objects with its arm (without using a tool) and learn the rolling properties of the objects from the resulting displacements.

Bogoni and Bajcsy describe a system that evaluates the applicability of differently shaped pointed objects for cutting and piercing operations [12,13]. A robot manipulator is used to move the tool into contact with various materials (e.g., wood, sponge, plasticine) while a computer vision system tracks the outline of the tool and measures its penetration into the material. The outlines of the tools are modeled by superquadratics and clustering algorithms are used to identify interesting properties of successful tools. This work is one of the few examples in the robotics literature that has attempted to study object functionality with the intention of using the object as a tool by a robot.

Several computer vision projects have focused on the task of recognizing objects based on their functionality [14,15]. Hand tools are probably the most popular object category used to test these systems. One problem with these systems, however, is that they try to reason about the functionalities of objects without actively interacting with the objects.

3   Behavior-Grounded Tool Representation

3.1   Robots, Tools, and Tasks

Several definitions for tool use have been given in the literature. Arguably, the most comprehensive definition is the one given by Beck [1, p. 10]:

> *"Tool use is the external employment of an unattached environmental object to alter more efficiently the form, position, or condition of another object, another organism, or the user itself when the user holds or carries the tool during or just prior to use and is responsible for the proper and effective orientation of the tool."*

The notion of robotic tool use brings to mind four things: 1) a robot; 2) an environmental object which is labeled a tool; 3) another environmental object to which the tool is applied (labeled an attractor); and 4) a tool task. For tool use to occur all four components need to be present. In fact, it is meaningless to talk about one without taking into account the other three. What might be a tool for one robot may not be a tool for another because of differences in the robots' capabilities. Alternatively, a tool might be suitable for one task (and/or object) but completely useless for another. And finally, some tasks may not be within the range of capabilities of a robot even if the robot is otherwise capable of using tools. Thus, the four components of tool use must always be taken into consideration together.

This is compatible with Gibson's claim that objects afford different things to people with different body sizes. For example, an object might be graspable for an adult but may not be graspable for a child. Therefore, Gibson suggests that a child learns "his scale of sizes as commensurate with his body, not with a measuring stick" [2, p. 235]. For example, an object is graspable if it has opposable surfaces the distance between which is less than the span of the hand [2, p. 133].

Because of these arguments, any tool representation should take into account the robot that is using the tool. In other words, the representation should be *grounded* in the behavioral and perceptual repertoire of the robot. The main advantage of this approach is that the tool's affordances are expressed in concrete terms (i.e., behaviors) that are available to the robot's controller. Note that this is in sharp contrast with other theories of intelligent systems reasoning about objects in the physical world [16,14]. They make the assumption that object properties can be expressed in abstract form (by a human) without taking into account the robot that will be using them.

Another advantage of the *behavior-grounded* approach is that it can handle changes in the tool's properties over time. For example, if a familiar tool becomes deformed (or a piece of it breaks off) it is no longer the same tool. However, the robot can directly test the accuracy of its representation by executing the same set of exploratory behaviors that was used in the past. If any inconsistencies are detected in the resulting observations they can be used to update the tool's representation. Thus, the accuracy of the representation can be directly tested by the robot.

3.2   Theoretical Formulation

The previous sections presented a justification for the *behavior-grounded* representation. This section formulates these ideas using the following notation.

Let $\beta_{e_1}, \beta_{e_2}, \ldots, \beta_{e_k}$ be the set of exploratory behaviors available to the robot. Each behavior, has one or more parameters that modify its outcome. Let the parameters for behavior β_{e_i} be given as a parameter vector $E_i = [e_1^i, e_2^i, \ldots e_{p(i)}^i]$, where $p(i)$ is the number of parameters for this behavior. The behaviors, and their parameters, could be learned by imitation, programmed manually, or learned autonomously by the robot. In this paper, however, the issue of how these behaviors are selected and/or learned will be ignored.

In a similar fashion, let $\beta_{b_1}, \beta_{b_2}, \ldots, \beta_{b_m}$ be the set of binding behaviors available to the robot. These behaviors allow the robot to attach tools to its body. The most common binding behavior is grasping. However, there are many examples in which a tool can be controlled even if it is not grasped. Therefore, the term *binding* will be used. The parameters for binding behavior β_{b_i} are given as a parameter vector $B_i = [b_1^i, b_2^i, \ldots b_{q(i)}^i]$.

Furthermore, let the robot's perceptual routines provide a stream of observations in the form of an observation vector $O = [o_1, o_2, \ldots, o_n]$. It is assumed that the set of observations is rich enough to capture the essential features of the tasks to which the tool will be applied.

A change detection function, $T(O(t'), O(t'')) \rightarrow \{0, 1\}$, that takes two observation vectors as parameters is also defined. This function determines if an "interesting" observation was detected in the time interval $[t', t'']$. In the current set of experiments $T = 1$ if the attractor object was moving during the execution of the last exploratory behavior. The function T is defined as binary because movement is either detected or it is not.

With this notation in mind, the functionality of a tool can be represented with an *Affordance Table* of the form:

Binding Behavior	Binding Params	Exploratory Behavior	Exploratory Params	O^s	O^e	Times Used	Times Succ

In each row of the table, the first two entries represent the binding behavior that was used. The second two entries represent the exploratory behavior and its parameters. The next two entries store the observation vector at the start and at the end of the exploratory behavior. The last two entries are integer counters used to estimate the probability of success of this sequence of behaviors.

Binding Behavior	Binding Params	Exploratory Behavior	Exploratory Params	O^s	O^e	Times Used	Times Succ
β_{b_1}	$\tilde{b}_1^1$	β_{e_3}	$\tilde{e}_1^3, \tilde{e}_2^3$	$\tilde{O}(t')$	$\tilde{O}(t'')$	4	3

The meanings of these entries are best explained with an example. Consider the following sample row in which the binding behavior β_{b_1} which has one parameter was performed to grasp the tool. The specific value of the parameter for this behavior was $\tilde{b}_1^1$ (a ˜ sign is used to represent a specific fixed value). Next, the exploratory behavior β_{e_3} was performed with specific values $\tilde{e}_1^3$ and $\tilde{e}_2^3$ for its two parameters. The value of the observation vector prior to the start of β_{e_3} was $\tilde{O}(t')$ and it value after β_{e_3} has completed was $\tilde{O}(t'')$. This sequence of behaviors was performed 4 times. It resulted in observations similar to the first time this row of the affordance table was created in 3 of these instances, i.e., its probability of success is 75%. Section 6 and Figure 5 provide more information about the organization of the affordance table.

Initially the affordance table is blank. When the robot is presented with a tool it performs a *behavioral babbling* routine which picks binding and exploratory behaviors at random, applies them to the tools and objects, observes their effects, and updates the table. New rows are added to the table only if $\mathcal{T}$ was on while the exploratory behavior was performed. During learning, the integer counters of all rows are set to 1. They are updated during testing trials.

4   Experimental Setup

All experiments were performed using the CRS+ A251 mobile manipulator shown in Figure 1. Five tools were used in the experiments: stick, L-stick, L-hook, T-stick, and T-hook (see Figure 1). The tools were built from pine wood and painted with spray paint. The choice of tools was motivated by the similar tools that Köhler's used in his experiments with chimpanzees [7]. An orange hockey puck was used as an attractor object. The experimental setup is shown in Figure 2 and is described in more detail below.

A Sony EVI-D30 camera was mounted on a tripod overlooking the robot's working area (see Figure 2). The robot's wrist, the tools, and the attractor were color coded so that their positions can be uniquely identified and tracked using

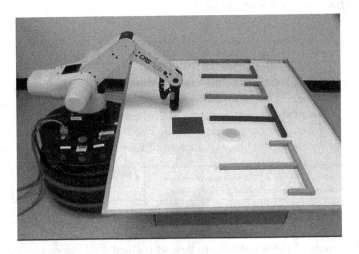

Fig. 1. The figure shows the CRS+ A251 mobile manipulator, the five tools, and the hockey puck that were used in the experiments

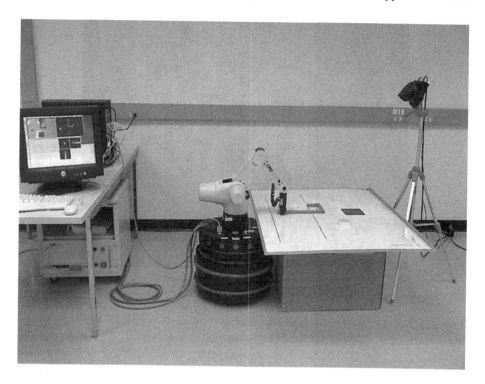

Fig. 2. Experimental setup

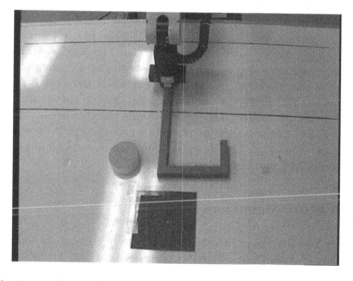

Fig. 3. The image shows the field of view of the robot through the Sony EVI-D30 camera. The robot's wrist, the attractor object, the tools, and the goal region were color coded and their positions were tracked using color segmentation (see Figure 4).

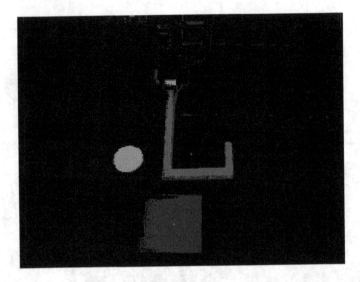

Fig. 4. Color segmentation results for the image frame shown in Figure 3. The positions of the color coded objects were calculated after calibrating the camera using Roger Tsai's method [17,18]. Although the shape of the tool can be extracted form this image it is not required and used by the behavior-grounded approach.

computer vision (see Figures 3 and 4). The computer vision code was run at 15Hz in 640x480 resolution mode.

To ensure consistent tracking results between multiple robot experiments the camera was calibrated every time it was powered up. A 6 × 6 calibration pattern was used. The pattern consists of small color markers placed on a cardboard, 5 inches apart, so that they form a square pattern. The pixel coordinates of the 36 uniformly colored markers were identified automatically using color segmentation. The centroid positions of the 36 color markers were used to calculate a mapping function which assigns to each (x,y) in camera coordinates a (X,Y,Z) location in world coordinates. This calculation is possible because the markers are coplanar and the equation of the plane in which they lie is known (e.g., Z=0 is the plane of the table). The mapping function was calculated using Roger Tsai's method [17,18] and the code given in [19].

5   Exploratory Behaviors

All behaviors used here were encoded manually from a library of *motor schemas* and *perceptual schemas* [3] developed for this specific robot. The behaviors result in different arm movement patterns as described below.

The first four behaviors move the arm in the indicated direction while keeping the wrist perpendicular to the table on which the tool slides. These behaviors have a single parameter which determines how far the arm will travel relative to its current position. Two different values for this parameter were used

Exploratory Behaviors	Parameters
Extend arm	offset_distance
Contract arm	offset_distance
Slide arm left	offset_distance
Slide arm right	offset_distance
Position wrist	x,y

(2 and 5 inches). The *position wrist* behavior moves the manipulator such that the centroid of the attractor is at offset (x, y) relative to the wrist.

5.1   Grasping Behavior

There are multiple ways in which a tool can be grasped. These represent a set of affordances which we will call first order (or *binding affordances*), i.e., the different ways in which the robot can attach the tool to its body. These affordances are different from the second order (or *output affordances*) of the tool, i.e., the different ways in which the tool can act on other objects. This paper focuses only on output affordances, so the binding affordances were specified with only one grasping behavior. The behavior takes as a parameter the location of a single grasp point located at the lower part of the tool's handle.

5.2   Observation Vector

The observation vector has 12 real-value components. In groups of three, they represent the position of the attractor object in camera-centric coordinates, the position of the object relative to the wrist of the robot, the color of the object, and the color of the tool.

Observation	Meaning
o_1, o_2, o_3	X,Y,Z positions of the object (camera-centric)
o_4, o_5, o_6	X,Y,Z positions of the object (wrist-centric)
o_7, o_8, o_9	R,G,B color components of the object
o_{10}, o_{11}, o_{12}	R,G,B color components of the tool

The change detection function $\mathcal{T}$ was defined with the first three components, o_1, o_2, o_3. To determine if the attractor is moving, $\mathcal{T}$ calculates the Euclidean distance and thresholds it with an empirically determined value (0.5 inches). The *times-successful* counter is incremented if the observed attractor movement is within 40 degrees of the expected movement stored in the affordance table.

6   Learning Trials

During the learning trials the robot was allowed to freely explore the properties of the tools. The exploration consisted of trying different behaviors, observing their results, and filling up the affordance table. The initial positions of the attractor and the tool were random. If the attractor was pushed out of tool reach by the robot then the learning trial was temporarily suspended while the attractor was manually placed in a new random position. The learning trials were limited to one hour of run time for every tool.

6.1   What is Learned

Figure 5 illustrates what the robot can learn about the properties of the T-hook tool based on a single exploratory behavior. In this example, the exploratory behavior is "Contract Arm" and its parameter is "5 inches." The two observation vectors are stylized for the purposes of this example. The information that the robot retains is not the images of the tool and the puck but only the coordinates of their positions as explained above. If a different exploratory behavior was selected by the robot it is possible that no movement of the puck will be detected. In this case the robot will not store any information (row) in the affordance table.

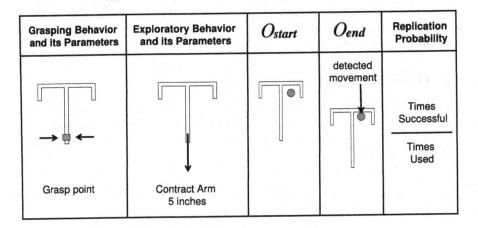

Grasping Behavior and its Parameters	Exploratory Behavior and its Parameters	O_{start}	O_{end}	Replication Probability
Grasp point	Contract Arm 5 inches		detected movement	Times Successful / Times Used

Fig. 5. Contents of a sample row of the affordance table for the T-hook tool

When the robot performs multiple exploratory behaviors a more compact way to represent this information is required. A good way to visualize what the robot learns is with graphs like the ones shown in Figure 6. The figures show the observed outcomes of the exploratory behaviors when the T-hook tool was applied randomly to the hockey puck. Each of the eight graphs shows the observed movements of the attractor object when a specific exploratory behavior was performed. The movements of the attractor object are shown as arrows. The start of each arrow corresponds to the initial position of the attractor relative to the wrist of the robot (and thus relative to the grasp point) just prior to the start of the exploratory behavior. The arrow represents the observed distance and direction of movement of the attractor in camera coordinates at the end of the exploratory behavior. In other words, each of the arrows shown in Figure 6

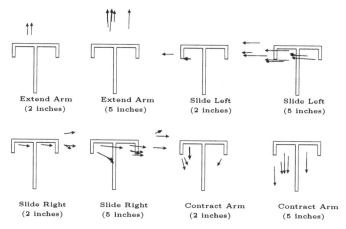

Extend Arm   Extend Arm   Slide Left   Slide Left
(2 inches)   (5 inches)   (2 inches)   (5 inches)

Slide Right   Slide Right   Contract Arm   Contract Arm
(2 inches)   (5 inches)   (2 inches)   (5 inches)

Fig. 6. Visualizing the affordance table for the T-hook tool. Each of the eight graphs show the observed movements of the attractor object after a specific exploratory behavior was performed multiple times. The start of each arrow corresponds to the position of the attractor in wrist-centered coordinates (i.e., relative to the tool's grasp point) just prior to the start of the exploratory behavior. The arrow represents the total distance and direction of movement of the attractor in camera coordinates at the end of the exploratory behavior.

represents one observed movement of the puck similar to the "detected movement" arrow show in Figure 5. The arrows in Figure 6 are superimposed on the initial configuration of the tool and not on its final configuration as in Figure 5.

This affordance representation can also be interpreted as a *predictive* model of the results of the exploratory behaviors. In other words, the affordances are represented as the expected outcomes of specific behaviors. This interpretation of affordances is consistent with the idea that biological brains are organized as predictive machines that anticipate the consequences of actions – their own and those of others [20, p. 1]. It is also consistent with some recent findings about the internal representation of the functional properties of novel objects and tools in humans. For example, "if the brain can predict the effect of pushing or pulling an object this is effectively an internal model of the object that can be used during manipulation"[6]. A recent result in the theoretical AI literature also shows that the state of a dynamic system can be represented by the outcomes of a set of tests [21,22]. The tests consist of action-observation sequences. It was shown that the state of the system is fully specified if the outcomes of a basis set of test called *core tests* are known in advance [22].

6.2   Querying the Affordance Table

After the affordance table is populated with values it can be queried to dynamically create behavioral sequences that solve a specific tool task. The behaviors in these sequences are the same behaviors that were used to fill the table. This subsection describes the search heuristic used to select the best affordance for

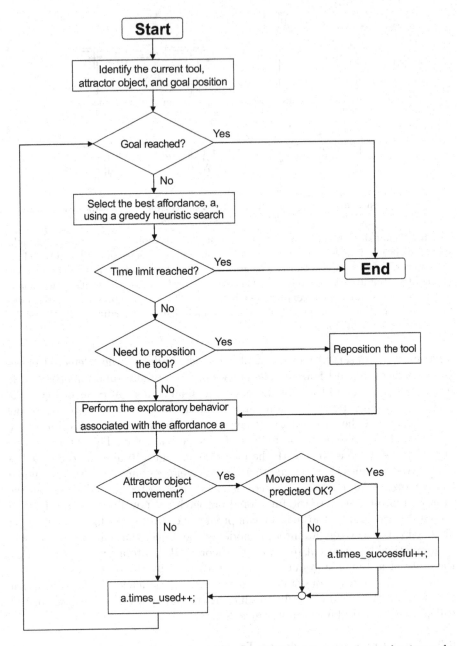

Fig. 7. Flowchart diagram for the procedure used by the robot to solve tool-using tasks with the help of the behavior-grounded affordance representation

the current task configuration. This heuristic is used by the procedure for solving tool-using tasks shown in Figure 7.

During testing trials, the best affordance for a specific step in a tool task was selected using a greedy heuristic search. The query method that was adopted uses empirically derived heuristics to perform multiple nested linear searches through the affordance table. Each successive search is performed only on the rows that were not eliminated by the previous searches. Four nested searches were performed in the order shown below:

1) Select all rows that have observation vectors consistent with the colors of the current tool and object.

2) From the remaining rows select those with probability of success greater than 50%. In other words, select only those rows that have a replication probability (times_successful/times_used) greater than $\frac{1}{2}$ (the reasons for choosing this threshold value are described below).

3) Sort the remaining rows (in increasing order) based on the expected distance between the attractor object and the goal region if the behavior associated with this row were to be performed.

4) From the top 20% of the sorted rows choose one row which minimizes the re-positioning of the tool relative to its current location.

As it was mentioned above the greedy one-step-lookahead heuristic was derived empirically. The performance of the heuristic was fine tuned for speed of adaptation in the presence of uncertainty which is important when multiple robot trials have to be performed. For example, the threshold value of 50% used in step 2 above was chosen in order to speed up the elimination of outdated affordances when the geometry of the tool suddenly changes (see the experiment described in Section 7.2). With this threshold value it takes only one unsuccessful behavioral execution in order to eliminate an affordance from further consideration. Future work should attempt to formulate a more principled approach to this affordance-space planning problem, preferably using performance data derived from tool-using experiments with animals and humans (e.g., [6]).

7   Testing Trials

Two types of experiments were performed to test the behavior-grounded approach. They measured the quality of the learned representation and its adaptation abilities when the tool is deformed, respectively.

7.1   Extension of Reach

In the first experiment the robot was required to pull the attractor over a color coded goal region. Four different goal positions were defined. The first goal position is shown in Figure 1 (the dark square in front of the robot). The second goal position was located farther away from the robot (see Figure 2). To achieve it the robot had to push the attractor away from its body. Goals 3 and 4 were placed along the mid-line of the table as shown in Figure 8.

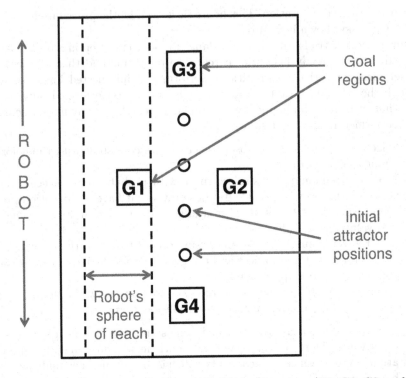

Fig. 8. The figure shows the positions of the four goal regions (G1, G2, G3, and G4) and the four initial attractor positions used in the extension of reach experiments. The two dashed lines indicate the boundaries of the robot's sphere of reach when it is not holding any tool.

In addition to that there were 4 initial attractor positions per goal. The initial positions are located along the mid-line of the table, 6 inches apart as shown in Figure 8. The tool was always placed in the center of the table. A total of 80 trials were performed (4 goals × 4 attractor positions × 5 tools). The table below summarizes the results. The values represent the number of successful solutions per goal, per tool. Four is the maximum possible value as there are only four initial starting positions for the attractor object.

Tool	Goal 1	Goal 2	Goal 3	Goal 4
Stick	0	2	4	4
L-stick	4	2	4	4
L-hook	4	3	4	4
T-stick	3	3	4	4
T-hook	4	4	4	4

As can be seen from the table, the robot was able to solve this task in the majority of the test cases. The most common failure condition was due to pushing

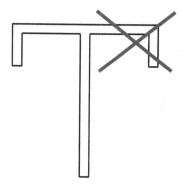

Fig. 9. A T-hook missing its right hook is equivalent to an L-hook

the attractor out of tool's reach. This failure was caused by the greedy one-step-lookahead heuristic used for selecting the next tool movement. If the robot plans the possible movements of the puck for 2 or 3 moves ahead these failures will be eliminated. A notable exception is the Stick tool, which could not be used to pull the object back to the near goal (G1). The robot lacks the required exploratory behavior (*turn-the-wrist-at-an-angle-and-then-pull*) that is required to detect this affordance of the stick. Adding the capability of learning new exploratory behaviors can resolve this problem.

7.2 Adaptation After a Tool Breaks

The second experiment was designed to test the flexibility of the behavior-grounded representation in the presence of uncertainties. The uncertainly in this case was a tool that can break. For example, Figure 9 shows the tool transformation which occurs when a T-hook tool loses one of its hooks. The result is a L-hook tool. This section describes the results of an experiment in which the robot was exposed to such tool transformation after it had already learned the affordances of the T-hook tool.

To simulate a broken tool, the robot was presented with a tool that has the same color ID as another tool with a different shape. More specifically, the learning was performed with a T-hook which was then replaced with an L-hook. Because color is the only feature used to recognize tools the robot believes that it is still using the old tool.

The two tools differ in their upper right sections as shown in Figure 9. Whenever the robot tried to use affordances associated with the missing parts of the tool they did not produce the expected attractor movements. Figure 10 shows frames from a sequence in which the robot tried in vain to use the upper right part of the tool to move the attractor towards the goal. After several trials the replication probability of the affordances associated with that part of the tool was reduced and they were excluded from further consideration. Figure 11 shows frames from the rest of this sequence in which the robot was able to complete the task with the intact left hook of the tool.

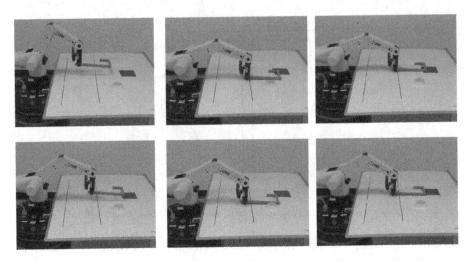

Fig. 10. Using a broken tool (Part I: Adaptation) - Initially the robot tries to move the attractor towards the goal using the missing right hook. Because the puck fails to move as expected the robot reduces the replication probability of the affordances associated with this part of the tool.

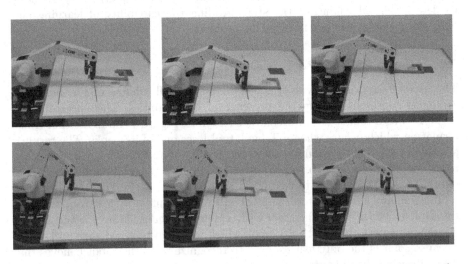

Fig. 11. Using a broken tool (Part II: Solving the task) - After adapting to the modified affordances of the tool, the robot completes the task with the intact left hook

A total of 16 trials similar to the one shown in Figure 10 were performed (i.e., 4 goal regions × 4 initial attractor positions). In each of these experiments the robot started the testing trial with the original representation for the T-hook tool and modified it based on actual experience. The robot was successful in all 16 experiments, i.e., the robot was able to place the attractor over the target goal region with the "broken" tool in all 16 experiments.

8   Conclusions and Future Work

This paper introduced a novel approach to representing and learning tool affordances by a robot. The affordance representation is *grounded* in the behavioral and perceptual repertoire of the robot. More specifically, the affordances of different tools are represented in terms of a set of exploratory behaviors and their resulting effects. It was shown how this representation can be used to solve tool-using tasks by dynamically sequencing exploratory behaviors based on their expected outcomes.

The behavior-grounded approach represents the tool's affordances in concrete terms (i.e., behaviors) that are available to the robot's controller. Therefore, the robot can directly test the accuracy of its tool representation by executing the same set of exploratory behaviors that was used in the past. If any inconsistencies are detected in the resulting observations they can be used to update the tool's representation. Thus, the accuracy of the representation can be directly tested by the robot. It was demonstrated how the robot can use this approach to adapt to changes in the tool's properties over time, e.g., tools that can break.

A shortcoming of the behavior-grounded approach is that there are tool affordances that are unlikely to be discovered since the required exploratory behavior is not available to the robot. This problem has also been observed in animals, e.g., macaque monkeys have significant difficulties learning to push an object with a tool away from their bodies because this movement is never performed in their normal daily routines [23]. This problem can be resolved, however, if the ability to learn new exploratory behaviors is added.

There are some obvious extensions to this work that are left for future work. First, the current implementation starts the exploration of a new tool from scratch even though it may be similar to an already explored tool. Adding the ability to rapidly infer the affordances of a new tool from its shape similarity to previous tools would be a nice extension.

Second, the current implementation uses a purely random behavioral babbling exploration procedure. Different strategies that become less random and more focused as information is structured by the robot during the exploration could be used to speed up the learning process.

Third, the behavior-grounded approach should be compared experimentally with planners for pushing objects (e.g., [24]). We expect that the behavior-grounded method would approach asymptotically the accuracy of these planners as the number and diversity of the exploratory behaviors is increased. We also expect, however, that our approach would excel in situations that cannot be predicted by the planners, e.g., tools that can break or objects whose center of mass can shift between trials.

References

1. Beck, B.B.: Animal Tool behavior: The use and manufacture of tools by animals. Garland STMP Press, New York (1980)
2. Gibson, J.J.: The ecological approach to visual perception. Houghton Mifflin, Boston (1979)

3. Arkin, R.: Behavior-based robotics. MIT Press, Cambridge (1998)
4. Power, T.G.: Play and Exploration in Children and Animals. Lawrence Erlbaum Associates, Publishers, Mahwah (2000)
5. Lorenz, K.: Innate bases of learning. In: Pribram, K.H., King, J. (eds.) Learning as Self-Organization, Lawrence Erlbaum Associates, Publishers, Mahwah (1996)
6. Mah, C.D., Mussa-Ivaldi, F.A.: Evidence for a specific internal representation of motion-force relationships during object manipulation. Biological Cybernetics 88(1), 60–72 (2003)
7. Köhler, W.: The mentality of apes, Harcourt, Brace, and Co. (1931)
8. Povinelli, D., Reaux, J., Theall, L., Giambrone, S.: Folk Physics for Apes: The Chimpanzee's theory of how the world works. Oxford Univ. Press, Oxford (2000)
9. Visalberghi, E., Trinca, L.: Tool use in capuchin monkeys: distinguishing between performing and understanding. Primates 30, 511–521 (1989)
10. Krotkov, E.: Perception of material properties by robotic probing: Preliminary investigations. In: IJCAI. Proceedings of the International Joint Conference on Artificial Intelligence, Montreal, pp. 88–94 (August 1995)
11. Fitzpatrick, P., Metta, G., Natale, L., Rao, S., Sandini, G.: Learning about objects through action - initial steps towards artificial cognition. In: ICRA. Proceedings of IEEE International Conference on Robotics and Automation, Taipei, Taiwan (May 12–17, 2003)
12. Bogoni, L., Bajcsy, R.: Interactive recognition and representation of functionality. Computer Vision and Image Understanding 62(2), 194–214 (1995)
13. Bogoni, L.: Identification of functional features through observations and interactions. PhD thesis, University of Pennsylvania (1995)
14. Stark, L., Bowyer, K.: Generic Object Recognition using Form and Function. Machine Perception and AI, vol. 10. World Scientific, Singapore (1996)
15. Rivlin, E., Dickinson, S.J., Rosenfeld, A.: Recognition by functional parts. Computer Vision and Image Understanding 62(2), 164–176 (1995)
16. Hayes, P.J.: The second naive physics manifesto. In: Formal Theories of the Commonsense World, Ablex Publishing, Greenwich (1985)
17. Tsai, R.Y.: An efficient and accurate camera calibration technique for 3D machine vision. In: CVPR. Proceedings of IEEE Conference on Computer Vision and Pattern Recognition, Miami Beach, FL, pp. 364–374 (1986)
18. Tsai, R.Y.: A versatile camera calibration technique for high-accuracy 3D machine vision metrology using off-the-shelf TV cameras and lenses. IEEE Journal of Robotics and Automation RA-3(4), 323–344 (1987)
19. Willson, R.: Tsai Camera Calibration Software (1995), the source code can be downloaded from http://www-2.cs.cmu.edu/~rgw/TsaiCode.html
20. Berthoz, A.: The brain's sense of movement. Harvard University Press, Cambridge (2000)
21. Singh, S., Littmn, M., Sutton, R., Stone, P.: Learning predictive state representations. Paper Draft (unpublished)
22. Littman, M.L., Sutton, R.S., Singh, S.: Predictive representation of state. Advances in Neural Information Processing Systems 14 (2002)
23. Ishibashi, H., Hihara, S., Iriki, A.: Acquisition and development of monkey tool-use: behavioral and kinematic analyses. Canadian Journal of Physiology and Pharmacology 78, 958–966 (2000)
24. Mason, M.T.: Mechanics of Robotic Manipulation. MIT Press, Cambridge (2001)

Function-Based Reasoning for Goal-Oriented Image Segmentation

Melanie A. Sutton[1] and Louise Stark[2]

[1] University of West Florida, Pensacola, Florida, USA
msutton@uwf.edu
[2] University of the Pacific, Stockton, California, USA

Abstract. Function-based object recognition provides the framework to represent and reason about object functionality as a means to recognize novel objects and produce plans for interaction with the world. When function can be perceived visually, function-based computer vision is consistent with Gibson's theory of affordances. Objects are recognized by their functional attributes. These attributes can be segmented out of the scene and given symbolic labels which can then be used to guide the search space for additional functional attributes. An example of such affordance-driven scene segmentation would be the process of attaching symbolic labels to the areas that afford sitting (functional seats) and using these areas to guide parameter selection for deriving nearby surfaces that potentially afford back support. The Generic Recognition Using Form and Function (**GRUFF**) object recognition system reasons about and generates plans for understanding 3-D scenes of objects by performing such a functional attribute-based labelling process. An avenue explored here is based on a novel approach of autonomously directing image acquisition and range segmentation by determining the extent to which surfaces in the scene meet specified functional requirements, or provide affordances associated with a generic category of objects.

1 Introduction

All computer vision systems require some type of representation. Function-based representation, such as that used in the **GRUFF** (Generic Recognition Using Form and Function) system [38], is a move toward more generic repesentation by capturing entire classes of objects with simple definitions of their functional requirements. The domain of objects GRUFF has concentrated on is man-made objects with functional attributes that can be derived by visual inspection. For any particular object category, there is some set of functional properties shared by *all* objects in that category.

Model-based vision systems proceed from the assumption that a model is available for each object. Alternately, function-based vision systems seek to categorize sets of scene surfaces as meeting the requirements for membership within a class of objects (e.g. dishes, furniture, handtools). This results in an approach that is more scaleable in terms of recognition of novel objects and simplificaton of path-planning for navigation in previously unencountered spaces. When

E. Rome et al. (Eds.): Affordance-Based Robot Control, LNAI 4760, pp. 159–172, 2008.
© Springer-Verlag Berlin Heidelberg 2008

function can be perceived visually from surfaces within a space for these goals, function-based computer vision is consistent with Gibson's theory of affordances [11]. Function-based recognition is not, however, consistent with Gibson's claim that we perceive affordance properties of the environment in a direct and immediate way. Processing must take place to make the association of the function to the structure. For example, in the GRUFF system, the definition of a generic object category is defined as the composition of the required functional attributes. For example:

arm chair ::= provides seating surface + provides stability
+ provides back support surface + provides arm support

Recognition is conceptualized as the labelling of the object, as depicted in Figure 1.

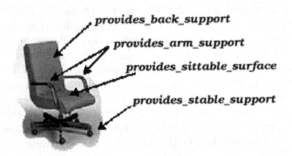

provides_back_support

provides_arm_support

provides_sittable_surface

provides_stable_support

Fig. 1. Object correctly classified as chair labelled for its functional properties

As previously suggested, representation systems which support *generic* object recognition offer several promising advantages over traditional model-based vision systems. In model-based approaches, the computer's task is to identify specific objects based on stored models that represent possible views of the objects to be recognized. Alternatively, in a function-based approach, specific structural models are disregarded, in favor of shape analysis to determine if the objects are usable within the constraints of particular category of objects. Figure 2 provides an image of two chairs as an example, showing how function-based reasoning is used to segment objects in the scene by attaching labels such as *provides sittable surface* and *provides back support*. The functional evidence described by these labels can then be combined to form final scene segmentation and labelling of image areas as *chairs*.

While the labelling concept may appear simple, issues such as non-uniform lighting, occlusion of various objects, and perceptual ambiguities make the selection of an "optimal" parameter set for image acquisition, segmentation, and recognition inherently difficult [13]. Although some existing research has explored the concept of "navigational functionalities" using motion, for example, to classify threats, obstacles, and landmarks [31], much of the existing literature has paid scant attention to the use of functional analysis to drive alternative image acquisition strategies or to clean-up initially noisy data so that a more representative set of symbolic labels is determined.

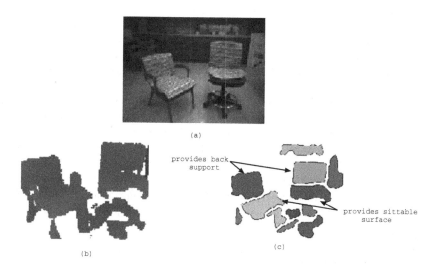

Fig. 2. (a) Left camera intensity image. (b) Derived range image. (c) Extracted 3-D surfaces with functional requirement-level labels.

The subfields of *active vision* and *scale-space theory* have been proposed in the computer vision community as methods to address some of these issues and improve system robustness. Active vision encompasses the controlled change of the parameters of the sensory system to facilitate vision [3,6], while scale-space theory describes the implications of scale of observation on developing methods for analyzing measured data [21,23,24]. Both approaches recognize that automation is the key; techniques which scale-up to more numerous and more complex environments are necessary to store, access, and process the volumes of information a vision system may acquire in as simple a task as navigating one floor of an office building. In our research, we are exploring utilizing measures of functional characteristics in a scene at various scales to drive parameter selection for further exploration.

The following sections provide background information on computer vision systems incorporating these concepts, as well as detailed descriptions of the Small Vision System (SVS) software [20] and Generic Recognition Using Form and Function (GRUFF) object recognition system [38] utilized in this work. Finally, an introduction to the design and testing strategies of GRUFF's new affordance-based automatic parameter selection mechanisms is presented.

2   Background

2.1   Active Vision and Attentional Scene Segmentation

Visual servoing (using visual sensors to control motion) in robotic applications is perhaps one of the simplest examples of active vision principles [16]. Early work in the area of incorporating function from motion includes Bogoni and Bajcsy's investigations of manipulatory interactions, such as piercing [5]. However, as computer vision systems endeavor to solve even more complex tasks, change of motion parameters alone is often insufficient. A system may in fact need to remain stationary and analyze its current position with alternative sensors, or process its current state of information in a different manner in order to navigate the environment in the most efficient or safe manner possible. Along these lines, Maver and Bajcsy have examined using occlusions as a guide to planning the next view [26].

More recently, Fitzpatrick and colleagues have explored system modes that support a "learning to act" paradigm for robotic exploration [10]. Their experiments in this area thus distinguish between a "discovery mode" where a visual system analyzes and processes the consequences of motor acts, and a "goal-directed mode" where a system utilizes the acquired knowledge to select the motor acts that map to specific visual events (e.g., movement in a particular direction).

Brown, Eklundh and colleagues have also investigated alternative strategies for selective perception and attentional scene segmentation [25,28]. The concept of goal-oriented resegmentation was explored in the development of the VISIONS Image-Understanding System, pioneered by Hanson and Riseman in the 1980's [13]. These systems analyzed outdoor scenes of houses and roads, and used attributes such as color, texture, shape, size, location, and relative location to drive scene segmentation.

2.2   Generic Object Recognition Utilizing Function-Based Reasoning

As opposed to an attribute-based or model-based matching method of performing scene segmentation, a function-based approach analyzes the functionality of surfaces, as they are oriented in the scene, to determine if specified sets of functional requirements can be met. The idea of using function to represent object categories for recognition purposes is not new. Binford and Minsky, among other researchers, have argued that object categories are better defined by focusing on the intended functionality of objects [4,27]. The concept of how the use of function could be integrated into a computer vision system has matured over the years. One body of work has looked at problems for which the assumed input is a complete symbolic description (e.g., a semantic network) of an object and its functionally relevant parts [42,43]. This well-known work by Winston *et al.* explores reasoning by analogy between parts and functional properties of objects. Rivlin *et al.* also integrated function and object parts "by combining a set of functional primitives and their relations with a set of abstract volumetric shape primitives and their relations" [30].

Another body of work has concentrated on producing and recognizing a function-oriented symbolic description of the object through reasoning about the "raw" shape description rather than decomposing the object into parts, with the assumption of a complete 3-D shape description (e.g., a boundary representation) of an object provided as input [9,19,34,35,39]. These works bypassed the "real" vision problem, at least to some extent, by assuming complete shape models as input. Functional information gained through an initial evaluation of an object can be also used to help guide interaction with the object. Interaction can then be performed based on hypothesized areas of functional significance [7,18,29,33,41]. Functionality in object recognition has continued to gain attention as an alternative to the strict model-based approach [37,38]. A broad sampling of other work that falls into this category can be found in the proceedings of the 1993 and 1994 AAAI Workshops on reasoning about object function [1,2] and the special issue of *Computer Vision and Image Understanding* on functionality in object recognition [5,8,12,14,30,31].

3   Experimental Platform and Overview of Data Flow

Figure 3 provides a summary of the GRUFF architecture and provides additional details on how its subsystems communicate. As noted by the numbering, the first step in the process is to invoke the Model Building Subsystem to extract surfaces (reporting information about the faces and vertices that can be used to build a 3-D model). The Shape-based Reasoning Subsystem is then invoked to use this information and apply concepts of physics and causation to the 3-D surfaces, using operations such as clearance and stability. The results of this analysis are reported in a text file. Finally, the Interaction-based Reasoning Subsystem reads this text file and is subsequently invoked multiple times, using operations to control robot arms and cameras and to perform image processing, in order to confirm the shape-suggested functionality of the surface model. The final results of this subsystem are also reported in a text file.

Such a design is similar in several respects to a blackboard architecture-based system, such as that used in the the road scene understanding system developed by Lapierre, *et al.* [22]. For example, in the GRUFF-I (GRUFF using interaction) system, a single "supervisor" program invokes independent model building, shape-based and interaction-based "specialist" programs, each of which provides a partial interpretation of the current scene, using different sensors and data formats. The controlling program focuses the activities of the sensors according to the success or failure of the interaction. As Lapierre pointed out, there are a number of advantages to this modular approach, such as the simplicity of adding new sensors and specialists, the ease of program maintenance and the support of software re-usability, in that well-designed specialists can be used to solve other problems.

The GRUFF system utilized in this research has been tested on hundreds of simulated and real objects and scenes and has been accepted in the literature as a viable and successful generic object recognition system [38,40,41,32]. For a sampling of real objects, see those in Figure 4, created from a variety of materials (Styrofoam, balsa wood, paper and sponge).

Knowledge in the GRUFF system is of three types:

- A category hierarchy which specifies superordinate, basic level and subordinate categories.

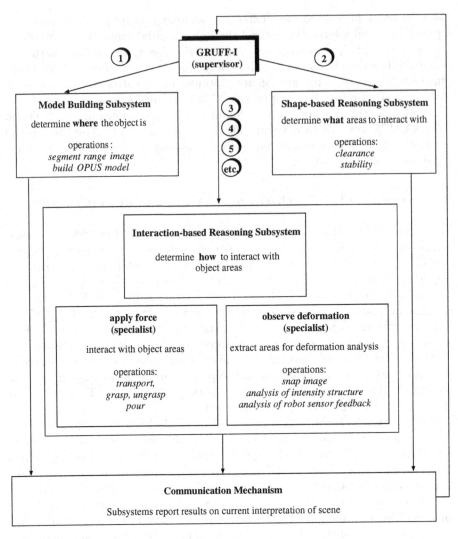

Fig. 3. Communication in the GRUFF-I system. The subsystems communicate via shared files which contain information about how each subsystem interprets the scene.

$$\text{furniture} \iff \text{chair} \iff \text{arm chair}$$

- Functional properties that define each category (provides_sittable_surface, provides_stability, ...).
- Knowledge primitives used to reason about shape

The GRUFF system is capable of providing the labels shown in Figure 2-c based on an understanding of generic categories of objects, stored internally within the system's *knowledge definition tree*. System developers have defined this tree for the generic sets of objects expected to be encountered by the GRUFF

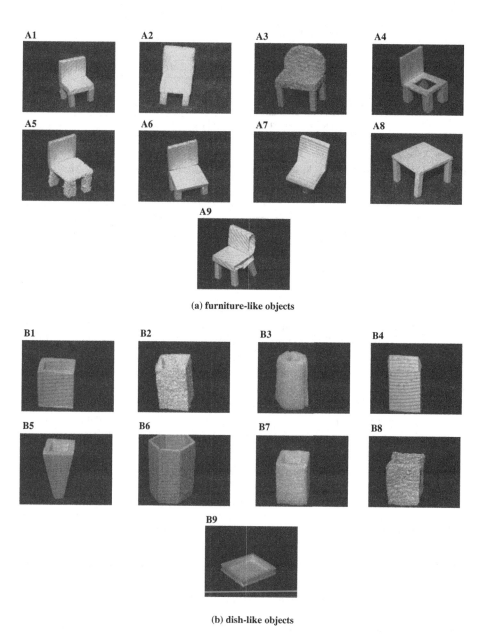

(a) **furniture-like objects**

(b) **dish-like objects**

Fig. 4. Functional and non-functional object models. Objects A1 and B1 represent functional objects. Alternately, the remaining objects fail for the following reasons: deformable (A2, A3, A5, A9, B2, B3, B4, B8), unstable (A7, B5), non-sittable (A4 due to hole in seat, A6 due to seat angle), inability to provide containment (B6 due to hole in side, B7 due to bottomless), and incompatible shape dimensions for average user (A8 due to seat area exceeding average, B9 due to limited height).

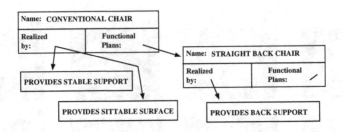

Fig. 5. Portion of GRUFF 's knowledge representation tree representing the generic object category *straight back chair*

Fig. 6. Flow of data from image acquisition to final function-based scene labelling

system. While not included in this paper, additional research exploring the effort and time for **GRUFF** to learn these parameters is explored in [38]. For example, as shown in Figure 5, to be recognized by GRUFF as a *straight back chair*, the list of 3-D surfaces derived from a range image of the scene must meet three functional requirements. The first requirement, *provides stable support*, cannot be confirmed without interaction. When evaluating real data extracted from a scene the assumption is that if a surface is observed in a certain location it is somehow being supported in that location. Satisfying the two additional requirements, *provides sittable surface* and *provides back support*, involves a search in the derived surface list for (1) a flat sittable surface parallel to the ground plane and (2) nearby back surface(s), perpendicular to the ground plane.

When the goal of the system is to find all "chairs" in a scene, the focus of attention can be limited to surface areas within a certain height range, while temporarily ignoring other data. If no surface within the proper height range to function as a seat can be found, no further evaluation of the current image is warranted, and the system can be directed to an alternative viewpoint. Alternatively, if the system's goal is to find a back support for a potential sittable surface that has already been discovered, the focus of attention can be restricted to the immediate area of the sittable surface. Each of these scenarios provide different cues that can be used by the object recognition system to best set the parameters to gain optimal data for the current task.

Figure 6 shows the flow of data as stereo image pairs are acquired and processed by the SVS software [20] and GRUFF subsystems. As indicated in Figure 6, greyscale images from the left and right cameras are combined into a disparity map. This map represents the disparity between the left and right images for corresponding points in the images and is calculated using an area-correlation algorithm within the SVS software. [20]. This information is then processed to

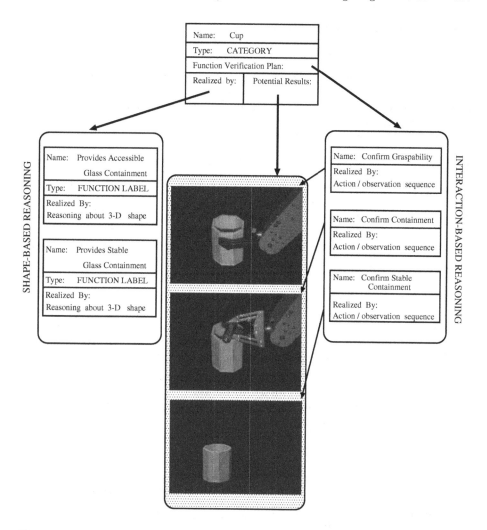

Fig. 7. Verifying the functional plan for a cup. This involves instructing the robot arm to interact with the object in a manner consistent with its shape-suggested functionality.

produce a range image where image locations include the 3-D coordinates of each point in the image. The 3-D points associated with the final range image are then segmented utilizing the YAR segmentation algorithm developed by Hoover, *et al.* [15]. Post-processing of the final segmentation includes erosion and dilation to extract a final list of planar, non-intersecting, "floating" scene surfaces that are provided as input to the GRUFF system.

The Interaction-based Reasoning Subsystem uses information derived from the vision and robot components in order to direct interaction with the object in the scene to confirm functionality. This subsystem begins by instantiating a function verification plan, which contains a representation of how reasoning about physical interaction should occur, as shown in Figure 7. The goal of this sub-system is to use the 3-D information derived from the visual sensors, along with the output of the shape-based analysis, to direct the robot arm to interact with particular locations on the object, defined in terms of the robot arm-centered coordinate system. The success or failure of this interaction is subsequently de-termined through analysis of 2-D intensity images and robotic sensor feedback obtained during the interaction.

3.1   Parameter Sets, Metrics and Measures

The hardware platform underlying the GRUFF system has varied over the years and has included both structured light scanners and numerous custom-built and off-the-shelf stereo vision systems. In general, across the structured light scanner-based systems, we observed about a 20-30% loss of usable data or models within each subsystem (model-building, shape-based reasoning, and interaction-based reasoning) [41]. Assessing our system to determine the "optimal" system param-eter set to mitigate these data losses, in terms of producing the most metrically accurate points for segmentations is the natural progression of our research. Using affordance-based criteria to drive this parameter selection means using functional attributes derived from preliminary processing to drive additional pa-rameter selections that yield metrically accurate data (low depth errors, minimal loss of observed data points, and low surface fitting differentiation compared to known ground truth). With each surface extraction, the GRUFF object recog-nition system returns an overall metric in the range 0.0 to 1.0 according to how well the extracted surfaces in the scene met the functional requirements of an object category, as follows [38]:

$$associationMeasure_{ObjectRec} = f(functionalReq_1, functionalReq_2, ...) \quad (1)$$

The final assessment of the goodness of fit for a parameter set for a given set of extracted surfaces is then based on an evaluation of the impact of all these metrics (decreased errors and data loss). By learning about how the choice of parmeter set determines the resulting extracted surfaces, we hope to at-tain a higher value for survival of surfaces with functional attributes leading to categorization.

4   Next Steps for GRUFF

As described in the previous section, the goal is to investigate automating param-eter selection to provide cleaner and more complete data for surface extraction that can be used for both recognition and successful navigation. Initial work in this area has been conducted using the SVS setup. After setting up the above described hardware and performing the calibration procedures outlined in the SVS software package, we undertook an additional set of experiments to deter-mine the overall accuracy of the collected data at various depths. This involved placing a test cube in the scene at incremental positions in front of the stereo head and recording the differences between manually acquired and SVS-derived distances measured to the n=6 corner points of this object. The distance differences were recorded to determine the initial impact of varying the *confidence*, *disparity*, *window*, and *x-offset* parameters. An observed mean percent error was calculated for each distance using the following equation:

$$depthErrorPercent_{PreEval} = \frac{\sum_{i=1}^{n_{corners}} \frac{(depth_i^{observed} - depth_i^{ground\ truth})}{depth_i^{ground\ truth}}}{n_{corners}} \qquad (2)$$

These errors proved to be low, with the lowest value being 0.4% and the highest percent error being 11.8%. The results of this test showed that the system was most accurate at distances less than 2.5 m.

In the next stage of analysis, we have begun testing the system in a task-driven mode, using the ideal starting parameter set derived above, and feedback from the final object recognition stage. As indicated in Figure 8, in this mode of operation, the system is presented with a new scene and autonomously corrects parameters to determine an "optimal" segmentation of the surfaces derived from the corresponding images, as determined by the final metric from the GRUFF system ($associationMeasure_{ObjectRec}$). The starting parameter set and initial recognition results are used to determine coarse locations of potential sittable surfaces. The center of these surfaces is then used to refine parameter set choices applicable for surfaces at the derived distance. The success of this mode of operation of the system is measured by how often the system self-adjusts a parameter set that subsequently leads to higher recognition results.

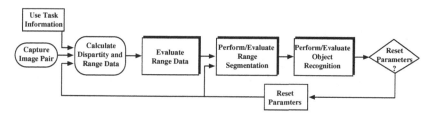

Fig. 8. Task-driven flow of data from function-based scene labelling to refinement of image acquisition and range segmentation parameters

The greatest disadvantage to stereo vision is that most planar surfaces do not appear in the range data because of the lack in texture [20]. However, the work presented here is extensible to other image acquisition systems, such as laser range finders or structured light scanners. Future work that we are exploring in this project includes indexing into our parameter sets to guide both rough (global) and fine (local) path planning for a navigation unit.

5   Conclusions

It was Gibson's assumption that we perceive in order to operate on the environment and that perception is designed for action. Affordances are the perceivable possibilities for action. Gibson's theory of affordances is consistent with function-based vision. An object *affords* support by being flat, horizontal and positioned at the proper height for sitting, all attributes that can be confirmed visually. The interesting result of using such an approach for object recognition is that the system will many times "recognize" or "categorize" objects that were not originally designed for the desired task, but can be used to fulfill a specified function. For example, when looking for a place to sit down, the **GRUFF** system incorrectly identified a trash can as a viable chair by simply turing it over and sitting on the bottom. Is the system wrong? Not necessarily. Gibson wisely argued that perception of an affordance was not the same as classifying the object [11]. This lends even greater support to function-based vision when the goal is task-oriented in an unknown environment.

The **GRUFF** object recognition system reasons about and generates plans for understanding 3-D scenes of objects by performing a functional attribute-based labelling process. Due to the sequence of processes that must take place, this approach is not considered direct or immediate perception of the affordance properties as Gibson claims we perceive such properties. The systematic steps, however, do not detract from the perception of many different possiblities for action that cannot be captured in most model-based recognition systems.

We have proposed a novel approach to acquiring and managing parameter set selection to guide initial and refined scene segmentations. Where you are looking for information in an environment and the final task of the system are just a few of the driving forces behind what determines the best parameter settings for an object recognition system to use.

Acknowledgments

The co-authors wish to acknowledge the support and participation of Drs. Ken Hughes and Adam Hoover on hardware and range segmentation aspects of this work.

References

1. Working notes of AAAI-93 Workshop on Reasoning About Function, Washington, D.C. (July 12, 1993)
2. Working notes of AAAI-94 Workshop on Representing and Reasoning About Device Function, Seattle, Washington (August 3, 1994)
3. Aloimonos, Y.: Active Perception. Advances in Computer Vision series, vol. I. Lawrence Erlbaum Associates, Mahwah (1993)
4. Binford, T.O.: Survey of model-based image analysis systems. International Journal of Robotics Research 1, 18–64 (1982)
5. Bogoni, L., Bajcsy, R.: Interactive recognition and representation of functionality. Computer Vision and Image Understanding, special issue on Functionality in Object Recognition 62(2), 194–214 (1995)
6. Christensen, H.I., Bowyer, K.W., Bunke, H.: Active Robot Vision. Scientific Press, Singapore (1993)

7. Connell, J.H.: Get me that screwdriver! Developing a sensory-action vocabulary for fetch-and-carry tasks. IBM Cyber Journal Research Report RC 19473 (April 1994)

8. Cooper, P., Birnbaum, L., Brand, E.: Causal scene understanding. Computer Vision and Image Understanding, special issue on Functionality in Object Recognition 62(2), 215–231 (1995)

9. Di Manzo, M., Trucco, E., Giunchiglia, F., Ricci, F.: FUR: Understanding FUnctional Reasoning. International Journal of Intelligent Systems 4, 431–457 (1989)

10. Fitzpatrick, P., Metta, G., Natale, L., Rao, S., Sandini, G.: Learning about objects through action - initial steps towards artificial cognition. In: ICRA. Proceedings of the IEEE International Conference on Robotics and Automation, Taipei, Taiwan (May 2003)

11. Gibson, J.J.: The Ecological Approach to Visual Perception. Houghton Mifflin Company, Boston, MA (1979)

12. Green, K., Eggert, D., Stark, L., Bowyer, K.: Generic recognition of articulated objects through reasoning about potential function. Computer Vision and Image Understanding, special issue on Functionality in Object Recognition 62(2), 177–193 (1995)

13. Hanson, A., Riseman, E.: The VISIONS image-understanding system. In: Brown, C. (ed.) Advances in Computer Vision I, Erlbaum, Hillsdale, NJ, pp. 1–114 (1988)

14. Hodges, J.: Functional and physical object characteristics and object recognition in improvisation. Computer Vision and Image Understanding, special issue on Functionality in Object Recognition 62(2), 147–163 (1995)

15. Hoover, A., Golgof, D., Bowyer, K.: Egomotion estimation of a range camera using the space envelope. IEEE Transactions on Systems, Man, and Cybernetics, Part B 33(4), 717–721 (2003)

16. Hutchinson, S., Hager, G.D., Corke, P.: Visual servoing: A tutorial. IEEE Transactions on Robotics and Automation 12(5) (1996)

17. Jain, A., Dorai, C.: 3-D object recognition: Representation and matching. Statistics and Computing 10(2), 167–182 (2000)

18. Kim, D., Nevatia, R.: A method for recognition and localization of generic objects for indoor navigation. In: IEEE Workshop on Applications of Computer Vision, pp. 280–288 (1994)

19. Kise, K., Hattori, H., Kitahashi, T., Fukunaga, K.: Representing and recognizing simple hand-tools based on their functions. In: Asian Conference on Computer Vision, Osaka, Japan, pp. 656–659 (November 1993)

20. Konolige, K., Beymer, D.: SRI Small Vision System: User's Manual Software Version 3.0a. SRI International (September 2003)

21. Koenderink, J.J.: The structure of images. Biological Cybernetics 50, 363–370 (1984)

22. Lapierre, I., Laurgeau, C.: A road scene understanding system based on a blackboard architecture. In: Bunke, H. (ed.) Advances in Structural and Syntactic Pattern Recognition, pp. 571–585. World Scientific, Singapore (1992)

23. Lindeberg, T.: Scale-Space Theory in Computer Vision. Kluwer Academic Publishers, Dordrecht (1994)

24. Lindeberg, T.: Feature detection with automatic scale selection. International Journal of Computer Vision 30(2), 79–116 (1998)

25. Maki, A., Nordlund, P., Eklundh, J.: Attentional scene segmentation: Integrating depth and motion. Computer Vision and Image Understanding 78(3), 351–373 (2000)

26. Maver, J., Bajcsy, R.: Occlusions as a guide to planning the next view. IEEE Transactions on Pattern Analysis and Machine Intelligence 15(5), 417–433 (1993)
27. Minsky, M.: The Society of Mind. Simon and Shuster, New York (1985)
28. Rimey, R.D., Brown, C.M.: Control of selective perception using Bayes nets and decision theory. International Journal of Computer Vision, special issue on Active Vision 12, 173–207 (1994)
29. Rivlin, E., Rosenfeld, A., Perlis, D.: Recognition of object functionality in goal-directed robotics. In: Working Notes on Reasoning About Function, pp. 126–130 (1993)
30. Rivlin, E., Dickinson, S., Rosenfeld, A.: Recognition by functional parts. Computer Vision and Image Understanding, special issue on Functionality in Object Recognition 62(2), 164–176 (1995)
31. Rivlin, E., Rosenfeld, A.: Navigational functionalities. Computer Vision and Image Understanding, special issue on Functionality in Object Recognition 62(2), 232–244 (1995)
32. Shapiro, L.G., Stockman, G.C.: Computer Vision. Prentice-Hall, Upper Saddle River (2001)
33. Stansfield, R.A.: Robotic grasping of unknown objects: A knowledge-based approach. International Journal of Robotics Research 10, 314–326 (1991)
34. Stark, L., Bowyer, K.W.: Achieving generalized object recognition through reasoning about association of function to structure. IEEE Transactions on Pattern Analysis and Machine Intelligence 3(10), 1097–1104 (1991)
35. Stark, L., Bowyer, K.W.: Indexing function-based categories for generic object recognition. In: CVPR 1992. Computer Vision and Pattern Recognition, Champaign, Illinois, pp. 795–797 (June 1992)
36. Stark, L., Hall, L.O., Bowyer, K.W.: Methods for Combination of Evidence in Function-Based 3-D Object Recognition. International Journal of Pattern Recognition and Artificial Intelligence 7(3), 573–594 (1993)
37. Stark, L., Bowyer, K.W., Hoover, A.W., Goldgof, D.B.: Recognizing object function through reasoning about partial shape descriptions and dynamic physical properties. Proceedings of the IEEE 84(11), 1640–1656 (1996)
38. Stark, L., Bowyer, K.: Generic Object Recognition using Form and Function. Series in Machine Perception Artificial Intelligence, vol. 10. World Scientific, New York (1996)
39. Sutton, M., Stark, L., Bowyer, K.W.: Function-based generic recognition for multiple object categories. In: Jain, A.K., Flynn, P.J. (eds.) Three-dimensional Object Recognition Systems, pp. 447–470. Elsevier Science Publishers, Amsterdam (1993)
40. Sutton, M.A., Stark, L., Bowyer, K.: GRUFF-3: Generalizing the domain of a function-based recognition system. Pattern Recognition 27(12), 1743–1766 (1994)
41. Sutton, M., Stark, L., Bowyer, K.W.: Function from visual analysis and physical interaction: A methodology for recognition of generic classes of objects. Image and Vision Computing 16(11), 745–763 (1998)
42. Winston, P., Binford, T., Katz, B., Lowry, M.: Learning physical description from functional definitions, examples, and precedents. In: AAAI 1983, pp. 433–439 (1983)
43. Winston, P., Rao, S.: Repairing learned knowledge using experience. In: Winston, P.H., Shellard, S.A. (eds.) AI at MIT: Expanding Frontiers, pp. 363–379. MIT Press, Cambridge (1990)
44. Clarke, F., Ekeland, I.: SAMPLE. Arch. Rat. Mech. Anal. 78, 315–333 (1982)

The MACS Project: An Approach to Affordance-Inspired Robot Control

Erich Rome[1], Lucas Paletta[2], Erol Şahin[3], Georg Dorffner[4],
Joachim Hertzberg[5], Ralph Breithaupt[1], Gerald Fritz[2], Jörg Irran[4],
Florian Kintzler[4], Christopher Lörken[5], Stefan May[1], and Emre Uğur[3]

[1] Fraunhofer IAIS, Sankt Augustin, Germany
[2] Joanneum Research, Graz, Austria
[3] Middle East Technical University, Ankara, Turkey
[4] Austrian Research Institute for Artificial Intelligence, Vienna, Austria
[5] University of Osnabrück, Germany

Abstract. In this position paper, we present an outline of the MACS approach to affordance-inspired robot control. An affordance, a concept from Ecological Psychology, denotes a specific relationship between an animal and its environment. Perceiving an affordance means perceiving an interaction possibility that is specific for the animal's perception and action capabilities. Perceiving an affordance does not include appearance-based object recognition, but rather feature-based perception of object functions. The central hypothesis of MACS is that an affordance-inspired control architecture enables a robot to perceive more interaction possibilities than a traditional architecture that relies on appearance-based object recognition alone. We describe how the concept of affordances can be exploited for controlling a mobile robot with manipulation capabilities. Particularly, we will describe how affordance support can be built into robot perception, how learning mechanisms can generate affordance-like relations, how this affordance-related information is represented, and how it can be used by a planner for realizing goal-directed robot behavior. We present both the MACS demonstrator and simulator, and summarize development and experiments that have been performed so far. By interfacing perception and goal-directed action in terms of affordances, we will provide a new way for reasoning and learning to connect with reactive robot control. We will show the potential of this new methodology by going beyond navigation-like tasks towards goal-directed autonomous manipulation in our project demonstrators.

1 Introduction

In Cognitive Science, the term *affordances* was first coined by the perceptual psychologist J.J. Gibson [1] to denote a resource or support that the environment offers an animal for action, and that the animal must be able to directly perceive and employ. The concept denotes a mutual relationship between animal and environment, and is related to modern concepts like "situatedness" and

E. Rome et al. (Eds.): Affordance-Based Robot Control, LNAI 4760, pp. 173–210, 2008.
© Springer-Verlag Berlin Heidelberg 2008

"embeddedness". The concept of affordances has, since its conception, proven to have a strong appeal in a wide range of fields, ranging from design [2] and neuroscience to robotics.

In robotics and artificial intelligence, affordances offer an original perspective on coupling perception, action and reasoning. However, despite its appeal, the use of affordances has mostly been confined to an inspiration source in robotics and that no systematic study on how this concept can be utilized in robot control has been made. The main reason behind this is the mist surrounding this elusive notion, created by the verbose definitions of affordances and its different, sometimes conflicting uses. Although a number of attempts were made towards formalizing this concept in Ecological Psychology [3,4] and in Computational Linguistics, none were provided a good basis over which this concept be utilized at different aspects of robot control.

After this characterization, we illustrate briefly why the concept of affordances may be beneficial for the use in robot control: Firstly, the concept of affordances links perception, action, learning and reasoning in an agent-specific way. Thus it bears the potential for a new engineering method for a biologically inspired, hybrid (reactive and deliberative) control architecture for mobile robots with manipulation capabilities. Secondly, the complementarity of the object and the affordance notions may allow a robot a greater flexibility for performing tasks. A robot system that uses object-centered perception may need to abort a mission if objects of a certain class that are required to reach a (sub-)goal are not available. In those cases where an affordance (like a function) of this object is more important than its sensorial appearance, affordance-based perception may be more appropriate, since it allows the robot to perceive and use objects with the same function that belong to a completely different object class, that is, it helps finding more alternatives for action.

The main objective of the MACS project is to explore and exploit the concept of *affordances* for the design and implementation of autonomous mobile robots acting goal-directedly in a dynamic environment. The aim is to develop affordance-inspired control as a method for robotics. That involves making affordances a first-class concept in a robot control architecture. By interfacing perception and action in terms of affordances, the project aims to provide a new way for reasoning and learning to connect with reactive robot control. The potential of this new methodology will be shown by going beyond navigation-like tasks towards goal-directed autonomous manipulation in the project demonstrators. All over, MACS aims at embedding its technical results into cognitive science.

In the MACS project, there is explicit support for the affordance concept in our architecture and the hypothesis is that the resulting performance of the robot will benefit in terms of robustness and generality. In fact, these are essentially the only criteria that can be used to evaluate empirically whether an affordance-based robotic system is better than a non-affordance-based one.

Thus, the main result of MACS will be a working, integrated robot system, based on the KURT3D robot, that serves as a proof of concept for the affordance-inspired robot control approach. Other results of the project will be a formal theory, a dedicated simulation environment, a specifically taylored learning approach for generating affordance representations, an affordance-based planner, feature extractors and other software for function-centered perception, plus dissemination of the results.

The remainder of the paper is organized as follows. We start with a brief analysis of the state of the art in affordances related research in (ecological) psychology, including brief reviews of recent formalizations and theories of affordances. The next section reviews briefly the state of the art in affordance-related research, both in Ecological Psychology and in Robotics. The following three sections describe the state of work and results in the areas of perceiving and learning affordances, and using affordance representations for goal-directed action and planning. The central section on architecture reviews related work, provides basic definitions of the MACS approach, including the definition of a *agent (or robot) affordance*, and outlines the affordance-inspired robot control architecture developed in MACS.

The architecture has been and is being tested both in simulation and a real demonstration testbed including the mobile robot KURT3D with its basic manipulation capabilities. Both facilities and some of the experiments are described in the next section. We conclude with a summary of our approach and the main results, and provide outlines of both the remaining work and possible future work.

2   Affordances in Ecological Psychology

J.J. Gibson (1904-1979) is one of the most influential psychologists of the 20th century, who aimed to develop a "theory of information pick-up" as a new theory of perception. He argued that an organism and its environment complement each other and that studies on the organism should be conducted in its natural environment rather than in isolation, ideas that later formed the basic elements of Ecological Psychology. The concept of affordance was conceived within this context.

Based on his studies of meaningful optical variables[1] and the Gestaltist conception of immediate perception of meanings of the things, J.J. Gibson built his own theory of perception and introduced the term *affordance* to refer to the action possibilities that objects offer to an organism, in an environment. The term affordances first appeared in his 1966 book [5], and is further refined in his later book [1]. In this book, the description of the affordance concept was discussed in a complete chapter, which generally laid out the fundamental aspects of affordances:

> "The affordances of the environment are what it offers the animal, what it provides or furnishes, either for good or ill. The verb to afford is found

---

[1] For example *optical center of expansion* of the visual field was such an optical variable which was meaningful for a pilot trying to land a plane, indicating the direction of the glide, and helping him to adjust the landing behavior.

in the dictionary, but the noun affordance is not. I have made it up. I mean by it something that refers to both the environment and the animal in a way that no existing term does. It implies the complementarity of the animal and the environment." (J.J. Gibson, 1979/1986, p. 127)

J.J. Gibson believed that affordances were directly perceivable (a.k.a. *direct perception*) by the organism, thus the meaning of the objects in the environment were directly apparent to the agent acting in it. This was different from the contemporary view of the time that the meaning of objects were created internally with further "mental calculation" of the otherwise meaningless perceptual data.

The discussions on the perception of object affordances naturally had some philosophical consequences on the much debated object concept.

"The theory of affordances rescues us from the philosophical muddle of assuming fixed classes of objects, each defined by it common features and then given a name. ... You do not have to classify and label things in order to perceive what they afford." (J.J. Gibson, 1979/1986, p. 134)

Gibson goes on to state that

"... If you know what can be done with a graspable object, what it can be used for, you can call it whatever you please. ... The theory of affordances rescues us from the philosophical muddle of assuming fixed classes of objects, each defined by its common features and then given a name. ... But this does not mean you cannot learn how to use things and perceive their uses. You do not have to classify and label things in order to perceive what they afford." [1, p. 134].

Thus, objects and affordances are complementary in the sense that one object class may offer a multitude of affordances, and one affordance may be offered by a multitude of object classes.

J.J. Gibson's view of studying organism and environment together as a system (including the concept of affordance) has been one of founding pillars of Ecological Psychology. Following the formulation of the theory of affordances, the Ecological Psychology community started to conduct experiments in order to verify that people are able to perceive the affordances of the environment and to understand the mechanisms underlying this perception. These experiments [6,7,8,9,10,11] aimed at showing that organisms (mostly human) can perceive whether a specific action is *do-able* or *not-do-able* in an environment. This implies that what we perceive are not necessarily objects (e.g. stairs, doors, chairs), but the action possibilities (e.g. climbable, passable, sittable) in the world. Although the number of these experiments is quite high, the diversity in them is rather narrow. They constitute a class of experiments characterized by two main points: taking the ratio of an environmental measure and a bodily measure of the human subject; and based on the value of this ratio, making a binary judgment of whether a specific action is possible or not.

The first point gives us a clue about how the experimenters interpreted affordances. Since affordances were roughly defined as the properties of the environment taken relative to the organism acting in it, the effort was to show that the ratio between an environmental measure and a bodily measure of the organism have consequences for behavior. This ratio must also be perceivable, so that the organism is aware of this measure which, in a way, determines its behavior's success.

Warren's stair-climbing experiments [6] have generally been accepted as a seminal work on the analysis of affordances, constituting a baseline for later experiments which seek to understand affordance-based perception. In these studies, Warren showed that organisms perceive their environment in terms of *intrinsic* or *body-scaled* metrics, not in absolute or global dimensions. He was able to calculate the constant, so called π proportions, that depend on specific properties of the organism-environment system. There exists one such ratio per each affordance, and they solely depend on the functionally relevant variables of corresponding actions. For instance, a humans judgment of whether he can climb a stair step is not determined by the global dimension of the height of the stair step, but by its ratio to his leg-length.

In [7], Warren and Whangs showed how the perception of geometrical dimensions such as size and distance is scaled relative to the "perceived eyeheight" [2] of the perceiver, in an environment where the subjects were to judge the affordance of walking through an aperture. Marks' surface sitting and climbing experiments [8] also incorporated a similar approach. Some of these studies[9,10] criticized former studies because they limited themselves to only one perceptual source, namely visual information. Instead of limiting themselves to visual perception, they studied haptic perception in infant traversability of surfaces and critical slant judgment for walking on sloped surfaces. While in these experiments human subjects were asked to judge whether a certain affordance exists or not in a static environment, Chemero[11] conducted other experiments, in order to prove that changes in the layout of affordances are perceivable in dynamic environments, and found out that the results are compatible with *critical ratio* values. Another important work is Oudejans et. al.'s [12] study of *street-crossing behavior* and perception of *critical time-gap* for safe crossing. This work is novel since it shows that not only static properties of the organism, but also its dynamic state is important when deciding on its actions.

An overview of the mentioned experiments shows that they are mostly focused on the perception aspect of affordances. Other cognitive processes such as learning, high level reasoning and inference mechanisms are not the subjects of these experiments, and the link between affordances and these higher level processes is not discussed.

3   An Affordance-Inspired Robot Control Architecture

3.1   Related Work

The concept of affordances is highly related to autonomous robot control and influenced studies in this field. We believe that for a proper discussion of the

---

[2] In [7], eyeheight is defined as the height at which a person's eyes would pass through the wall while walking and looking straight in a natural and comfortable position.

relationship of the affordance concept to robot control, the similarity of the arguments of J.J. Gibson's theory and reactive/behavior-based robotics should be noted first.

The concept of affordances and behavior-based robotics emerged in very similar ways as opposing suggestions to the dominant paradigms in their fields. J.J. Gibson constructed his theory based on the criticism of the then dominant theory of perception and cognition, which favoured modeling and inference. Likewise, behavior-based robotics was motivated by the criticism of the then dominant robotic architectures, which favoured modeling and inference. This parallelism between the two fields suggests that they are applications of the same line of thinking to different domains ([13, p. 244]; [14]). Opposing to modeling and inference, J.J. Gibson defended a more direct relationship between the organism and the environment and suggested that a model of the environment and costly inferential processes were not needed. In a similar vein, behavior-based robotics advocated a tight coupling between perception and action. Brooks, claiming that "the world is its own best model", suggested an approach that eliminated all the modeling and internal representation [15]. As a result, one can see the underlying concepts of affordances in existence in robot control architectures such as subsumption architecture [16], the robot-schema architecture [17] and AuRA [18].

Some roboticists have already been explicitly using ideas on affordances in designing behavior-based robots. For example, Murphy [19] suggested that robotic design can benefit from ideas in the theory of affordances such that complex perceptual modeling can be eliminated without loss in capabilities. She tried to prove her point with three case studies and drew attention to the importance of the ecological niche in the design of behaviors. Likewise, Duchon et al. [14] benefited from J.J. Gibson's ideas on direct perception and optical flow in the design of behaviors and termed Ecological Robotics to be the practice of applying ecological principles to the design of mobile robots.

The use of affordances within Autonomous Robotics is mostly confined to behavior-based control of the robots, and that its use in deliberation remains a rather unexplored area. This is not a coincidence, but indeed a consequence of the lacks in J.J. Gibson's theory. The reactive approach could not scale up to complex tasks in robotics, in the same way that the theory of affordances in its original form was unable to explain some aspects of perception and cognition. The need to hybridize robotic control architectures can be considered similar to the attempts in Cognitive Psychology to view affordances as part of a complete cognitive model. While some cognitive models relate affordances only with low-level processes [20], others consider their role in cognitive processes as well [21,22,23]. Similarly in robotics, some hybrid architectures inherit properties related to affordances only at their reactive layer [18,24], while other studies exploit how affordances reflect to high-level processes such as learning [25,26,23,27,28], decision-making [29], and planning [30]. Recently a number of robotic studies focused on the learning of affordances in robots. These studies mainly tackled two major aspects. In one aspect, affordance learning is referred to as the learning of consequences of a certain action in a given situation [27,28,30]. Stoytchev's [28,30] and Fitzpatrick et al.'s [27] work uses affordances as a higher-level concept, which a developing cognitive agent learns about by interacting with the objects in its environment. The robots in both studies execute certain actions on certain objects, and observe and learn the change in the environment as the consequence of the action. In other studies the focus lies on the learning of invariant properties of environments that afford a certain behavior [23,26,29]. In [23], MacDorman proposes an architecture, where the robot learns a sensory-motor mapping of its actions, and uses this learned model to make plans at the deliberative level. The learned model is then used to predict the affordances of objects in the environment. However, MacDorman defines affordances only in terms of internal values of the robot (like "tasty" and "poisonous" things), and not the physical changes it can create in the environment separating the process of predicting the outcome of actions, from the process of predicting affordances.

Some hybrid architectures inherit the properties of reactive architectures in their reactive components. For example, AuRA [18] is said to be influenced from J.J. Gibson's theory of affordances for using action-oriented perception in the reactive component. In AuRA, each motor schema is associated with a perceptual schema, which extracts the sensory input relevant for the particular behavior. Similarly, in the SSS [24] architecture, the communication of lower and upper layers is based on the idea of matched filters, which suggests that certain sensor states are equivalent if they call for the same motor response. Although not explicitly stated, we can further relate affordances to some deliberative processes in hybrid architectures. For instance, the AuRA [18] architecture can be said to perform deliberative modulation of perception, since plan execution occurs by activating motor schemas and the relevant perceptual schemas specified by the plan. Another example is the SFX [31] architecture in which the symbolic world model depends on the current behavior, as a consequence of action-oriented sensor fusion.

We would like to note, that the affordance theory of J.J. Gibson was mostly used as a source of inspiration in autonomous robotics. As a result, only certain aspects of the theory were used, and that no attempts to consider the implications of the whole theory towards autonomous robot control were made. In this sense, the development of an "affordance-inspired robot control architecture" that is designed to learn, detect, and use the affordances in the environment [32] will be an important contribution to the field.

3.2 The MACS Approach to Affordance-Inspired Robot Control

The vast majority of robot perception approaches are either close perception-action couplings for reactive behavior or oriented towards object recognition on higher control levels. Also, object recognition is in many cases based on general computer vision methods that do not account for the specifics of the robot at hand, i.e. its sensory system and its actuator system. Only very few robot perception approaches deal with recognition of functions that the environment offers (cf. Sec. 5).

We can state that a function-centered perception approach will realize a view of the environment that is orthogonal to object-centered perception. Such function-centered perception would potentially allow a robot to find more alternatives for acting in its environment. A robot mission that requires to find—based on appearance only—and use certain objects in the environment will fail if one or more of these objects cannot be found. But often the identity or appearance of an object may not be relevant for completing a task. A task could, for instance, also be completed if the robot finds an alternative object that offers the same functions as the original one (in J.J. Gibson's terminology, one would say: it affords the same action possibility). An affordance-inspired robot control with a function-centered perception would allow a robot more flexibility in plan execution and thus increase the likelihood of successfully completing a mission. Thus, it would enhance a robot's abilities to perceive and utilize the potential for action that the environment offers, i.e. enable a robot to make use of affordances. This is the central hypothesis of MACS.

MACS aims at realizing affordance-inspired control in a hybrid architecture that allows goal-directed behavior based on function-centered perception, with functions related to and grounded in the robot's action capabilities. Affordance support in the sense sketched in the previous sections will be built into several levels of the architecture. In order to use affordance support for deliberate action, i.e. for planning, we will need an explicit representation of the potential for action or the functions that the enviroment offers, respectively. The formalization that is the basis for such representations is described in [33]. In summary, a number of formalizations have been proposed to clarify the concept of affordance in the field of Ecological Psychology. To summarize briefly, Turvey [34] defined affordances as 'dispositions' in the environment that get actualized with the interaction of the organism and the environment. Different from Turvey's formalism, which attached affordances to the environment, Stoffregen [35] and Chemero [3] defined affordances as relations within the organism-environment system. Independent from these formalizations in Ecological Psychology, Steedman [36] formalized affordances in Linguistics by providing an explicit link to action possibilities offered by the environment, and by proposing the use of the concept in planning. The authors are not aware of other robot control methods that make use of explicit, symbolic affordance representations.

In order to distinguish our use of the term "affordance" from the use in Ecological Psychology, we introduced the definition of an agent (or robot) affordance [33,32] [3]:

Definition 1 ((Agent) Affordance). *An* (agent) affordance *is a relation between an agent and its environment which affords a capability. The agent/environment relation affords a capability if the agent*

1. *has the capacity to recognize that it is in such a relation between itself and its environment, and it*
2. *has the ability to act to bring about that capability.*

---

[3] A similar but alternative formalization of affordances was also proposed in [37].

This definition states that the affordance is a perceivable relation between the subjective capabilities of an agent and the features of its surroundings. The agent affordance definition is used whenever we are referring to or describing the robot's situation in its environment, e.g. in examples of the robot's behavior or in descriptions of experiments. For this purpose, we use the notions of entity, (observed) behavior, and (observed) outcome. An example shall illustrate the meaning of these notions. Given our mobile robot KURT3D with its basic electromagnetic gripper as manipulation device, and given that there are magnetic cans in its environment, we could say: "The robot has successfully lifted the blue can.", where some features of the blue can comprise the entity, lifting is the observed behavior, and the successful execution resulting in the can attached to the robot's electromagnet is the observed outcome. The entity can be represented by a set of features perceived prior to the lifting behavior, the lifting behavior can be represented as a sequence of basic actions, and the outcome can be represented by a set of features perceived after the lifting behavior has been executed. This leads to a straightforward definition of an (agent) affordance representation [32]:

Definition 2 (Affordance Representation). *An* affordance representation *or* affordance triple *is a data structure:*

$$(\text{cue descriptor}, \text{behavior descriptor}, \text{outcome descriptor}). \qquad (1)$$

Here, a cue descriptor or an outcome descriptor is specified as a list of attribute value pairs. A behavior descriptor consists of one or more behavior identifiers. Optionally, parameters for these behaviors can be specified.

Such representations can either be handcrafted or learned during an extended initial learning phase as described in Sec. 6. The cue part of the representation can be used to hypothesize the presence of a certain affordance in the environment that the robot searches for achieving the planned outcome. The feature set comprising a cue needs only be sufficient for making such a hypothesis. It is neither required that the feature set is a sufficient representation of the manipulated object, nor that all the cue features belong to this object.

After a certain amount of affordance representations have been created, the robot shall make use of this information for deliberate action as described in Sec. 4. A mission defined by a human operator could be the task of searching "liftables" and stack these in an arbitrary location. The planner would create operators that employ affordance representations, and an execution control would monitor, as usual, the progress of task completion.

In order to implement these concepts, the proposed affordance-inspired control architecture consists of two branches. A bottom-up branch goes from sensors via a perception module (cf. Sec. 5) to a learning module (cf. Sec. 6) that generates affordance representations. A top-down branch goes from a deliberation module via execution control down to a behavior system that provides some basic robot skills, including but not limited to driving, braking, map-building and lifting, or moving and controlling the magnet.

3.3   Architectural Building Blocks

The proposed affordance-inspired control architecture scheme is depicted in Fig. 1. In this diagram, a red, solid arrow between components A and B in the diagram is of type control flow. The arrow indicates that the control is passed from A to B. The arrow does say nothing about the situations in which the control is passed, nor about the data that might be exchanged when passing control. The designations close to such an arrow indicate qualitatively the nature of the control flow, e.g. information request, configuration request etc. A blue, dashed arrow between components A and B in the diagram is of type data flow. The data flow arrow does not say anything about the circumstances, that is, the current control states, under which the data are transferred. The designations close to such an arrow indicate qualitatively the types of data that are passed from A to B. Bold arrows indicate flows between modules, thin arrows intra module flows. Data passed from module A to B are available to all components inside B. Orange colored boxes are specific affordance support oriented components that are usually not found in other control architectures.

The main architectural building blocks in this diagram are:

User Interface. Displays status information and allows a user both to guide a robot manually through an action sequence and to just specify a mission goal for the robot. The

Deliberation module. Converts a mission goal into an executable affordance-based mission plan which is passed to the

Execution module. This module executes the mission plan, monitors its execution, including successful or unsuccessful acting upon affordances. The Execution module's new *Event and Execution monitor* checks the existence of affordance support cues and compares expected outcome with actual outcome of an executed behavior control routine. The Execution control triggers behaviors of the

Behavior System. This module provides a number of pre-programmed behavior control routines that can be viewed as basic skills of the robot. Some behavior control routines are parametrizable and can be configured by other modules, if necessary. The behaviors make use of

Actuators. That enable the robot to move about and to interact with its environment. They include the drive motors, the sensor servos, and the crane arm motors. The

Sensors. Enable the robot to perceive its environment and its internal states, Virtual sensors provide software state information, real sensors yield data from the environment. All sensory data are first handled by the

Perception module. It relays sensory data, extracted features and status information (like active behaviors and their parameters) to the Learning module, Execution module, Behavior System and Deliberation module. It can be configured to look just for certain features that relate to searched affordance support cues. Its *Entity Structure Generation Module* converts sensory data into appropriate data structures for architectural affordance support.

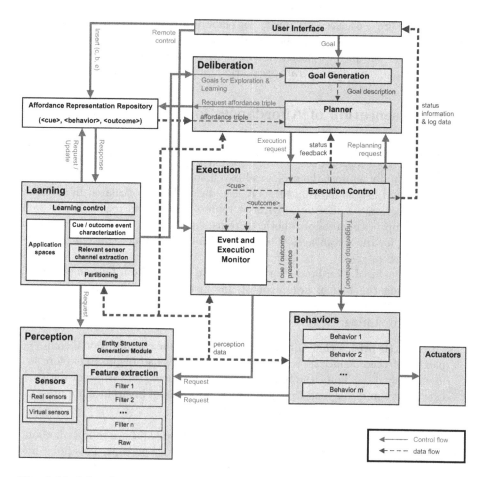

Fig. 1. Modules, data and control flow of the MACS control architecture. A solid arrow between components A and B indicates control flow, a dashed arrow data flow. White boxes are specific affordance support oriented components.

Learning module. Takes input from the Perception module and generates affordance representations (affordance triples) to populate the new

Affordance Representation Repository. This repository is new and specific to our affordance-based approach. It provides affordance representations for use with the affordance-based Planner for goal-oriented, affordance-based mission planning.

This architecture is implemented in such a way that it can be connected both to the physical robot and the simulated robot via the same interface, just by pushing a button. This enables us to test the system both in simulated and in real environments.

In the next three sections, the affordance-based approaches of the main building blocks within this architecture, namely planning (Sec. 4), perception (Sec. 5)

and learning (Sec. 6), are explained. An elaborate description of the behavior system and its basic skills can be found in [38]. Before we conclude this article, we present the physics-based simulator MACSim and the experimentation environment, i.e. the demonstrator scenario and its elements in Sec. 7.

4   Representation of Affordances for Deliberation

Literature is rather sparse when it comes to more or less formal definitions for representations of affordances. This is not surprising as representing them explicitly is actually against the ecological psychologist's interpretation of directly perceivable and usable affordances as it has always been postulated by Gibson. While such a view on affordance without representation and reason has as well been picked up in the area of robotic systems, e.g. by [19], we dissent from this view arguing for the advantages of a clearly defined affordance concept throughout the MACS project.

For the benefit of affordances for robotics, we diverge from Gibson's original view, following the line of argument of, for instance, MacDorman who justifies learning and the explicit recognition, and thus implicit representation, of affordances by stating:

"It is not surprising that Gibson underestimated the computational complexity of vision, since he wrote before researchers had begun to explore it seriously. [...] Thus, the brain may need to process sensorimotor data extensively and to spend time learning what kinds of invariance are useful in recognizing affordances." [39, p. 1003]

We are furthermore of the opinion that it makes indeed sense to reason about affordances instead of acting directly upon an affordance percept. This point has as well been picked up by [14] as they explicitly argue that an agent does not merely respond to a directly perceived stimulus by applying the action that is afforded in that situation. It is not controlled by the environment. It can rather use the information provided by the affordances of a situation and reason about them in a goal-directed manner selecting those afforded actions that will lead to its goal.

The demand put on the MACS project was now to define an explicit, symbolic affordance representation that the whole architecture and all its various components are based on. Some of the following goes back to work done in [33] and has already been introduced in [38]. The overall idea, however, is primarily inspired by the work of Chemero [3] who first described an affordance as a perceivable relation between an agent and its environment or, as we interpret it, between the subjective capabilities of an agent and the features of its surroundings. We extended this idea by introducing the definitions of an (agent) affordance and an affordance representation (Definitions 1 and 2, Sec. 3).

Regarding Def. 2 of the affordance representation, one can understand its attributes as features of the environment or even internal states of the robot while the values are not restricted to distinct values but can also represent value ranges.

The *cue descriptor* holds that filtered or raw sensory information that supports the existence of the represented affordance whereas the *outcome descriptor* contains the data as it was perceived by the robot while previously executing the behavior referenced in the *behavior descriptor*. That descriptor, on the other hand, refers to a robot behavior and a set of parameters that were used with this robot behavior when the according cues and outcomes were monitored.

To subsume this definition an affordance is represented by:

- The *cues* for an affordance, that support it. These are the perceivable features or attributes of the environment or the agent and their values or value ranges. Attribute value pairs stored in a cue descriptor can thus be, for instance, the relative distance to a test object, its color, or the different currents propagated to the robot's motors.
- The behavior descriptor refers to the behavior or sequence of behaviors the robot has applied when this representation was created. To stick with the last example this would be a lift action combined with the parameters like motor current or crane movement that were used for the particular action.
- The *outcome* of any action or behavior executed upon the affordance. The outcome represents the changes of the agent and the environment as far as they can be perceived by the agent. Examples would be, that a blue colored blob is being perceived at a higher position, relatively to the agent, if it has applied a lifting action.

The different affordance representation triples that can both be hand-coded or learned (see Sec. 6) are then used during runtime of the system to build up and maintain a world model of the robot's surroundings that is represented as an affordance map. The different map regions hereby hold the information whether a particular affordance type has been perceived in that area.

Given such a representation it is left to describe how affordances can be exploited for robotics by reasoning about them. The approach followed in the MACS project, it is really only one approach to this matter, is to ground plan operators by means of affordances. The idea behind this is that there are situations where one wants to achieve something but one does not actually care about how or with the help of what object to reach the desired goal. For instance, when one wants to weigh down a pile of paper one can do this by putting a rock, a cup, or a book on that pile achieving the same effect with each of these items. In other words, you only have to select *any* item that affords the weighing action. This is the point where the affordance concept nicely comes together with the approach to deliberation and planning within the MACS project.

The MACS planning system is based on a complete domain and problem definition specified in the Planning Domain Definition Language (PDDL) [40]. The planner's world model contains knowledge of where what kind of affordance has been perceived and uses the availability of an affordance in a certain region of the environment to plan an action in that region (cf. Fig. 10). Take the example that the robot has to open a door by putting some weight on a switch. The generated plan will be a sequence of operators to drive to a region where the liftability affordance has been perceived, to lift a liftable item there, to drive to the switch and put the item, whatever it may be, on the switch. The plan will thus contain a *lift* operator that gets implemented or grounded only during the execution phase of the plan. The robot simply has to select an affordance representation triple that belongs to the type of the liftability affordance and whose cues of its cue descriptor can currently be perceived. By acting as specified in that triple's behavior descriptor, the robot implicitly chooses the next available liftable item and lifts it; be it a rock, a cup, or a book.

The deliberation part of the MACS architecture thus reasons about affordances in the sense that it goal-directedly selects the kind of affordance to act upon; i.e. it decides to use the liftability affordance and not, for instance, a pushability affordance. For a complete specification of the MACS deliberation module refer to [41].

5 Perception of Affordances

In the context of ecological perception , as it was created by J.J. Gibson [1], visual perception would enable agents to experience in a direct way the opportunities for action. However, J.J. Gibson remained unclear about how this concept could be used in a technical system. Neisser [42] replied to this concept with the notion of a perception-action cycle that shows the reciprocal relationship of the knowledge (i.e., a schema) about the environment directing exploration of the environment (i.e., action), which samples the information available for pick up in the environment, which then modifies the knowledge, and so on. This cycle describes how knowledge, perception, action, and the environment all interact in order to achieve goals. Our work on affordance-like perception is in the context of technical systems based on a notion of affordances that 'fulfill the purpose of efficient prediction of interaction opportunities'.

In the project MACS we provide a refined concept of affordance perception by proposing two processing stages in terms of a predictive module, an interaction and an evaluation module (cf. Sec. 5.2). Affordance-like perception aims at supporting control schemata for perception-action processing in the context of rapid and simplified access to agent-environment interactions. Furthermore, we argue that has not yet been sufficiently addressed, in particular with respect to cue selection.

5.1 Related Work

Previous research on affordance based *perception* focused on heuristic definitions of simple feature-function relations to facilitate sensor-motor associations in robotic agents. Human cognition embodies visual stimuli and motor interactions in common neural circuitry (Faillenot et al. [43]). Accordingly, the affordance-based context in spatio-temporal observations and sensor-motor behaviors has been outlined in a model of cortical involvement in grasping by Fagg and Arbib [44], highlighting the relevance of vision for motor interaction [45]. Reaching and grasping involves visuomotor coordination that benefits from an affordance-like mapping from visual to haptic perceptual categories (Wheeler et al. [46]). Within this context, the MIT humanoid robot Cog was involved in object poking and proding experiments that investigate the emergence of affordance categories to choose actions with the aim to make objects roll in a specific way (Fitzpatrick et al. [27]). The research of Stoytchev [30] analyzed affordances on an object level, investigating new concepts of object-hood in a sense of how perceptions of objects are connected with visual events that arise from action consequences related to the object itself. Although this work innovatively demonstrated the relation between affordance triggers and meaningful robot behaviors, these experiments involve computer vision still on a low level, and do not consider complex sensor-motor representation of an agent interaction in less constrained, even natural environments.

Affordance based visual object representations are per se function based representations. In contrast to classical object representations, functional object representations (Stark and Bowyer [47], Rivlin et al. [48]) use a set of primitives (relative orientation, stability, proximity, etc.) that define specific functional properties, essentially containing face and vertex information. These primitives are subsumed to define surfaces and form the functional properties, such as 'is sittable' or 'provides stable support'. Bogoni and Bajcsy [49] have extended this representation from an active perception perspective, relating observability to interaction with the object, understanding functionality as the applicability of an object for the fulfillment of some purpose. However, so far, function-based representations were basically defined by the engineer, and not learned from interaction.

5.2   Stages in Affordance Perception

We developed a refined concept on affordance perception [50] by proposing (i) an interaction component (affordance recognition: recognizing relevant events in interaction via perceptual entities) and (ii) a predictive aspect (affordance cueing: predicting interaction via perceptual entities). This innovative conceptual step enables firstly to investigate the functional components of perception that make up affordance-based prediction, and secondly to lay a basis to identify the interrelation between predictive features and predicted event via machine learning technology [51,52,50,53].

Fig. 2 illustrates the various stages within the affordance based perception process for the example of the affordance *fill-ability* in the context of the opportunities for interaction with a coffee cup. Fig. 2(a) schematically illustrates the detection of perceptual entities that would provide affordance cues in terms of verifying the occurrence of a cup that is related to the prediction of being fill-able in general. Fig. 2(b) shows in analogy entities that would underlie the process of interaction of an agent with the cup by actually filling it up. Finally, Fig. 2(c) represents the entities corresponding to the final state of the interaction with the outcome of a successfully filled coffee cup. These figures illustrate that affordance cueing and affordance recognition must be conceptually separated and would involve different perceptual entities in general. While

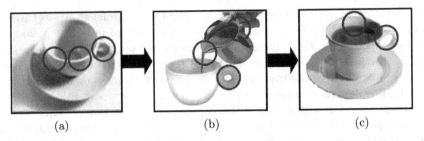

(a)   (b)   (c)

Fig. 2. Affordance recognition in affordance based perception for the example of the affordance fill-able with respect to the impact of selecting appropriate features. The seemingly simple interaction of filling up a coffee cup can be partitioned into various stages in affordance based perception, such as, (a) affordance cueing by predictive features that refer to a fill-able object, (b) identifying perceptual entities that represent the process of the affordance related interaction (e.g., flow of coffee), and (c) recognizing the final state by detecting perceptual entities that represent the outcome of interaction (e.g., level of coffee in cup).

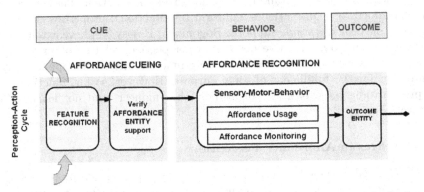

Fig. 3. Concept of affordance perception, depicting the key components of affordance cueing and recognition embedded within (left) an agents perception-action cycle (cf. Sec. 2, Def. 2)

affordance recognition actually involves the recognition of the interaction process and its associated final state, affordance cueing will be solely determined by the capability to reliably predict this future event in a statistical sense.

Fig. 3 depicts the innovative concept of feature based affordance perception worked out in the MACS project (cf. Sec. 2, Def. 2). We identify first the functional component of *affordance recognition*, i.e., the recognition of the affordance related visual event that characterizes a relevant interaction, e.g., the capability of lifting (lift-ability) an object using an appropriate robotic actuator. The recognition of this event should be performed by identifying a process of evaluating spatio-temporal information that leads to a final state. This final state should be unique in perceptual feature/state space, i.e., it should be characterized by the observation of specific feature attributes that are abstracted from the stream of sensory-motor information.

The second functional component of *affordance cueing* encompasses the key idea on affordance based perception, i.e., the prediction aspect on estimating the opportunity for interaction from the incoming sensory processing stream. In particular, this component is embedded in the perception-action cycle of the robotic agent. The agent is receiving sensory information in order to build upon arbitrary levels of feature abstractions, for the purpose of recognition of perceptual entities. In contrast to classical feature and object recognition, this kind of recognition is *purposive* in the sense of selecting exactly those features that efficiently support the evaluation of identifying an affordance, i.e., the perceptual entities that possess the capability to predict an event of affordance recognition in the feature time series that is immediately following the cueing stage of affordance based perception. The outcome of affordance cueing is in general a probability distribution on all possible affordances, providing evidence for a most confident affordance cue by delivering a hypothesis that favors the future occurrence of a particular affordance recognition event. This cue is functional in the sense of associating the related feature representation with a specific utility with respect to the capabilities of the agent and the opportunities provided by the environment, thus representing *predictive features* in the affordance based perception system.

5.3   Implementation: Perception Module

The *perception module* includes an *Entity Structure Generation Module* (Fig. 1, cf. also [33]) that generates appropriate data structures from sensory data in a framework of entity structures. Starting from simple structures (e.g. raw sensory data) these data structures are processed via transformation and/or combination into more abstract ones, describing the scene (e.g. regions of different colors and their relation) as well as affordances (e.g. regions with attributes like liftable, traversable, etc.). The concept of *computational units* is employed to process these structures within an overall abstraction hierarchy. Computational units use *Entity Trajectory Streams* (i.e. series of entity structures over time) as input and produce entity trajectory streams as output. These entity trajectory streams provide input for the learning module, which learns suitable combinations of computational units for affordance cueing. For an example, several entity trajectory streams are combined in a final computational unit that classifies a particular region in the camera images into 'liftable' or 'non-liftable'. This classifier is encapsulated in the concept of the computational unit, with the benefit of a clear interface to other modules in the architecture of the system.

For finding salient locations that might be interesting during the robot's learning and mission phases, we employ a visual attention system called VOCUS [54]. VOCUS allows 'bottom up' detection of salient features in the environment as well as a 'top-down' search for certain features related to affordance cues [55]. The VOCUS system was also enhanced to work with two cameras in order to allow a triangulation of the position of salient regions relative to the robot. In order to accelerate VOCUS and to reduce CPU workload, it has been reimplemented such that it can run on a GPU. The latter variant can compute foci of attention at 60 fps, i.e. it can detect salient regions in both camera images at frame rate with little CPU usage [56]. This frees the CPU for other control tasks.

VOCUS is mainly employed by a basic skill for perceiving interesting locations. It computes foci of attention based on a saliency measure applied to elementary features like color, brightness and orientation contrasts. The feature vector describing a salient location in an image is also provided as a computational unit, i.e., VOCUS' output can also be used by the learning module.

5.4   Learning in Affordance Perception

There are affordances that are explicitly innate to the agent through evolutionary development and others that have to be learned [1]. Learning the chains of affordance driven actions can lead to learning new, more complex affordances (cf. Sec. 6). In contrast to previous work on functional feature and object representations, we stress the fact that functional representations must necessarily contain purposive features, i.e., represent perceptual entities that refer to interaction patterns and thus must be selected from an existing pool of features by means of machine learning.

In this context we demonstrated the learning of causal relationships between visual cues and predictable interactions, using both 3D and 2D information [51,52]. We verified the concept with a concrete implementation applying state-of-the-art visual descriptors [57] and regions of interest that were extracted from a simulated robot scenario and prove that these features were successfully selected for their relevance in predicting opportunities of robot interaction by means of decision trees [58].

Fig. 4(a) shows the application of local (SIFT) descriptors for the characterization of regions of interest in the field of view. For this purpose, we first segment the color based visual information within the image, and then associate integrated descriptor responses sampled within the regions to the region feature vector. The integration is performed via a histogram on local descriptors that are labeled with 'rectangular' and 'circular' attributes, respectively.

On-going work is in the direction of extending the scope of predictability via visual cueing using reinforcement learning [53]. Reinforcement learning [59,60] as an on-line version of Markov decision processes (MDP) [61] is able to determine a specific perceptual state that owns the predictive characteristics for the representation of an affordance-like visual cue. The learning process is applied to bridging two basic components characterizing the interaction component, i.e., affordance recognition, and the predictive aspect, i.e., affordance cueing, respectively. [62] presents the underlying theory and the experimental results from a robotic system scenario demonstrating how affordance recognition can provide the reinforcement signal to drive the propagation of reward information back in the affordance perception process. Upon convergence of the stochastic learning algorithm, we are able to identify an early perceptual state that enables to discriminate the capability to predict a future interaction opportunity with high confidence.

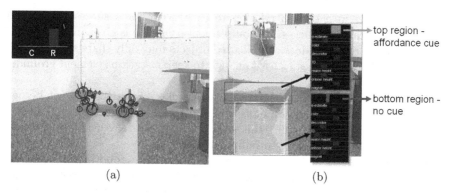

(a)   (b)

Fig. 4. Affordance based cueing of region determined perceptual states from learned predictive cumulative rewards. (a) On the basis of a color blob detector, local descriptors are classified into rectangular/circular (R/C) ones and the associated histogram feeds here into the recognition of an affordance cue (with respect to lift-ability). (b) Analyzed top and bottom regions are correspondingly classified as cues for lift-ability or non-lift-ability, visualized in terms of green and red bars with bar sizes correlating to positive or negative reward, respectively (monitoring boxes, top), anticipating a lift-able event.

There is huge potential in research on affordance perception towards extending the feature based representations towards object driven affordance-based interaction, grounding the work on the visual descriptor information presented here. Furthermore, the learning of affordance cues can be viewed in the frame of developmental learning of meaningful sequences of affordance triplets [63], opening a broad avenue for future research.

6   Learning of Affordances

The learning approach that was developed within the MACS project is an approach to acquire knowledge about relations that determine the interaction possibilities between an agent and its environment. Within this approach an artificial agent starts with basic interactions and uses more and more complex interactions over time and thus gathers experience about what happens before, during and after these interactions. These experiences are generalized by the agent, enabling it to act also in novel situations. Therefore the robot used starts with an initial set of reflex like actions and is designed to be able to deal with a growing set of (learned) actions. Thereby the approach is not limited to a special kind of actions.

The set of basic reflex-like actions shall enable the robot to stack building blocks. Whether two objects can be stacked or not dependents on the top region surface of the element that should provide the base, and depends on the bottom region surface of the element that should be stacked on this base. The two surfaces must be in a certain relation to each other for a successful stacking trial. In simple cases the necessary complementary shape is given over the entire top and bottom regions. More complicated objects may only share some of those complementary regions, but at least enough to keep a stacking element grounded on the base.

When objects are provided to an agent, the relevant surfaces cannot be perceived directly. Nevertheless humans are able to assume whether an object is stackable or not, without seeing this surface. They do it by using several cues based on their own experience to fulfill this task.

Consequently, in the MACS project, affordances within a robotic system are represented by relations between *cues*, *behaviors*, and *outcomes*. The space of learned affordances is thus a multi-relational repository from which *cue-behavior-outcome* triples can be derived. To be able to extract these triples is not only crucial for learning by self-experience and for planning but also for learning by imitation to match observed *cue* and *outcomes* to previously made self-experience. That means that triples, which are *1:1:1* relations, are derived from that *o:m:n* relations database.

The *cues* and *outcomes*, their inter-relations as well as the relation to the causing actions are learnt from the incoming perceptual data stream. For a detailed description of the learning approach see paper *Learning of Interaction Possibilities* in this volume.

The schema in Fig. 5 depicts the key components of the developed *Learning Module* that is connected to and interacts with the overall affordances based architecture (see Sec. 3). The image shows which modules are required and how they are interconnected to realize the required data and control flow. The depicted modules, the used data structures, and the data / control flow are described in the following sub-sections.

6.1   Application Spaces Module

The agent applies actions to the environment. While doing that the agent permanently monitors its environment and the internal states before, during and after the application. The sets of resulting time series are stored within behavior specific *Application Spaces* in the *Application Spaces Module* to be available for the learning processes. The begin and the end of the application of the actions must be marked within each stored time series. To be able to learn a cue for the existence of an affordance and the concerning outcomes (consequences of using an affordance), the recorded time series have to include data from a certain time interval before and after the application of the behavior.

During the learning process, the *Application Spaces* are divided into partitions. This partitioning information, i.e. a *Partitioner Object*, as created by the *Partitioning Module* (see Sec. 6.2), is stored in relation to its corresponding application space.

The relevant sensor channel information that is extracted during the learning process (see Sec. 6.3) as well as the characterization of these sensor channels (see Sec. 6.4) are to be stored within the *Application Spaces* as well.

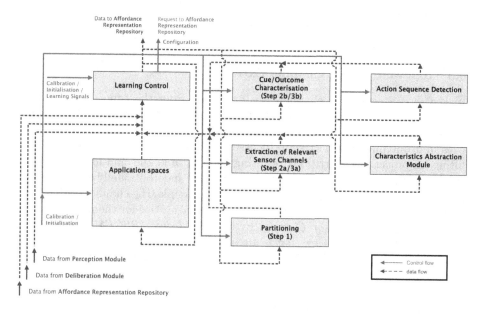

Fig. 5. The key components of the developed learning architecture, its modules, and the data (dashed lines) and control flows (solid lines) between the components

6.2   Partitioning

In the application space of an action sets of similar action application results should exist after a sufficient number of trials. For example in case of the application space of action "close gripper", the following subsets could emerge:

– a set of results where the involved objects were gripped,
– a set of results where the objects slipped away,
– a set of results where the objects were not grippable at all.

As input the *Partitioning Module* receives the data of an Application Space. This *Application Space* contains a set of time series, resulting from several applications of the same action. The *Partitioning Module* provides a mechanism to discriminate these different types of action application results from each other.

The output of the *Partitioning Module* is a *Partitioner Object* that is stored and linked to the belonging application space. The *Partitioner Object* provides a function to decide for a given time series to which partition it belongs. A partition is thus defined as the set of all time series that are mapped to the same partition identifier.

When there is already a *Partitioner Object* assigned to an *Application Space* and the agent acquired new experiences concerning the related behavior (new time series are stored within the *Application Space*) the partitioner must be adapted to these new experiences, if they deviate from the previous made ones. This re-learning process could change the *Partitioner Object* and thus could cause previously recorded time series to change their partition. It is also possible that new partitions emerge.

6.3   Relevant Sensor Channel Extraction

In the next step sensor channels are extracted from the time series of each partition of an application space that are representative for these partitions. Representative means, that these channels are in direct relation with the differing cues and outcomes, respectively. In case of performing an action that causes lifting an object, the partitions resulting from liftable and non-liftable objects will differ in the height (y-position time series) and (optionally) in the force sensor channel. For learning cues in this given example, the channel of the color blob filter (y-position of the blobs) could be representative for the partitions. As input, the *Relevant Sensor Channel Extraction Module (RSCEM)* receives the data of an *Application Space* that is already partitioned.

To find characteristic channels concerning cues, the same process is applied to the pre-application part of the recorded time series of a partition. These partitions are sub-partitioned further.

As output, the *RSCEM* provides

- for each partition a set of channel identities of the relevant sensor channels concerning the cue events for the Application Space
- for each partition a set of channel identities of the relevant sensor channels concerning outcome events for the Application Space

These sets are stored in the relevant application space.

When there is already a *Partitioner Object* assigned to an Application Space and the two sets of relevant sensor channels, and the agent acquired new experiences in applying the related action (new data time series are stored within the *Application Space*) an adaptation of the set of relevant sensor channels for the partitions could be necessary in the case, that e.g.

- the previously gained knowledge was incomplete (new environmental configurations, e.g. new objects occurred)
- the configuration of the sensors or actuators has changed (e.g. broken or altered because of growth or enhancement)
- the partitioning has changed (e.g. partitions altered or new partitions emerged, see Sec. 6.2).

6.4   Event Characterization

After the extraction of the relevant sensor channel(s), descriptions of what is characteristic for the relevant channel(s) of the partitions are to be derived, i.e. *cue characteristics* and *outcome characteristics*. These characteristics are used to enable the agent to recognize affordances (in case of characterizing cue related channels) or to monitor the outcome of the application of an action (in case of characterizing outcome related channels).

As input, the *Event Characterizer Module (ECM)* receives data of an *Application Space* in which the sets of relevant sensor channels for each partition (derived by the *Relevant Sensor Channel Extraction Module*, section 6.3) are stored.

As output the *Event Characterizer Module* provides

– for each partition a set of cue characteristics for the *Application Space*,
– for each partition a set of outcome characteristics for the Application Space.

Similar considerations to above with respect to new experiences apply.

6.5 Characteristics Abstraction

The task of the *Characteristics Abstraction Module (CAM)* is first to find similarities between the elements of a given set of outcome characteristics. Two or more characteristics could share a subset of characteristics, e.g. two different outcomes (different ball trajectories) of two behaviors applied to a ball (beating and kicking) share the characteristics, that the ball is moved and that the space in front of the agent is free after the behavior application. On an abstract level of observation, looking at these examples regarding the "change location" characteristic and neglecting the different time series that occur, both action applications and the corresponding outcomes are equal.

The described abstraction process, and the storage of this gathered abstracted outcome information in the *Application Space*s, enable an artificial agent to treat two or more actions as equal, with regard to the expected outcome of applying these actions in the context of the related cue characteristics. Regarding the above mentioned example where two different behaviors (beating and kicking) are applied on the same object (a ball), the two different behaviors are equal for reaching the outcome described by the derived abstracted "change location" characteristic.

Additionally, objects or entities can be treated as equal, regarding the outcome that occurs by applying such *equal actions*. Even if objects or entities do not share visual features, they can be treated as equal under the context of applying those *equal actions* and gaining the abstracted outcome characteristics.

The outcome of the characterization process together with the extraction of abstracted characteristics by using similarity measurements on the level of characteristics (done by the *CAM*) enables the agent to measure similarities between entities on the abstract level of functionality. Thus the agent is enabled to achieve a level of semantic similarity measurement based on its perceptional similarity measurement abilities together with its behavioral experiences, which provides one method of solution to the complex problem of semantic similarity measurement in robotics [64].

7 Simulator and Demonstrator

We have described a demonstrator scenario and sketched a number of proof-of-concept experiments [65] that are suited to demonstrate the novelty of the MACS approach. The experiments will be performed with a six-wheeled mobile robot with a simple crane arm manipulator, named KURT3D. The robot is available both in a physics-based simulation, MACSim, and as a physical system (four units). With the integrated system, we plan to conduct a number of experiments in stack building, where we use a variety of test objects, from specifically made objects to everyday objects, that the robot shall use for building stacks. The robot shall learn the functions of stacking bases, middle stack elements and top stack elements, and, optionally, learn stability cues. The stack height should only be limited by the maximum height of the crane arm magnet above ground and the number and heights of stackable test objects. The robot will experiment with many of these test objects and learn cues for the presence of certain functions or affordances. Cues in this sense may be invariants across a wide range of test objects with different appearances. The robot shall learn how to use these test objects for the stacking task. The final challenge will be the use of new test objects that offer the same functions but have different appearances than the test objects that have been employed in the initial learning phase. Separate real-world experiments have been conducted with all modules of the architecture (perception of affordances, learning of affordances, planning using affordances, basic skills). Also, various experiments have been conducted in the simulator MACSim. In this section, we will describe the physical demonstrator and the simulator, and we will provide an overview on the experiments we have conducted so far and which are described in several publications.

7.1 Physical Demonstrator

The main elements of the physical demonstrator are a mobile robot, KURT3D, an experimentation arena called the demonstrator environment, and test objects for perception and manipulation experiments.

The MACS version of the KURT3D mobile robot platform consists of the KURT2 base platform, the KURT3D sensory enhancements, the MACS rack and a newly developed crane manipulator. The KURT2 base platform is a six-wheeled mobile robot platform of roughly one by one foot width and depth, and eight inches height. The robot has three wheels on each side, which are connected by a tooth-belt. Per side, a single DC motor drives all wheels via the tooth-belt. The drives and other low-level functions are controlled via a C167 and a TMC 200 controller board and special firmware. These microcontrollers are connected via CAN bus to an on-board notebook computer that runs the high-level control programs under Linux. The standard sensory equipment consists of tilt sensors and a number of distance transducers along the perimeter of the robot.

The KURT3D configuration consists of two additional enhanced sensor systems: a 3D Laser scanner and a stereo pan-tilt camera system, which both were developed at Fraunhofer IAIS. An additional rack has been mounted on top of the robot in order to support a reversible notebook mount and the MACS crane arm (Fig. 6).

The crane arm has three degrees of freedom. The arm itself can be rotated around a vertical axis. A small lorry can be moved horizontally along the crane's

Fig. 6. The mobile robot KURT3D, equipped with a crane arm manipulator and a magnetic gripper

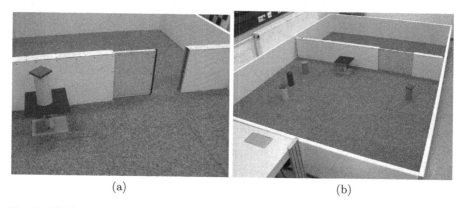

(a)   (b)

Fig. 7. (a) The physical test arena, called demonstrator scenario, including a separating wall, a sliding door, and a (red) switch to open the door. (b) The switch can be operated by putting a weight on it, which will open the door. Removing the weight will close the door. This particular set-up has been chosen to train the robot to observe effects of its manipulation actions.

extension arm, and a magnetic griper can be raised and lowered along a rope that is hanging from the movable lorry. This construction allows most simple manipulation tasks, namely trying to 'grip' items in the environment with the electromagnetic gripper and lift them.

The demonstrator environment setup consists of a defined mission area with the dimensions of 2.5m x 3.5m. The area is surrounded by walls that are 40cm high and 5cm wide, made of heavy and robust wooden elements (Fig. 7(a)). As first passive elements to be manipulated by the crane arm we use tin cans with different colors, sizes and top designs. Some of them are magnetizable, some are not. Their weight can easily be altered by butting in heavy material at any time.

The demonstrator scenario contains also active components: a movable dividing wall with a motor driven sliding door that can divide the mission area into two separate rooms. The door can be opened and closed via a switch. The switch is operated depending on the weight put on it by the robot (Fig. 7(b)). The switch has a weighing area of 25x25cm, is working on a high sensitive pressure sensor (strain gauge element) and is adjustable to trigger on weights between 15g and 7kg. This particular setup has been chosen to train the robot to observe effects of its manipulation actions.

The demonstrator environment and the test objects have been constructed both physically and in simulation (Fig. 8).

(a)   (b)

Fig. 8. (a) Simple experimentation environment, showing robot KURT3D (FhG/AIS). (b) Total view of the demonstrator environment in MACSim.

7.2   Simulator MACSim

MACSim (Fig. 9) is a high fidelity simulation environment that models the KURT3D robotic platform and its environment. Built on top of a commercial quality open-source engine, ODE[4] (Open Dynamics Engine), MACSim accurately simulates the objects, robot parts, and their dynamics in a 3D world.

The simulation model of our mobile robot provided in MACSim closely matches the real KURT3D robot in many aspects. Based on their physical properties, such as mass, size, and center of mass, all parts that constitute the robot are modelled as rigid bodies. Later, junction locations of these components were measured, and they were assembled with appropriate joints to acquire the complete simulated robot. In order to simulate different actuators of the robot, such

---

[4] http://ode.org

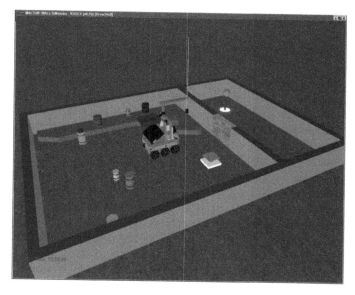

Fig. 9. A snapshot from MACSim where the KURT3D robot is modeled in an environment which is created for the demonstrator scenario

as wheel systems or camera servo motors, the joints are virtually constrained and motorized with the parameters obtained from the real robot.

Realistic sensor modelling is also very crucial, since robot actions and control rely on the robot's perception of the world. While ODE provides excellent support for modelling rigid body dynamics based on laws of physics, similar to many low level engines, virtual sensors are not explicitly supported. For example, there is no ready-to-use acoustic signal or infra-red beam that could be sent or received. For laser scanner and infrared proximity sensors, ODE's ray geometry and collision detection routines are utilized, and ray intersection method is used. For color cameras, OpenGL's backbuffer data is employed. Moreover, in order to close the gap between reality and simulation, sensor and actuator parameters are calibrated, based on the "same setup experiments" in virtual and real worlds.

The reality of the simulator is further verified in [66,67], where the robot controllers trained in the simulator are successfully transferred to the real robot. For example, in [66], a large set of training data (approximately 3000 samples) obtained from interactions of the robot with its environment is required to learn the perception of traversability affordances. MACSim is utilized in a training phase to decrease the time and cost of the learning process and to remove any risk of physical damage that might occur on the real robot. It is later shown that the robot is able to perceive the same affordances offered by the environment when encountered with same situations either in simulated or real world. Moreover, the physical effects created in the simulator and real world are compatible when the robot executes a certain action in that particular situation.

7.3   First Experiments

The final demonstrator scenario will be employed for the final proof of concept of the MACS approach to affordance-inspired robot control. In this final scenario, our robot shall demonstrate the capabilities of its integrated affordance-inspired control architecture, where the planner creates affordance related operators using affordance maps (Fig. 10), and tasks related to learning and goal-directed use of affordances are performed based on these operators. However, for demonstrating and evaluating the benefits of our new robot control approach we do not rely on the final demonstrator alone. Instead, we decided to provide also proofs of concept for several significant steps during the development process. For this purpose, we defined a framework for selected experiments allowing us to analyse the performance of our approach in an isolated and well defined way, starting with simple tasks and increasing the complexity step by step towards the final demonstrator scenario [65,68]. In the phase of the project where the basic skills and perceptual feature detectors necessary for performing affordance related tasks were developed, specific experiments were performed to prove the explicit support for our affordance concept.

For introducing affordance support into robot perception, we first examined the generation of a traversability map based on laser scanner input and a pre-programmed classification of traversable areas in the environment [33]. Next, we developed feature filters based on SIFT descriptors that enable 'top down' and 'bottom up' detection and classification of simple image features. This enables the robot to distinguish features in the top, body and bottom regions of test objects in the environment. These filters work equally well on simulated and real camera data [69,70,71,72].

A desired basic skill of our robot is the autonomous exploration of its environment. One question here was: Based on simple features alone, how can the robot find interesting spots in its environment that potentially contain items that it can manipulate, and thus enable it to learn from its actions. For this purpose, a special variant of the visual attention system VOCUS ([54], cf. Sec. 5.3) has been successfully employed. For driving towards the salient location, the robot's Behavior System provides basic navigational skills, namely driving through free space that is computed based on data of the 3D Laser scanner. The combination of basic navigational skills with salient region detection by VOCUS enables the robot to explore its environment by selecting potentially interesting areas and driving towards them until they are in range of the robot's manipulator. We have informally named this combination 'curiosity drive' behavior. For the creation of an appropriate Behavior System, we also performed experiments in autonomous navigation and map generation with basic support for affordance information [38,73].

Based on these concepts and results, the next development phase was dedicated to the integration of the architecture components and to the introduction of learning mechanisms. The latter ones are mainly employed to determine the descriptive feature sets that are either cues for a certain affordance, or descriptors of the outcomes of the robot's acting upon an affordance. The results of

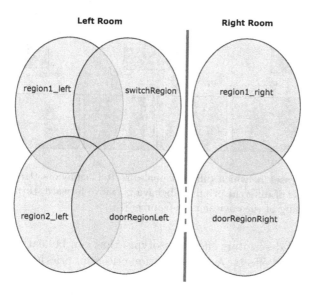

Fig. 10. Affordance Map. The world (cf. Fig. 9) is separated into several regions. If the robot perceives an affordance within one of those regions the affordance type is added to the map. Plans are made based on the constructed affordance map.

reinforcement learning experiments of predictive cues in affordance-based perception were presented in [62,53,51,52]. Learning mechanisms for environmental cues needed for perceiving the traversability affordance were demonstrated in [74,66] and used in 'curiosity drive' experiments in [67]. Here, we tried to formally define the 'curiosity' notion beyond saliency measures by introducing an SVM based measure that helps the robot to decide whether an interaction possibility is worthwhile exploring (cf. also below). In this phase, we have used extensively both the MACSim simulator and synthetic data for our developments and experiments related to learning, which was beneficial.

Exploiting affordance perception and learnt knowledge for goal-directed behavior is the focus of the last phase of our development. In our recent experiments we accomplished the transition of primitive behaviors to goal-directed behavior by using learnt behavior-effect relations and situation awareness to achieve more complex behaviors [66,76,77,78]. In this study, the robot interacts with its environment by executing a set of primitive behaviors and collecting interaction samples. Based on these experiences, the robot discovers the different effects it can create in the environment, and associates an observed effect with the primitive behaviors and environmental situations that resulted in this effect. The robot then uses the learnt relations to achieve more complex behaviors. In our experiment, we used three primitive behaviors (turn-left, turn-right, and move-forward) and the learnt affordance relations of these behaviors to achieve three different goal-directed behaviors (traverse, approach, and avoid). Since the robot learns the affordance relations from its own experiences, it is not trivial for a human observer to specify a goal that 'makes sense' to the robot. One solution

Fig. 11. Three cases in which different goal-directed behaviors (traverse, avoid, approach) make use of different primitive behaviors (move-forward, turn-right, turn-left) in the same setting of the environment (source: [75]).

is to use as goal descriptors effect prototypes that can be learned from a range of similar observed effects. As an evaluation criterion, priorities can be assigned to learnt effect prototypes. This enables the robot to select and execute a primitive behavior that would result in an effect similar to the goal, i.e. to the effect prototype having the highest priority. The results of this study are sketched in Fig. 11.

The learned affordance relations can also be used as operators for planning, since they provide the capability to predict the effects of behaviors as discussed in the context of *cue-outcome based planning* [41]. In a recent study [79], we used these predictions to generate totally ordered plans which are composed of sequences of primitive behaviors. Forward chaining is used for this purpose. The robot starts with perceiving the present entity, and predicts the effects that each of its (five) primitive behaviors will create. Next, it estimates the five future entities that the robot will perceive after execution of corresponding behaviors by summing up the predicted effects and current entity. The robot then proceeds by predicting the effects of behaviors on those future entities and estimating next entities. This process can be viewed as the breath-first construction of a plan tree where the branching factor is the number of behaviors. Planning stops when any future entity or total predicted effect of the behavior sequence satisfies the desired goal. Fig. 12 shows a number of sample plans generated using learned affordance relations for different goals in various environments.

In another series of experiments, we studied the learning of traversability affordances and investigated how the required number of interactions with the environment can be minimized with minimal degradation on the learning process. Specifically, we applied a two step learning process which consists of bootstrapping and curiosity-based learning phases. In the bootstrapping phase, a small set of initial interaction data were used to find the relevant perceptual features for the affordance, and were used to train a Support Vector Machine classifier. In the curiosity-driven learning phase it was determined whether a given interaction opportunity is worth exploring or not [67] (see Fig. 13 below).

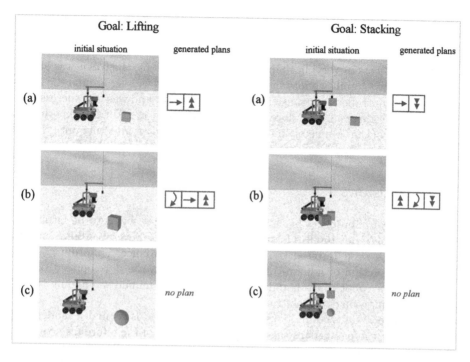

Fig. 12. The generated plans are shown as sequences of primitive behaviors. For lifting and stacking tasks the goals are defined as increase in the crane rope tension and decrease in the distance features on middle grids of the scan image, respectively. The primitive behaviors used in these experiments are turn-left, turn-right, and move-forward, lift, and release. (source: [80]).

Fig. 13. This sequence shows how the perception of traversability affordance are used to navigate in blocked situations. The initial position of the robot is shown in the left-most figure. The robot first goes forward, then turns left since trash-bin does not afford traversability. Third snapshot shows the robot driving over the spherical object. The path of the robot is shown in the last figure. (source: [67]).

The effects of two parameters of our learning system that serve as the curiosity threshold and the number of bootstrap samples were examined in systematic experiments. Selecting a small threshold keeps the system away from interacting with interesting situations, and selecting a large one slows down learning, since uninteresting samples are used for training. As for the number of bootstrap samples, small values degrade the performance of the system and large values beyond a certain threshold do not improve the performance. The affordance perception system, trained using optimized parameters, was tested in our scenario cluttered with objects of varying shapes. In this environment, the robot was able to predict the traversability affordances of the objects and wander around the room. The trained controller was transferred to the real robot and was also successful in predicting the traversability affordance of real world objects. Further experiments will make use of the completely integrated robot control architecture until the full complexity of the final demonstrator scenario tasks will be achieved.

8   Conclusion

The concept of affordances has a strong appeal, since it seems to be intuitively understandable and applicable to a variety of areas. Several groups and researchers have been inspired by the concept of affordances. Affordances have been used in design of human-computer interfaces, in the development of new approaches for robot control, and in investigations of human wayfinding strategies in large man-made infra-structures [81].

In all these areas, the major problem for utilization is to find a model that is suitable for the particular usage or implementation of the affordance concept. One major difficulty for finding operational models of the affordance concept is the vast generality of J.J. Gibson's affordance definition which he simply defined for all "animals". The questions arose whether it is really applicable to beings as different as crickets and humans, and whether is applicable to animals at different levels of individual development.

In this article, we have presented a comprehensive approach to affordance-inspired robot control. The approach is based on our own operational model of affordances in the context of Robotics. It is built on a representational concept, the affordance representation triples, consisting of cue–behavior–outcome descriptors. Such representations are generated during an initial learning phase by analysing the streams of basic and complex perceptual features and applying a three stage learning approach. This comprises the "bottom-up" part in the proposed architecture. The "top-down" part of the architecture foresees the use of affordances for deliberate action, i.e. mission planning and execution. Thus, affordance support is built into all components of the proposed architecture.

The learned representations are grounded in the robot's actions and perceptions, thus they "make sense" for the robot. However, for a human observer, the comprehensability of the learned affordance representations currently remains an open problem. Schönherr [82] presented a solution for a similar case by letting a human assign a symbol to a set of features designating a "situation". A similar solution could be applied to assign "meaning" to affordance representations.

The presented approach to affordance-based planning foresees the goal-directed selection of the proper kind of affordance to act upon. This first version of the planner uses PDDL to define the plan operators. A second version, if feasible, shall introduce new operators that use the full range of cue-behavior-outcome descriptors.

The final stage of the MACS project will be dedicated to extensive experimentation and evaluation of the approach. Regarding the benefit of affordance-inspired control, the hypothesis is that it will provide a systematic way to detect agent-specific possibilities and alternatives for action based on function-oriented perception. A working implementation would enable a robot to find more action alternatives than pure appearance-based perception approaches, since current state-of-the-art appearance-based robot perception approaches typically can handle only about 100 everyday objects, which clearly limits interaction possibilities.

However, there are many situations where (object) recognition capabilities are required. Neisser [83] proposed an approach that includes both affordance-related perception and object recognition. To date this approach has not been realized in robot control either. Thus, as a long term research question, the interaction between affordance perception and object recognition seems to be worthwhile to pursue. Investigating the little explored affordance-inspired perception and control is a prerequisite for a combined system along Neisser's considerations.

Acknowledgements

Being a general MACS position paper, this article is based on contributions of many of the MACS project staff. The authors would like to thank the following current and previous project members: Andreas Bartel[5], Maya Çakmak[3,11], Mehmet Doğar[3], Patrick Doherty[6], Simone Frintrop[1,7], Fredrik Heintz[6], Dirk Holz[8], Martin Hülse[1,9], Maria Klodt[1,7], Torsten Merz[6,12], Frank Meyer[5], Jens Poppenborg[5], Piotr Rudol[6], Göktürk Üçoluk[3], Björn Wingman[6], Rainer Worst[1], Mariusz Wzoreck[6], and Keyan Ghazi-Zahedi[1,10].

This work was partly funded by the European Commission's 6th Framework Programme IST Project MACS under contract/grant number FP6-004381. The Commission's support is gratefully acknowledged.

---

[1]Fraunhofer IAIS, Sankt Augustin, Germany; [2]Joanneum Research, Graz, Austria; [3]Middle East Technical University, Ankara, Turkey; [4]Austrian Research Institute for Artificial Intelligence, Vienna, Austria; [5]University of Osnabrück, Germany; [6]University of Linköping, Sweden; [7]University of Bonn, Germany; [8]University of Applied Sciences Bonn-Rhein-Sieg, Sankt Augustin, Germany, [9]University of Wales, Aberystwyth, UK, [10]Max Planck Institute for Human Cognitive and Brain Sciences, Leipzig, Germany, [11]Georgia Institute of Technology, Atlanta, GA, USA, [12]CSIRO ICT Centre, Brisbane, Australia.

References

1. Gibson, J.J.: The Ecological Approach to Visual Perception. Houghton Mifflin, Boston, MA (1979), also: Lawrence Erlbaum Associates, London (1986)
2. Norman, D.A.: The Psychology of Everyday Things. Basic Books, New York (1988)

3. Chemero, A.: An outline of a theory of affordances. Ecological Psychology 15(2), 181–195 (2003)
4. Steedman, M.: Formalizing affordance. In: Proceedings of the 24th Annual Meeting of the Cognitive Science Society. Conference Fairfax VA, August 2002, pp. 834–839. Lawrence Erlbaum, Washington D.C (2002)
5. Gibson, J.J.: The senses considered as perceptual systems. Houghton Mifflin, Boston (1966)
6. Warren, W.H.: Perceiving affordances: Visual guidance of stair climbing. Journal of Experimental Psychology 105(5), 683–703 (1984)
7. Warren, W.H., Whang, S.: Visual guidance of walking through apertures: body-scaled information for affordances. Journal of Experimental Psychology 13(3), 371–383 (1987)
8. Mark, L.S.: Eyeheight-scaled information about affordances: A study of sitting and stair climbing. Journal of Experimental Psychology: Human Perception and Performance 13(3), 361–370 (1987)
9. Gibson, E.J., Riccio, G., Schmuckler, M.A., Stoffregen, T.A., Rosenberg, D., Taromina, J.: Detection of the traversability of surfaces by crawling and walking infants. Journal of Experimental Psychology 13(4), 533–544 (1987)
10. Kinsella-Shaw, J.M., Shaw, B., Turvey, M.T.: Perceiving walk-on-able slopes. Ecological Psychology 4(4), 223–239 (1992)
11. Chemero, A.: What events are. Ecological Psychology 12(1), 37–42 (2000)
12. Oudejans, R., Michaels, C., van Dort, B., Frissen, E.: To cross or not to cross: The effect of locomotion on street-crossing behavior. Ecological Psychology 8(3), 259–267 (1996)
13. Arkin, R.C.: Behavior Based Robotics. MIT Press, Cambridge, MA (1998)
14. Duchon, A.P., Warren, W.H., Kaelbling, L.P.: Ecological robotics. Adaptive Behavior 6(3), 473–507 (1998)
15. Brooks, R.A.: Intelligence without representation. Artificial Intelligence 47, 139–159 (1991)
16. Brooks, R.A.: A robust layered control system for a mobile robot. IEEE Journal of Robotics and Automation 2(1), 14–23 (1986)
17. Lyons, D., Arbib, M.: A formal model of computation for sensory-based robotics. IEEE Transactions on Robotics and Automation 5(3), 280–293 (1989)
18. Arkin, R.C., Balch, T.: AuRA: Principles and practice in review. Journal of Experimental and Theoretical Artificial Intelligence 9(2), 175–189 (1997)
19. Murphy, R.R.: Case studies of applying Gibson's ecological approach to mobile robots. IEEE Transactions on Systems, Man, and Cybernetics 29(1), 105–111 (1999)
20. Norman, J.: Ecological psychology and the two visual systems: Not to worry! Ecological psychology 13(2), 135–145 (2001)
21. Gibson, E.J.: Perceptual learning in development: Some basic concepts. Ecological Psychology 12(4), 295–302 (2000)
22. Neisser, U.: Multiple systems: A new approach to cognitive theory. The European Journal of Cognitive Psychology 6, 225–241 (1994)
23. MacDorman, K.F.: Responding to affordances: Learning and projecting a sensori-motor mapping. In: Proc. of 2000 IEEE Int. Conf. on Robotics and Automation, San Fransisco, California, USA, pp. 3253–3259 (2000)
24. Connell, J.H.: SSS: a hybrid architecture applied to robot navigation. In: ICRA 1992. Proceedings of the 1992 IEEE International Conference on Robotics and Automation, Nice, France, May 12–14, 1992, vol. 3, pp. 2719–2724. IEEE Computer Society Press, Los Alamitos, CA (1992)

25. Cooper, R., Glasspool, D.W.: Learning action affordances and action schemas. In: French, R.M., Sougne, J.P. (eds.) Connectionist Models of Learning, Development and Evolution. Sixth Neural Computation and Psychology Workshop, London. Perspectives in Neural Computing, pp. 133–142. Springer, Heidelberg (2001)
26. Cos-Aguilera, I., Canamero, L., Hayes, G.M.: Using a SOFM to learn object affordances. In: Proceedings of the 5th Workshop of Physical Agents, Girona, Catalonia, Spain (March 2004)
27. Fitzgerald, P., Metta, G., Natale, L., Rao, S., Sandini, G.: Learning about objects through action – initial steps towards artificial cognition. In: ICRA. Proceedings of the 2003 IEEE International Conference on Robotics and Automation, pp. 3140–3145 (2003)
28. Stoytchev, A.: Toward learning the binding affordances of objects: A behavior-grounded approach. In: Proceedings of AAAI Symposium on Developmental Robotics, Stanford University (March 2005)
29. Cos-Aguilera, I., Canamero, L., Hayes, G.M.: Motivation-driven learning of object affordances: First experiments using a simulated khepera robot. In: ICCM 2003. Proceedings of the 9th International Conference in Cognitive Modelling, Bamberg, Germany, pp. 57–62 (April 2003)
30. Stoytchev, A.: Behavior-grounded representation of tool affordances. In: ICRA. Proceedings of IEEE International Conference on Robotics and Automation, Barcelona, Spain, April 18–22, pp. 3071–3076 (2005)
31. Murphy, R.R., Arkin, R.C.: SFX: An architecture for action-oriented sensor fusion. In: IROS 1992. Proc. of the IEEE/RSJ International Conference on Intelligent Robots and Systems, Raleigh, NC, pp. 1079–1086 (July 1992)
32. Rome, E., Şahin, E., Breithaupt, R., Irran, J., Kintzler, F., Paletta, L., Çakmak, M., Uğur, E., Üçoluk, G., Doğar, M.R., Rudol, P., Fritz, G., Dorffner, G., Doherty, P., Wzoreck, M., Surmann, H., Lörken, C.: Evaluation of existing control architectures for using affordances. Technical Report MACS/2/2.2 v1, Fraunhofer Institut für Intelligente Analyse- und Informationssysteme (IAIS), Sankt Augustin, Germany (2006)
33. Doherty, P., Merz, T., Rudol, P., Wzorek, M.: Tentative proposal for a formal theory of affordances; Tentative proposal for an affordance support architecture; Prototype: Affordance-based motion planner. Technical Report MACS/4/2.1 v1, Linköpings Universitet, IDA Group, Linköping, Sweden (2005)
34. Turvey, M.: Affordances and prospective control: An outline of the ontology. Ecological Psychology 4, 173–187 (1992)
35. Stoffregen, T.A.: Affordances are enough: Reply to chemero et al. Ecological Psychology 15(1), 29–36 (2003)
36. Steedman, M.: Plans, affordances, and combinatory grammar. Linguistics and Philosophy 25(5–6), 723–753 (2002)
37. Şahin, E., Çakmak, M., Doğar, M.R., Uğur, E., Üçoluk, G.: To afford or not to afford: A new formalization of affordances towards affordance-based robot control. Adaptive Behavior 15(4), 447–472 (2007)
38. Lörken., C.: Introducing affordances into robot task execution. In: Kühnberger, K.-U., König, P., Ludewig, P. (eds.) Publications of the Institute of Cognitive Science (PICS), vol. 2, University of Osnabrück, Osnabrück, Germany, (May 2007) ISSN 1610-5389.
39. MacDorman, K.F.: Grounding symbols through sensorimotor integration. Journal of the RSJ (The Robotics Society of Japan) 17(1), 5 (1999)
40. McDermott, D.: PDDL – The planning domain definition language. Technical report, Yale University (1998)

41. Lörken, C., Hertzberg, J.: A specification for a propositional planner and its interface to the MACS execution control module. Deliverable MACS/2/3.2, University of Osnabrück, Institute of Computer Science, Osnabrück, Germany (2007)
42. Neisser, U.: Cognition and Reality: Principles and Implications of Cognitive Psychology. W.H. Freeman and Co., New York (1976)
43. Faillenot, I., Toni, I., Decety, J., Grégoire, M.-C., Jeannerod, M.: Visual pathways for object-oriented action and object recognition: functional anatomy with pet. Cerebral Cortex 7(9), 77–85 (1997)
44. Fagg, A.H., Arbib, M.A.: Modeling parietal–premotor interactions in primate control of grasping. Neural Networks 11(7-8), 1277–1303 (1998)
45. Edwards, M.G., Humphreys, G.W., Castiello, U.: Motor facilitation following action observation: a behavioural study in prehensile action. Brain Cognition 53, 495–502 (2003)
46. Wheeler, D.S., Fagg, A.H., Grupen, R.A.: Learning prospective pick and place behavior. In: Proc. 2nd International Conference on Development and Learning, Cambridge, MA, June 2002, pp. 197–202. IEEE Computer Society Press, Los Alamitos (2002)
47. Stark, L., Bowyer, K.W.: Function-based recognition for multiple object categories. Image Understanding 59(10), 1–21 (1994)
48. Rivlin, E., Dickinson, S.J., Rosenfeld, A.: Recognition by functional parts. Computer Vision and Image Understanding: CVIU 62(2), 164–176 (1995)
49. Bogoni, L., Bajcsy, R.: Interactive recognition and representation of functionality. Computer Vision and Image Understanding: CVIU 62(2), 194–214 (1995)
50. Paletta, L., Fritz, G., Rome, E., Dorffner, G.: A computational model for visual learning of affordance-like cues. In: ECVP 2006. Proc. 29th European Conference on Visual Perception, St. Petersburg, Russia (August 2006)
51. Fritz, G., Paletta, L., Breithaupt, R., Rome, E., Dorffner, G.: Learning predictive features in affordance-based robotic systems. In: IROS 2006. Proc. of the IEEE/RSJ International Conference on Intelligent Robots and Systems, Beijing, China, pp. 3642–3647. Springer, Heidelberg (October 2006)
52. Fritz, G., Paletta, L., Kumar, M., Dorffner, G., Breithaupt, R., Rome, E.: Visual learning of affordance based cues. In: Nolfi, S., Baldassarre, G., Calabretta, R., Hallam, J.C.T., Marocco, D., Meyer, J.-A., Miglino, O., Parisi, D. (eds.) SAB 2006. LNCS (LNAI), vol. 4095, pp. 52–64. Springer, Heidelberg (2006)
53. Fritz, G., Paletta, L.: Reinforcement learning for the selection of predictive cues in affordance-based perception. In: ECVP 2006. Proc. 29th European Conference on Visual Perception, St. Petersburg, Russia (August 2006)
54. Frintrop, S.: VOCUS: A Visual Attention System for Object Detection and Goal-Directed Search. LNCS (LNAI), vol. 3899. Springer, Heidelberg (2006) (also: PhD thesis, University of Bonn)
55. Frintrop, S., Hülse, M., Rome, E., Paletta, L.: Saliency detection with visual attention. Technical Report MACS/3/1.3 v1, Fraunhofer Institut für Autonome Intelligente Systeme, Sankt Augustin, Germany (2005)
56. May, S., Klodt, M., Rome, E., Breithaupt, R.: Gpu-accelerated affordance cueing based on visual attention. In: IROS 2007. Proc. of the IEEE/RSJ International Conference on Intelligent Robots and Systems, San Diego, CA (2007)
57. Lowe, D.G.: Distinctive image features from scale-invariant keypoints. International Journal of Computer Vision 60, 91–110 (2004)
58. Quinlan, J.R.: C4.5 Programs for Machine Learning, Morgan Kaufmann, San Mateo, CA (1993)

59. Sutton, R.S., Barto, A.G.: Reinforcement Learning: An Introduction (Adaptive Computation and Machine Learning). MIT Press, Cambridge, MA (1998)
60. Whitehead, S.D., Ballard, D.H.: Learning to perceive and act by trial and error. Machine Learning 7(1), 45–83 (1991)
61. Puterman, M.L.: Markov Decision Processes. John Wiley & Sons, New York (1994)
62. Paletta, L., Fritz, G.: Reinforcement learning of predictive features in affordance perception. In: Rome, E., Hertzberg, J., Dorffner, G. (eds.) Towards Affordance-based Robot Control – Proceedings of Dagstuhl Seminar 06231. LNCS (LNAI), vol. 4760, Springer, Heidelberg (February 2008)
63. Paletta, L., Fritz, G., Kintzler, F., Irran, J., Dorffner, G.: Learning to perceive affordances in a framework of developmental embodied cognition. In: ICDL 07. Proc. 6th International Conference on Development and Learning, London, UK (July 2007)
64. Janowicz, K.: Extending semantic similarity measurement by thematic roles. In: Rodríguez, M.A., Cruz, I., Levashkin, S., Egenhofer, M.J. (eds.) GeoS 2005. LNCS, vol. 3799, Springer, Heidelberg (2005)
65. Breithaupt, R., Frintrop, S., Hertzberg, J., Rome, E., Müller, B.S.: Specification of final demonstrator. Technical Report MACS/6/1.1 v2, Fraunhofer Institut für Autonome Intelligente Systeme, Sankt Augustin, Germany (2004)
66. Uğur, E., Doğar, M.R., Çakmak, M., Şahin, E.: The learning and use of traversability affordance using range images on a mobile robot. In: ICRA 2007. Proc. of the IEEE International Conference on Robotics and Automation, Conference: Rome, Italy, April 10–14, pp. 1721–1726. IEEE, Los Alamitos (2007)
67. Uğur, E., Doğar, M.R., Çakmak, M., Şahin, E.: The curiosity-driven learning of traversability affordance on a mobile robot. In: ICDL 2007. Proc. of the IEEE International Conference on Development and Learning, Conference: London, UK (July 11–13, 2007)
68. Breithaupt, R., Frintrop, S., Şahin, E., Hertzberg, J., Pölz, P., Rudol, P., Uğur, E., Doherty, P., Rome, E., Müller, B.S.: Report on experiment design. Technical Report MACS/6/4.1 v1, Fraunhofer Institut für Autonome Intelligente Systeme, Sankt Augustin, Germany (2004)
69. Paletta, L., Fritz, G., Kumar, M., Hertzberg, J., Schönherr, F.: Top-down and bottom-up symbol grounding. Technical Report MACS/3/1.1 v3, Joanneum Research Institute of Digital Image Processing Computational Perception (CAPE), Graz, Austria (2005)
70. Paletta, L., Fritz, G., Şahin, E., Kumar, M.: Affordance recognition from visual cues. Technical Report MACS/3/1.2 v1, Joanneum Research Institute of Digital Image Processing Computational Perception (CAPE), Graz, Austria (2005)
71. Paletta, L., Fritz, G., Rome, E., Frintrop, S., Hertzberg, J., Kumar, M.: Prototypical affordance based object detection for MACS scenario. Technical Report MACS/3/1.4 v1, Joanneum Research Institute of Digital Image Processing Computational Perception (CAPE), Graz, Austria (2005)
72. Rome, E., Paletta, L., Fritz, G., Surmann, H., May, S., Lörken, C.: Multi-sensor affordance recognition. Technical Report MACS/3/2.1 v2, Fraunhofer Institut für Autonome Intelligente Systeme, Sankt Augustin, Germany (2006)
73. Holz, D., Lörken., C.: Continuous 3d environment sensing for autonomous robot navigation and mapping. In: Proc. of the 9. Fachwissenschaftlicher Informatik-Kongress, Bonn, Germany, Lecture Notes in Informatics (LNI), pp.39–42 Gesellschaft für Informatik (GI) (March 2007)

74. Uğur, E.: Direct perception of traversability affordance on range images through learning on a mobile robot. M.Sc. thesis, Middle East Technical University, Kovan Laboratory, Ankara, Turkey (2006)

75. Doğar, M.R., Çakmak, M., Uğur, E., Şahin, E.: From primitive behaviors to goal-directed behavior using affordances. Technical Report METU-CENG-TR-2007-02, Middle East Technical University, Kovan Laboratory, Ankara, Turkey, Short version published for ICDL (2007)

76. Uğur, E., Doğar, M.R., Çakmak, M., Şahin, E.: From primitive behaviors to goal-directed behavior using affordances. In: IROS 2007. Proc. of the IEEE/RSJ International Conference on Intelligent Robots and Systems, San Diego, CA, USA (2007)

77. Uğur, E., Doğar, M.R., Çakmak, M., Şahin, E.: Report on experimental results in simulator. Technical Report MACS/6/4.2 v1, Middle East Technical University Dept. of Computer Engineering, Ankara, Turkey (2007)

78. Doğar, M.R., Çakmak, M., Uğur, E., Şahin, E.: Report on experimental results in demonstrator. Technical Report MACS/6/4.3 v1, Middle East Technical University Dept. of Computer Engineering, Ankara, Turkey (2007)

79. Çakmak, M., Doğar, M.R., Uğur, E., Şahin, E.: Affordances as a framework for robot control. In: EpiRob 2007. Proc. of the International Conference on Epigenetic Robotics, Conference Piscataway, NJ, USA (November 5–7, 2007)

80. Çakmak, M.: Robot planning based on learned affordances. M.Sc. thesis, Middle East Technical University, Kovan Laboratory, Ankara, Turkey (2007)

81. Raubal, M.: Agent-based Simulation of Human Wayfinding: A Perceptual Model for Unfamiliar Buildings. PhD thesis, Institute for Geoinformation, Vienna University of Technology, Vienna, Austria (2001)

82. Schönherr, F.: Verankerung der Semantik veränderlicher Situations-Fakten und symbolischer Aktionen in der hybriden Roboterkontrollarchitekur DD&P, Fraunhofer series in information and communication technology 2004, 8. Shaker, Aachen (2004)

83. Neisser, U.: Cognitive Psychology. Prentice-Hall, Englewood Cliffs, NJ (1967)

Author Index

Lecture Notes in Artificial Intelligence (LNAI)

Vol. 4694: B. Apolloni, R.J. Howlett, L. Jain (Eds.), Knowledge-Based Intelligent Information and Engineering Systems, Part III. XXIX, 1126 pages. 2007.

Vol. 4693: B. Apolloni, R.J. Howlett, L. Jain (Eds.), Knowledge-Based Intelligent Information and Engineering Systems, Part II. XXXII, 1380 pages. 2007.

Vol. 4692: B. Apolloni, R.J. Howlett, L. Jain (Eds.), Knowledge-Based Intelligent Information and Engineering Systems, Part I. LV, 882 pages. 2007.

Vol. 4687: P. Petta, J.P. Müller, M. Klusch, M. Georgeff (Eds.), Multiagent System Technologies. X, 207 pages. 2007.

Vol. 4682: D.-S. Huang, L. Heutte, M. Loog (Eds.), Advanced Intelligent Computing Theories and Applications. XXVII, 1373 pages. 2007.

Vol. 4676: M. Klusch, K.V. Hindriks, M.P. Papazoglou, L. Sterling (Eds.), Cooperative Information Agents XI. XI, 361 pages. 2007.

Vol. 4667: J. Hertzberg, M. Beetz, R. Englert (Eds.), KI 2007: Advances in Artificial Intelligence. IX, 516 pages. 2007.

Vol. 4660: S. Džeroski, L. Todorovski (Eds.), Computational Discovery of Scientific Knowledge. X, 327 pages. 2007.

Vol. 4659: V. Mařík, V. Vyatkin, A.W. Colombo (Eds.), Holonic and Multi-Agent Systems for Manufacturing. VIII, 456 pages. 2007.

Vol. 4651: F. Azevedo, P. Barahona, F. Fages, F. Rossi (Eds.), Recent Advances in Constraints. VIII, 185 pages. 2007.

Vol. 4648: F. Almeida e Costa, L.M. Rocha, E. Costa, I. Harvey, A. Coutinho (Eds.), Advances in Artificial Life. XVIII, 1215 pages. 2007.

Vol. 4635: B. Kokinov, D.C. Richardson, T.R. Roth-Berghofer, L. Vieu (Eds.), Modeling and Using Context. XIV, 574 pages. 2007.

Vol. 4632: R. Alhajj, H. Gao, X. Li, J. Li, O.R. Zaïane (Eds.), Advanced Data Mining and Applications. XV, 634 pages. 2007.

Vol. 4629: V. Matoušek, P. Mautner (Eds.), Text, Speech and Dialogue. XVII, 663 pages. 2007.

Vol. 4626: R.O. Weber, M.M. Richter (Eds.), Case-Based Reasoning Research and Development. XIII, 534 pages. 2007.

Vol. 4617: V. Torra, Y. Narukawa, Y. Yoshida (Eds.), Modeling Decisions for Artificial Intelligence. XII, 502 pages. 2007.

Vol. 4612: I. Miguel, W. Ruml (Eds.), Abstraction, Reformulation, and Approximation. XI, 418 pages. 2007.

Vol. 4604: U. Priss, S. Polovina, R. Hill (Eds.), Conceptual Structures: Knowledge Architectures for Smart Applications. XII, 514 pages. 2007.

Vol. 4603: F. Pfenning (Ed.), Automated Deduction – CADE-21. XII, 522 pages. 2007.

Vol. 4597: P. Perner (Ed.), Advances in Data Mining. XI, 353 pages. 2007.

Vol. 4594: R. Bellazzi, A. Abu-Hanna, J. Hunter (Eds.), Artificial Intelligence in Medicine. XVI, 509 pages. 2007.

Vol. 4585: M. Kryszkiewicz, J.F. Peters, H. Rybinski, A. Skowron (Eds.), Rough Sets and Intelligent Systems Paradigms. XIX, 836 pages. 2007.

Vol. 4578: F. Masulli, S. Mitra, G. Pasi (Eds.), Applications of Fuzzy Sets Theory. XVIII, 693 pages. 2007.

Vol. 4573: M. Kauers, M. Kerber, R. Miner, W. Windsteiger (Eds.), Towards Mechanized Mathematical Assistants. XIII, 407 pages. 2007.

Vol. 4571: P. Perner (Ed.), Machine Learning and Data Mining in Pattern Recognition. XIV, 913 pages. 2007.

Vol. 4570: H.G. Okuno, M. Ali (Eds.), New Trends in Applied Artificial Intelligence. XXI, 1194 pages. 2007.

Vol. 4565: D.D. Schmorrow, L.M. Reeves (Eds.), Foundations of Augmented Cognition. XIX, 450 pages. 2007.

Vol. 4562: D. Harris (Ed.), Engineering Psychology and Cognitive Ergonomics. XXIII, 879 pages. 2007.

Vol. 4548: N. Olivetti (Ed.), Automated Reasoning with Analytic Tableaux and Related Methods. X, 245 pages. 2007.

Vol. 4539: N.H. Bshouty, C. Gentile (Eds.), Learning Theory. XII, 634 pages. 2007.

Vol. 4529: P. Melin, O. Castillo, L.T. Aguilar, J. Kacprzyk, W. Pedrycz (Eds.), Foundations of Fuzzy Logic and Soft Computing. XIX, 830 pages. 2007.

Vol. 4520: M.V. Butz, O. Sigaud, G. Pezzulo, G. Baldassarre (Eds.), Anticipatory Behavior in Adaptive Learning Systems. X, 379 pages. 2007.

Vol. 4511: C. Conati, K. McCoy, G. Paliouras (Eds.), User Modeling 2007. XVI, 487 pages. 2007.

Vol. 4509: Z. Kobti, D. Wu (Eds.), Advances in Artificial Intelligence. XII, 552 pages. 2007.

Vol. 4496: N.T. Nguyen, A. Grzech, R.J. Howlett, L.C. Jain (Eds.), Agent and Multi-Agent Systems: Technologies and Applications. XXI, 1046 pages. 2007.

Vol. 4483: C. Baral, G. Brewka, J. Schlipf (Eds.), Logic Programming and Nonmonotonic Reasoning. IX, 327 pages. 2007.

Vol. 4482: A. An, J. Stefanowski, S. Ramanna, C.J. Butz, W. Pedrycz, G. Wang (Eds.), Rough Sets, Fuzzy Sets, Data Mining and Granular Computing. XIV, 585 pages. 2007.

Vol. 4481: J. Yao, P. Lingras, W.-Z. Wu, M.S. Szczuka, N.J. Cercone, D. Ślęzak (Eds.), Rough Sets and Knowledge Technology. XIV, 576 pages. 2007.

Vol. 4476: V. Gorodetsky, C. Zhang, V.A. Skormin, L. Cao (Eds.), Autonomous Intelligent Systems: Multi-Agents and Data Mining. XIII, 323 pages. 2007.

Vol. 4460: S. Aguzzoli, A. Ciabattoni, B. Gerla, C. Manara, V. Marra (Eds.), Algebraic and Proof-theoretic Aspects of Non-classical Logics. VIII, 309 pages. 2007.

Vol. 4457: G.M.P. O'Hare, A. Ricci, M.J. O'Grady, O. Dikenelli (Eds.), Engineering Societies in the Agents World VII. XI, 401 pages. 2007.

Vol. 4456: Y. Wang, Y.-m. Cheung, H. Liu (Eds.), Computational Intelligence and Security. XXIII, 1118 pages. 2007.